Performing care

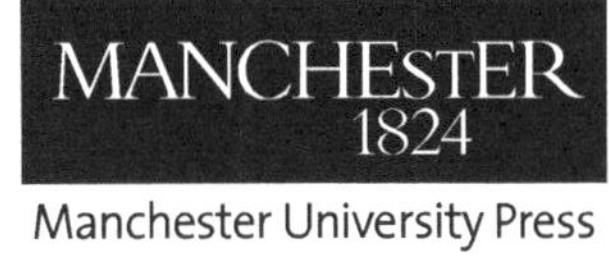

Manchester University Press

Performing care

New perspectives on socially
engaged performance

**EDITED BY AMANDA STUART FISHER
AND JAMES THOMPSON**

Manchester University Press

Published by Manchester University Press
Oxford Road, Manchester M13 9PL
www.manchesteruniversitypress.co.uk

British Library Cataloguing-in-Publication Data is available

ISBN 978 1 5261 4680 9 hardback
ISBN 978 1 5261 4681 6 open access
ISBN 978 1 5261 6396 7 paperback

First published by Manchester University Press in hardback 2020

This edition first published 2022

The publisher has no responsibility for the persistence or accuracy of URLs for any external or third-party internet websites referred to in this book, and does not guarantee that any content on such websites is, or will remain, accurate or appropriate.

Typeset by Newgen Publishing UK

To James' daughters Hannah and Leah and Amanda's daughters Beatrice and Tilly, who have taught us so much about care.

Contents

Illustrations

Contributors

Jen Archer-Martin (Ngāpuhi, Ngāti Pākeha) is a spatial designer, thinker and educator from Aotearoa (New Zealand). Her creative research practice explores the performance of mutually caring relationships between beings, materials and places. Recent works include: 'Performing Bitumen, Materialising Desiré' (2019, with Julieanna Preston, *Architectural Materialisms*); 'Notes on Caring Labours' (2018, *Performance Research*); 'Magical Agents: The Powers of Care Are Not Ours Alone' (2017, *Does Design Care … ?*); and 'Taking Note(s)_Performing Care' (2017, *Performing, Writing*, takingnotes. performingwriting.com). Jen is Senior Lecturer of Spatial Design at Massey University, New Zealand.

Sylvan Baker, FRSA, is Lecturer in Community Performance Applied Theatre at Royal Central School of Speech and Drama. He is an associate artist of the award-winning arts and health project *Performing Medicine* and former associate director of the Arts and Social Justice Research Centre, People's Palace Projects. The focus of his research is creative methods to stimulate co-creation and inclusion among marginalised communities. As a lead investigator of the AHRC-funded research project, *The Verbatim Formula*, he works with care-experienced young people to support adults in providing better care and education (see www.theverbatimformula.org.uk).

Dave Calvert is Senior Lecturer in Drama, Theatre and Performance at the University of Huddersfield, where he is a member of the Research Centre for Performance Practices (ReCePP). His primary research area is performance and learning disability and he has published on such artists and companies as Heavy Load, Mind the Gap, Susan Boyle and Back to Back. He has also written about various troupes in popular entertainment, including the British Pierrot tradition and the Rat Pack. He is currently chair of the UK-based theatre company Dark Horse.

Pat Deeny is Senior Lecturer in Nursing at Ulster University and Senior Fellow with the Higher Education Academy in the UK. He specialises in simulation and human-factor training for nurses and helps prepare health care professionals and postgraduate journalist students for work in disaster and conflict zones.

Kathleen Gallagher is Distinguished Professor at the University of Toronto. In 2017, she won the inaugural University of Toronto President's Impact Award for research impact beyond the academy. In 2018, she won the David E. Hunt Award for Excellence in Graduate Teaching. Dr Gallagher has published several award-winning books and articles on theatre, youth, pedagogy, methodology and gender, and travels widely giving international addresses and workshops for practitioners. Her multi-sited, collaborative ethnographic research continues to focus on questions of youth civic engagement and artistic practice and the pedagogical and methodological possibilities of theatre.

Maurice Hamington is Professor of Philosophy and Affiliate Faculty in Women, Gender and Sexuality Studies at Portland State University. He is a care ethicist who has authored or edited twelve books including: *Care Ethics and Poetry* (2019, co-written with Ce Rosenow); *Care Ethics and Political Theory* (2015, edited with Daniel Engster); *Applying Care Ethics to Business* (2011, edited with Maureen Sander-Staudt); *Socializing Care* (2006, edited with Dorothy C. Miller); and *Embodied Care* (2004). For more information on his other works see pdx.academia.edu/MauriceHamington.

Sara Houston is Principal Lecturer in Dance at the University of Roehampton, UK. Her primary research interest is in community dance and specifically the experience of dancing for those marginalised or excluded in society. Her work on dance and Parkinson's won her a BUPA Foundation Prize in 2011 and she was a finalist in the National Public Engagement Awards in 2014 in recognition of how she engaged the public internationally with that research. Her monograph, *Dancing with Parkinson's*, was published in 2019. Sara chairs the Board of People Dancing, the UK's national support organisation for community dance.

Maggie Inchley is Senior Lecturer in Drama, Theatre and Performance at Queen Mary University of London. Her publications include *Voice and New Writing: 1997–2007* (2015), which is concerned with the inclusion, representation and performance of marginalised voices in British theatre. She researches the intersections of aesthetics, gender and other aspects of identity in vocal performance. As principal investigator of AHRC-funded research project, *The Verbatim Formula*, she works with care-experienced young people to support adults in providing better care and education (see www.theverbatimformula.org.uk).

Matt Jennings is Lecturer in Drama at Ulster University. Based in Northern Ireland since 2001, Matt has worked as an artist and teacher in Australia, Ireland, the UK and France. In 2010, he completed a PhD on the impact of community drama in Northern Ireland since 1998. Matt also provides communication training for health professionals, particularly within the Ulster University School of Nursing.

Jayne Lloyd is course leader of the MA in Inclusive Arts Practice at the University of Brighton. She is an artist and researcher working across sculpture, drawing, film and performance. She has over fifteen years of experience delivering creative projects in a range of health and social care, education and community settings. In 2016 she completed a practice-based PhD at Royal Holloway, University of London, which explored the role of participatory art practices in the lives of care home residents living with dementia.

Caoimhe McAvinchey is Professor of Socially Engaged and Contemporary Performance at Queen Mary University of London. Prior to this, she established the MA Applied Drama programme at Goldsmiths, University of London. Publications include: *Theatre & Prison* (2011); *Performance and Community: Case Studies and Commentary* (2013); and *Phakama: Making Participatory Performance* (2018, with Lucy Richardson and Fabio Santos). Caoimhe is currently working on a monograph marking forty years of Clean Break theatre company.

Ella Parry-Davies is a British Academy postdoctoral fellow at the Royal Central School of Speech and Drama, University of London, where her research addresses relationships between performance, urban space and memory making in contexts of transnational migration. She holds a PhD jointly funded by King's College London and the National University of Singapore. She is editor of *Contemporary Theatre Review*'s *Interventions* platform and a BBC/AHRC New Generation Thinker. She is a founding co-convenor of the After Performance research group, and of the PSi working group on performance and critical social praxis.

Julieanna Preston explores the vitality of natural and synthetic materials in site-responsive live art performances. This artistic research often finds another form in performance writing as artist pages, essays, poems, scripts and scores. Recent works include: *Vital Tones* (2019, Sweden); *RPM Hums* (2018, NZ); *Murmur* (2017, UK); 'On Duration/On During' (2018, *Performance Research*); 'Performing Bitumen, Materialising Desiré' (2019, with Jen Archer-Martin, *Architectural Materialisms*); and 'Four Castings' (2018, *Performance Research*). She is Professor of Spatial Practice at Massey University, New Zealand.

Amanda Stuart Fisher is a reader in contemporary theatre and performance at Royal Central School of Speech and Drama. Her research interests focus around the relationship between performance and care and the dramaturgy of testimonial and verbatim theatre. She has published articles in *Performance Research, Research in Drama Education: The Journal of Applied Theatre and Performance, Studies in Theatre and Performance* and *TDR*. Her monograph *Performing the Testimonial: Rethinking verbatim dramaturgies* will be published in 2020 by MUP.

James Thompson is Professor of Applied Theatre at the University of Manchester. He researches all aspects of applied theatre, recently focusing on care and performance. He was the founder of *In Place of War* – a project supporting arts programmes in war and disaster zones and he has developed and run theatre projects in Africa and South Asia (principally DR Congo and Sri Lanka). He has written widely on socially engaged arts and his most recent books are *Performance Affects* (2009) and *Humanitarian Performance* (2014).

Karl Tizzard-Kleister is a PhD researcher in drama and nursing at Ulster University. His research explores how drama can be used in nursing education. Recently his research has explored how applied drama creates creative spaces to experience risk and vulnerability for student nurses.

Rachel Turner-King is Assistant Professor of Creativity, Performance and Education at the Centre for Education Studies, University of Warwick. She is course leader of the MA in Drama and Theatre Education. Her main research interests are: eco-pedagogy and education for sustainable development using drama; the theory and practice of hospitality and conviviality in public spaces; devising performance with young people, specifically the creative processes of collaborative theatre making. Her research on youth theatre practice has been published in edited works by Kelly Freebody and Michael Finneran (2016), Michael Anderson and Michael Finneran (2019) and in *Research in Drama Education: The Journal of Applied Theatre and Performance* (2018).

Acknowledgements

The ideas informing this edited collection were initially developed at a round table event in 2016 and the editors would like to thank Maurice Hamington, Caoimhe McAvinchey, Jonathan Petherbridge, Pam Smith, Robert Stern and Lois Weaver for their participation, being such good critical friends and so generously responding to our invitation to join us in this highly productive dialogue about the relationship between performance and care ethics. We would also like to thank all those who contributed to the Performing Care Symposium at the Royal Central School of Speech and Drama in December 2016, particularly Maurice Hamington who gave such an engaging keynote. We would also like to thank Maria Delgado, Dan Hetherington and Central's research office for their invaluable support for these events and the development of the edited collection. Our thanks are also extended to Sally Baggott for her excellent editing skills, to Adelina Ong and James Rawson for their help with the referencing and indexing process and to Tony Fisher for being a source of support throughout in so many ways. We would also like to thank David Harradine for his thoughtful input and Fevered Sleep for granting us permission to use the wonderful image from *Men & Girls Dance*. Our thanks also go to *Research in Drama Education: The Journal of Applied Theatre and Performance*, for kindly permitting us to republish James Thompson's article. Finally, we would like to send our warmest thanks to Matthew Frost and Manchester University Press for working with us on this project and supporting our desire to ground this book in an interdisciplinary interrogation of performance and care.

Caoimhe McAvinchey would like to thank Clean Break for supporting her access to the company, particularly Lucy Perman for her generous reflections and Anna Herrmann and Deborah Bruce for kindly giving permission to quote from the unpublished text, *Hear* (2016).

Ella Parry-Davies would like to thank Dima el Mabsout for sharing such generous insight into her work over several years and for her comments on Ella's critical responses to it. Ella also extends her thanks to Zeina Assaf, Kélina Gotman, Jane Rendell, Fiona Wilkie, Liang Peilin and Matthew

Yoxall for their comments at various stages of the writing of her chapter, and to interlocutors at PSi 2015 in Lebanon and PSi 2016 in Australia.

Matt Jennings, Pat Deeny and Karl Tizzard-Kleister would like to thank Luke Merritt and Harrison McCallum, who contributed to the development of Chapter 11 and Mary Findon-Henry, Lecturer in Mental Health and Forensic Healthcare, School of Nursing, Ulster University for her support and guidance with the project.

Introduction: caring performance, performing care

Amanda Stuart Fisher

> **Kate:** Ok, so the Home Office are saying you're more than 16.
> **Tariq:** I am 16.
> **Kate:** They think that the way you look and behave makes you older than
> that. So you'd be an adult, not a minor.
> *Tariq frowns, shakes his head.*
> **Kate:** you know what that means, yeah? That we wouldn't need to look
> after you, give you the same support. If you were a grown-up living here
> [at this supported accommodation] we'd ask you to leave.
> […]
> **Tariq:** You think I am lying too?
> **Kate:** It doesn't matter what I think. I am on your side – they have to be
> apart – objective. That means making the right decisions without their
> emotions all muddying it. (Extract from *Dear Home Office*, Harrison
> *et al.,* 2016: 20–1)

Devised and performed by unaccompanied minor refugee actors, *Dear Home Office* was the inaugural production of the newly founded Phosphoros Theatre.[1] In the extract above, we see Kate, a key worker at the housing association that supports Tariq, trying to explain the UK asylum system's assessment processes and the culture of suspicion and distrust that pervades it. It is a poignant moment in the play, highlighting both the somewhat arbitrary limits of the UK's care and support of young asylum seekers and the practical difficulties that confront any young accompanied minor refugee who is required to prove they are under the age of eighteen, and are therefore technically a child and 'vulnerable' in the eyes of the law.[2] In the production of *Dear Home Office* at the Pleasance Theatre in 2016, the actor playing Tariq appeared visibly to be an adolescent, caught somewhere in-between a boy and a young man. The real identity of the actor playing Tariq heightened the poignancy of the scene. Tariq emerged as a typical teenage boy, concerned not so much about the important legalities of the asylum system but of what Kate, his key worker, thought of him. The scene is all the more affecting because we, as audience members, are aware that the actor playing Tariq is likely to have also confronted these kinds of issues in 'real life', where, of course, the stakes are so much higher. In real life, a wrong answer or a false step can mean all care being removed, deportation back to punishing and brutal political regimes or a precarious existence living on the streets.

The character of Kate in this scene was played by Kate Duffy, one of the directors, who, at the time the play was made, was a key worker for a housing association that supports refugees and migrants from different parts of the world resettle in the UK. Throughout *Dear Home Office*, we learn more about the lived experience of the protracted, complex and highly politicised assessment processes of Britain's asylum system to which Tariq is subject and in which Kate and her colleagues are implicated. Audiences witness the carelessness of this process through the eyes of the young men, who are not only living it in 'real life' but who have become the actors in this play to share their experiences and stories with us. The stories are personal, moving and on occasion shocking as the focus shifts from arrival in the UK to accounts of life in the young men's home countries, where they were the victim of forced illegal conscription into armies, imprisonment without trial and beatings. There were also moments of humour as we witness the many errors the young men themselves made during the asylum process, such as mixing up the number of the day and month on a form and ending up appearing one year older. These simple but potentially catastrophic mistakes are very familiar to anyone who lives with teenagers, who are prone to slip-ups as they find their way in the world, and, in the play, these moments also serve effectively to remind us just how young and vulnerable these young men actually are.

The personal narratives of refugeeism and asylum are juxtaposed with video footage revealing the creation of the project itself. The footage depicts a residential trip for the cast to Derbyshire, where the young actors are seen rehearsing, walking and playing together in the countryside. Through glimpses of teenage buffoonery and moments of the cast relaxing and experiencing some quirky British cultural traditions together, such as an impromptu Christmas dinner and an Easter egg hunt, new and multidimensional representations of unaccompanied minor refugees emerge. These representations and the narratives accompanying them serve to challenge and replace the all too often threatening and negative stories about child refugees that have tended to dominate popular media in recent years.[3] In this way, the play dismantles the label of 'unaccompanied minor', transforming these young men into people with whom we can relate and, crucially, *care for*. Furthermore, the play moves beyond simple representations of acts of caring. Methodologically and dramaturgically, *Dear Home Office* performs a mode of care for its actors and a deep respect for these young men's experiences. Borrowing from theatre maker Peter Sellars the play moves beyond 'the furtive and presumptuous look of the culture of surveillance' and instead generates an 'eye-to-eye meeting of equal beings' (2016: viii), inviting audiences to recognise unaccompanied minors simply as young people they can relate to and who are in need of their support. In this sense, caring within this play emerges not only as part of its material content but also as an aesthetic practice. The caring structures of the play's development process, visible through the video footage, also reveal how performance of care can enact a mode of resistance to 'care-less' state processes that are structured around the concept of care as quantifiable economy and are designed to be measured and distributed only according to tightly predetermined formulas.

Refugees and asylum seekers are, of course, not the only care receivers to be subjected to this form of bureaucratised form of state care. As governmental care services across the world are increasingly being determined not by need or quality of care but by a politics of austerity and cost reduction, it is a timely moment to reflect not on how care is to be distributed and measured, but how care might be understood as an embodied, practised and artful phenomena.

Theorisation developed by care ethicists defines care as incorporating both 'practice and value' (Held, 2006) and, while the concept of care denotes certain affective labours, acts and gestures, it also therefore incorporates intrinsic values, determining how we *ought* to act in relation to other people. In her work with Berenice Fisher, Joan Tronto defined four 'ethical elements of care', which are useful to our exploration of how care and performance can operate together and that incorporate: 'attentiveness, responsibility, competence, and responsiveness' ([1993] 2009: 127). Pointing to interrelational modes of being, care ethics acknowledges the value of inter-human relationality and dependency, invoking the affective qualities of 'attentiveness, sensitivity, and responding to needs' (Held, 2006: 39).

Placing care in dialogue with performance, in the critical engagements that follow, contributors examine how some performance work that addresses itself to the care and support of other people enacts a form of resistance to the 'care-lessness' of contemporary life. The contributors to this edited collection are interested in how performances can be caring, responsive and attentive but also how social, medical and ecological practices of care can be understood as being artful, aesthetic, rehearsed and performative. Correlatively, the critical discussions in this book also call for reflection on performance practices that are *uncaring*, that are not constructed around an affective attentiveness towards the other and that devalue relationships of interdependence; for example, practices that instrumentalise participation or that inadvertently predetermine or enforce certain narratives of change and transformation upon unsuspecting communities. In this sense, this edited collection also considers how theories and practices of care might challenge some of the assumptions made about socially engaged performance and the way efficacy is defined and measured within this field.

This introduction now turns to further consider some definitions of care by examining some of the theorisation in this area developed within care ethics. Building on the concept of care as 'embodied' knowledge (Hamington, 2004) and a form of 'emotional labour' (Hochschild, 2012), the discussions of care in this edited collection position care both as a form of labour and a mode of performance. Care is something enacted both by social actors (such as nurses and social workers) and by performers in socially engaged performance projects. However, this is not to suggest that giving and receiving care is always an unquestionably positive experience. Through an engagement with disability studies and scholarship around performance and mental health, this introduction examines the more troubling aspects of caring, such as the capacity for care to become oppressive and manipulative and the challenges of generating meaningful caring encounters within contexts where care is in short supply. The deficits of care in contemporary societies present certain political and ethical challenges to socially engaged performance, which can find itself co-opted by neoliberal agendas that are determined by the values of autonomy and self-realisation rather than dependency and interrelationality. These challenges are considered in the final section of this introduction, which outlines the exposition of the edited collection as a whole and the way care and performance is explored within the wide range of international interdisciplinary projects examined here.

Care as performance/performance as care

Care ethics is a moral philosophy that emerged in the last two decades of the twentieth century and that has been highly influential to many theorisations of care that have been developed since then. Conceived as a normative moral theory that determines how we ought to comport ourselves in relation to other people, care ethics was advanced by feminist philosophers such as Carol Gilligan (1982), Nel Noddings ([1984] 2013), Virginia Held (1993), Joan Tronto ([1993] 2009) and Eva Feder Kittay (1999). By coupling 'care' with 'ethics', these theorists were not concerned with the development of an abstract moral principle of care but rather with concrete questions about how we relate to one another and how we think about particular situations, settings and relationships. As theatre scholar Nicholas Ridout points out, ethical theory denotes a practical approach to philosophy, addressing the central question: 'How shall I act?' (2009: 5). Of course, as Ridout goes on to argue, the question 'How shall I act?' has a double meaning in the context of theatre and performance because it not only asks how should I act in my everyday life, but also how should I act on stage? Or, what kind of theatre should I make? Or, in the context of socially engaged performance, in particular, how should I engage this community in theatre making and what might this performance *do* for this particular context?

When trying to answer the question of 'how to act', ethicists have tended to start with the premise that the person acting in the world is an autonomous subject who answers this question by engaging in a rational process of decision making and acting accordingly. Dominant ethical theories that position subjects as *autonomous* beings tend to view people, as care ethicist

Virginia Held points out, as 'self-sufficient independent individuals' (1993: 13). For Kantians, for example, autonomy points to the moral law that is internal to the subject, demonstrating the subject's freedom from the world, its influences and its own desires. Kant identifies morality with disinterestedness and thus the subject's ethical detachment from worldly cares and concerns. As Held indicates, Kantian subjects 'refrain from actions that they could not will to be universal laws to which all fully rational and autonomous agents could agree' (1993: 13). In contrast, care ethicists tend to view people 'as relational and interdependent, morally and epistemologically' (Held, 1993: 13). In this sense, the ethics of care 'respects rather than removes itself from the claims of particular others with whom we share actual relationships' (Held, 1993: 11). Yet, while care ethics acknowledges the interdependency of human relationships, it also 'sees many of our responsibilities as not freely entered into but presented to us by the accident of our embeddedness in familial and social and historical contexts' (Held, 1993: 14). This has led some care ethicists, such as Joan Tronto ([1993] 2009), to address a *politics of care* and to consider how certain structures of social injustice and 'inequalities of power and privilege' determine how the labour of caring is distributed and who undertakes it (Tronto, [1993] 2009: 101). Rather than viewing the obligation to care as a duty or as a rational decision-making process, care ethicists take account of the experience of caring and being cared for and the role of emotions and empathy in the structure of these encounters.

While contemporary conceptualisations of care owe much to the work of the feminist care ethicists in the 1980s, a number of other disciplinary fields have also explored both the concept and practice of care and how caring structures might determine our relationship with others. In *The Emotional Labour of Nursing: Its Impact on Interpersonal Relations, Management and Educational Environment* (1992), for example, Pam Smith examines the caring work of nursing as a mode of emotional labour. Positioning care as a mode of professional labour that incorporates practical skill and various modes of empathic engagement with others, Smith's thesis draws on Arlie Hochschild's theorisation around 'emotional labour' as developed in her book, *The Managed Heart: Commercialization of Human Feeling* (2012), where she considers the unacknowledged caring work of air hostesses. The emotional labour of caring has also been explored in other disciplinary contexts, such as social work, albeit in a differently nuanced way. For example, the issue of care, stress and emotional 'burn out' forms the focus Kate van Heugten's book *Social Work Under Pressure: How to Overcome Stress, Fatigue and Burnout in the Workplace* (2011).

The work of the care ethicists in the 1980s and 1990s did much to highlight the importance of care to the management and sustainability of medical and social practices. However, caring labour itself, at least in contemporary Western societies, remains as Joan Tronto aptly described it, a form of labour that is continually 'gendered, raced, classed' ([1993] 2009: 112). In contemporary societies, where care continues to be perceived largely as women's work, it is positioned as the remit of lowly paid workers who are largely drawn from lower socio-economic income groups. Domestic care is often outsourced to migrant women workers, who leave their own communities to undertake caring responsibilities for families in the developed countries of the West. While care might be crucial to the successful functioning of a society as a whole, its value is persistently denigrated and 'the work of caring for young and old seems to have moved down in honour and monetary reward' becoming 'work to get out of, to pass on to someone who can't get a better job' (Hochschild, 2003: 2).

Care has therefore become something of a commodity, something we 'buy in' rather than something we expect to *do*. The devaluation of care and the gendering of caring labour has been a long-standing concern of feminist theorists and is a problem in which many of us find ourselves implicated. While feminism has celebrated increased equality and the inclusion of more women in the workplace, the question of who now becomes responsible for childcare and the care of elderly family members remains a thorny issue. Furthermore, the 'advancement' of professional women in the West, as Premilla Nadasen argues, 'is dependent upon the labour – and often the exploitation – of poor women to carry out the work of social reproduction' (2016).

Although primarily theorised in relation to ethics and emotional labour, in *The Encyclopaedia of Bioethics* (1995), Warren T. Reich shows that the term 'care' itself has a much longer and broader history – one that discloses a much wider range of connotations and meanings. In his etymological account of care, Reich takes us back to the figure of the 'vengeful Cares' (*ultrices Curae*) that appear in Virgil – guarding the 'entrance to the underworld' (1995: 349), which he argues etymologically connects our understanding of care today with an association with loss and grieving. Here we encounter the dual meaning of the word 'care', since, as Reich points out, it is a term that denotes both *anxieties* and *concerns* as in 'care as burden', but also a sense of *engagement* with the other, as in 'care as solicitude' (1995: 350). The different meanings and inferences associated with the concept of care highlighted by Reich's etymological work usefully draw attention to care's multitudinous meanings and the different ways care is theorised and understood. For the editors and contributors of this edited collection, 'care' is a term that has many interconnected dimensions: it has a practical and emotional element (how we practically engage with other people); it has an ethical and political dimension (disclosing values that determine how we should act in the world and within the limited resources we might have available to us); and, crucially, it has an aesthetic component (determining how artistry and the feeling evoked by an engagement with the arts frames inter-human relationships in solicitous ways).

This edited collection's engagement with performance and care, in many ways, sets out to challenge Joan Tronto's assertion in *Moral Boundaries: A Political Argument for an Ethic of Care* ([1993] 2009) that 'to create a work of art, is not care' ([1993] 2009: 104). Tronto's refusal to see art as a mode of care emerges from her reading of the 'Aristotelian idea of nested ends', and her argument that an activity or a practice becomes conceived as a form of 'care' when it is 'aimed at maintaining, continuing, or repairing the world' ([1993] 2009: 104). The work of art, for Tronto at least, is viewed as something that is created to be an end in and of itself and is associated with self-fulfilling activities such as: 'pleasure, creative activity, production, destruction' ([1993] 2009: 104). Notably, in a footnote to this discussion of art, Tronto moves to a slightly more equivocal position where, drawing on the example of dance therapy that she positions as both creative but also therapeutic, she argues that some creative activities can be used 'to a caring end' ([1993] 2009: 204). However, what is omitted from Tronto's account of art are creative practices that are generated through an interrelated engagement with artistic creation and social responsibility and obligation; it is precisely these types of performance practices that we seek to interrogate in this edited collection. Rather than seeing creative practices as simply having a 'caring end', as Tronto suggests, we offer a conceptualisation of socially engaged performance that moves beyond social utility and positions performance as a mode of care that emerges somewhere in-between art and social practice. In this sense, we agree with the performance theorist Shannon Jackson's view, when she says: '[w]hether cast in aesthetic or social terms, freedom and expression are not opposed to obligation and care, but in fact depend upon each other' (2011: 14).

The relationship between care and performance examined within the chapters in this edited collection varies from project to project, but tends to be underpinned by a shared interest in the possibility of some interdependence between these two embodied concepts. Care emerges as being constitutively implicated within the concept of performance. After all, it is impossible to conceive of caring practice outside the parameters of how it is performed. In this sense, care, like live and theatrical performance, exists only as a live encounter and within a specific juncture of time and space. Furthermore, as with performance, care also involves forms of embodied knowledge. Feminist performance theorist Diana Taylor defines performance as an 'embodied practice', which also has an epistemological function because, as she goes on to argue, performance is not only something that we do, it is additionally a 'way of knowing' (2016: 3). Similarly, it is through the caring encounter that the givers and receivers of care learn what caring is and how it feels. Like live performance that is presented to an audience, the caring encounter is determined both by the repeated, practised gestures of the caregiver, but also, crucially, by the kinds of responses this elicits in the care receiver. In this sense, caring practice is not simply concerned with caring actions but with how these actions are experienced by another person. Borrowing from Richard Schechner's writing on performance, we suggest that caring practice – like performance – is 'made from bits of restored behaviour' (2013: 30); in other words, while caring is transient and live, it also requires technical reproducibility. Quality care relies on the capacity to practise and perform a task, making it repeatable and 'practised' and, like live performance, care also has a distinctive singular quality to it because each caring encounter is performed in the moment and is therefore always 'different from every other' (Schechner, 2013: 30). By thinking of care as performance and live performance as a mode of care, we recognise however that we must navigate a pathway through the many different meanings denoted by the term 'performance'.

Because socially engaged performance rarely takes place in theatre-specific spaces, the discussions of performance as care examined in this edited collection tend to interconnect with the caring labour of what sociologist Erving Goffman describes as the performance of the 'social actor' (1990). For this reason, the various performances of care explored within this edited collection often emerge from a nexus of theatre makers and social actors who work together, variously taking on each other's roles and exploring the tensions and synergies that emerge between the interchangeability of the performer and the performed. Within this edited collection, 'performance' emerges as a wide-reaching term that is applied to many different contexts. While our focus is performance in the sense of theatre making, the term 'performance' is also adopted to describe social performance, where it signifies a set of live, and different kinds of 'restored behaviours'. Performance then becomes a term that refers to different embodied practices that, to borrow from Diana Taylor, '[move] between the AS IF and the IS' and 'between pretend and new constructions of "the real"' (2016: 6, original emphasis).

Through the establishment of a dialogue between performance and care in this edited collection, the contributors consider how socially engaged performance work can enhance our understanding of care as a performed encounter in a wide range of different social and health contexts and, crucially, what this tells us about the caring potential of performance. The chapters that follow offer new interventions within recent debates that address care and the lack of quality care within contemporary societies, while also examining performances that enact a mode of care, as well as those that are uncaring or that fail to establish structures that are attentive to the needs of the other.

Care and its discontents: performing caring in sites of contestation and crisis

As indicated above, we find ourselves in an era when caring labour is increasingly sidelined and undervalued. Furthermore, the sense of an uncaring politics and an uncaring economic system has become pervasive, leading some social commentators, such as the Canadian social activist Naomi Klein, to call for radical change, and for '[a] society where the work of our care givers, and of our land and water protectors, is respected and valued. A world where no one and nowhere is thrown away – whether in firetrap housing estates, or on hurricane-ravaged islands' (2017).

Concerns about the lack of available caregivers today are having far-reaching impacts across the world, leading some to argue that the West is in the midst of a global crisis in health and social care (see Glenn, 2010; Fraser, 2016). Certainly, within the interconnected fields of applied theatre and arts and health, scholars and practitioners have recently begun to address how an engagement with the arts can ameliorate health and well-being in a range of social and settings (see Leonard *et al.*, 2016; Baxter and Low, 2017; Willson and Jaye, 2017). However, while some performance practices are designed to contribute to the process of healing and improved health, what interests the contributors in this edited collection is performance's engagement with care itself and the possibility for certain kinds of performance work to examine the connections and gaps between the processes of caregiving and the experience of being cared for.

In her book *Madness, Art, and Society: Beyond Illness* (2018), theatre scholar Anna Harpin draws attention to some of the deleterious side effects of care. Some medicalised caring practices, she argues, lack humanity and serve ultimately to disempower those being cared for. In her critique of medicalised approaches to the care of people living with mental health conditions, Harpin draws attention to 'the erasure of agency in medical care' and 'the failure of listening and dialoguing in certain current care practices' (2018: 2). Artistic intervention in this context, she argues, 'offers valuable ways of reconsidering the performative, aesthetic, and political implications of how therapeutic encounters and experiences are structured' (2018: 5). For Harpin, then, and for many of the contributors within this edited collection, art possesses the means to break down and rethink the diagnostic models of medicalised care, which, as Harpin argues, tend to be determined by a fixed concept of identity '[implying] this is what you *are*' (2018: 5, original emphasis). Art encourages a shift towards a more dialogic approach, acknowledging the person rather than the condition and 'explores what you are currently *experiencing*' (2018: 5, original emphasis). In this sense, art – and we would suggest certain approaches to performance in particular – humanises what otherwise can be experienced as the transactional, alienating and mechanistic processes of medicalised care. This critique of care has a resonance with the accounts of care that Patrick Anderson describes in his book *Autobiography of a Disease* (2017), where care in 'contemporary medical practice' is often experienced as 'Endless imaging technologies, documentary protocols, interventional procedures and surgeries, occupational training, independent living schemes and countless other social practices gathered under the headings "convalescence" and "recovery"' (2017: viii).

The potentiality for caring practice to be encountered as an uncaring, oppressive or controlling force is an issue that has also been much debated within disabilities studies. For people living with a disability, care can be viewed with some suspicion. Often associated with paternalistic forces, unequal power-based relationships and coercive processes that ultimately delimit the possibilities for autonomous, independent and empowered living, care for many disabled people, as Canadian disability scholar Kelly Fritsch points out, has 'often been a site of oppression, disempowerment, physical and sexual abuse, and negligence' (2010: 3). One reason for this is that within the context of disability, the term 'care' is often associated with 'dependency'. Detached from the possibility of a sense of reciprocity and interdependence, care in this context can be experienced as a transaction where the caregiver and care receiver become eternally trapped in their predetermined roles. In this context, the caregiver has agency and the person with a disability can then feel themselves to be positioned as helpless or even 'burdensome' (Fritsch, 2010: 4). These ideas have been critiqued at length by the care ethicist Eva Kittay, who in her book *Love's Labor: Essays on Women, Equality, and Dependency* (1999), argues for the need to recognise 'dependency' as a state of being shared by everyone at some point in their lives. Rather than perceiving dependency as being relegated to people who are vulnerable or those living with disabilities, Kittay calls for a repositioning of the concept of dependence as a 'feature of the human condition' (1999: 28). As many contributors to the edited collection argue, the process of making performance is always determined by relationships of interdependence and, therefore, performance making can become a means of recognising the value and necessity of interdependent relationships as a critical component of creative endeavour.

Importing the values and practices of care into performance, however, can also become a mode of critique, offering a way of reading and interrogating practices that feel careless or that seem to exploit rather than attend to the suffering of its participants and co-creators. As most of the performance work explored in this edited collection has been developed in collaboration with participants and partners from non-performing arts settings, the discussions of care that emerge must be seen as interdisciplinary and trans-sectoral in nature and relational in structure. In this sense, we see this edited collection as contributing to debates in applied and social theatre by seeking to move discourse in this area on from questions that address the measuring of efficacy and change. Instead, along with many of the other contributors in this edited collection, we pick up on James Thompson's call for an 'end' to the over instrumentalisation of performance in *Performance Affects: Applied Theatre and the End of Effect* (2009) and, rather than focusing on an evaluation of efficacy, this edited collection considers how caring performance can be artful and responsive, and how performance that cares might ultimately contribute to more artful caring processes and more caring societies. The following section of this introduction examines how the labour of caring has been developed in different disciplinary contexts and within some of the chapters in this book and considers how performance might respond to what has been described as a 'deficit' and a 'crisis' of care.

Performing the labour of caring: questions of implications and resistance

In her examination of the caring work of nurses, in *The Emotional Labour of Nursing Revisited: Can Nurses Still Care?* (2012), Pam Smith picks up recent concerns expressed in Britain about the lack of care and compassion in our

National Health Service, particularly in relation to the care of the elderly.[4] Reflecting on whether care is the product of 'labour' or 'love', Smith asks: 'Is it natural or is it a skill? Is it about feelings or tasks? Does it come from the heart, the head or the hand?' (2012: 18). These important questions not only get to the heart of what constitutes effective care in nursing contexts, but also address the structure and experience of care in other contexts, such as when we care for children or when we care for young people or community participants within a drama or dance workshop setting. By raising these questions, Smith asks us to consider whether good care should be understood as a set of skills that can be acquired and taught, or whether it is more to do with the way we emotionally engage with others and the kinds of emotional responses this caring elicits. Arlie Hochschild positions the work of caring for others as a form of hidden emotional labour, where the management of feelings is undertaken 'to sustain the outward countenance that produces the proper state of mind in others [such as] the sense of being cared for in a convivial and safe place' (2012: 7). Adapting Hochschild's research in this area, Smith recognises emotional labour and develops an account of the emotional aspect of nursing care, which she describes as a form of 'emotion work' (2012) that is productive and a fundamental element to good nursing.

The use of 'emotion work' when engaging with others crosses over into socially engaged performance practice that is often undertaken in partnership with vulnerable participant-performers. Writing about the practice of facilitation in applied theatre contexts, Sheila Preston engages with Hochschild's research in her consideration of the 'emotional labour of the facilitator' (2016: 50). Drawing on Hochschild's accounts of 'deep' and 'surface' acting, Preston considers how applied theatre facilitators adopt various performative strategies as a means of 'inducing and producing a playful and positive emotional state in others' (2016: 51). While, of course, facilitation is only one meaning-making process within a participatory performance project, Preston's research usefully draws attention to the complexity and problematics of using emotion work as a drama facilitator, where one must bring 'one's own personhood into the space' (Balfour, 2016: 153). In performances that take place in social or health care settings, the 'personhood' of the facilitators and indeed the performers themselves can be placed under intense pressure as project leaders and participants engage with and respond to the sometimes inadequate caring processes that are present within the particular social, community or medical context in which the project is based.

In this sense, socially engaged performance often finds itself dealing head-on with the lived experiences of individuals and communities who are directly encountering what Hochschild has described as 'care deficits' (2003), a critical moment when 'the *need* for care' has increased 'while contracting the supply of it' (2003: 214, original emphasis). The care deficits emerging in societies across the world today not only point to the lack of care available within the domestic sphere of the home (for older family members or children, for example), but also to the way that caring labour in other sectors of public life (such as education, social work, nursing and medicine) is being persistently devalued and overlooked. The lack of investment in caring infrastructures by governments and a general resistance to acknowledge the value of the caring labour undertaken by low-paid (or unpaid) workers, has led researchers from many different disciplinary contexts to consider the ethical and political implications of this 'crisis of care' (Fraser, 2016).

Performance that engages with different caring processes and settings, or that seeks to enact a mode of care for others, often finds itself involved within a tricky negotiation of the lived experience of participants marked by a *lack* of care and care services that are struggling to make ends meet. This presents socially engaged performance practitioners with a series of complex ethical and political challenges, precisely because these kinds of practices are often positioned as vehicles for overcoming shortfalls of care and for providing (temporary) solutions to this. As Jenny Hughes and Helen Nicholson point out, these kinds of performance practices are often conceptualised 'in ways that serve neoliberalism well' (2016: 4). In this sense, if we position performance as a mode of care for other people, we must also acknowledge the political dimension of this work. We must, as Hughes and Nicholson argue, recognise the need for artists to 'seek out a presence in those networks that complements the resistant practices that are immanent there rather than adopting more acquiescent relations that flatten out practice and reflection' (2016: 4).

For many of the contributors to this edited collection, care has the potential not only to be a form of emotion work but also to enact a mode of resistance. This final section of the introduction now moves on to consider some of the political and ethical dimensions of performance as care before offering some tentative proposals about how we might start to frame the ethico-political dimensions of socially engaged practices that are structured around caring processes.

Performing care: an ethico-political framework for socially engaged performance today

As indicated at the outset of this introduction, this edited collection positions care as being intrinsically bound to performance: first, because care can only be experienced as a live, embodied encounter; and, second, because it is comprised of repeated or 'restored' practices and behaviours. In this sense, care should be understood not as pre-existing the caring encounter, but as becoming itself through the demands of the relationship that emerges between the caregiver and care receiver. Care is, therefore, always situational and relational; but while it is constitutionally formulated through reperformed gestures or caring, it also has value attached to it. As Held explains, '[c]are is not reducible to the behaviour that has evolved and can be adequately captured in empirical descriptions' (2006: 39), rather care describes a set of values to which we, as individuals and as a society, should aspire. Care ethicists are not simply concerned with describing caring practices that already exist in the world 'as they have evolved under actual historical conditions of patriarchal and other domination' (Held, 2006: 39). Rather, care ethicists '[evaluate] such practices and [recommend] what they morally ought to be like' (Held, 2006: 39). In this sense, care 'is not the same as benevolence' but is 'more the characterisation of a social relation' (Held, 2006: 42), promoting a way of thinking and being in the world that determines (caring) action. Furthermore, while care ethics tends to focus on individuated, personal caring encounters, many care ethicists seek to shift personal moral decisions into wider sociopolitical contexts and consider how care ethics can address questions of justice, inequality, and social injustice (Held, 2006; Tronto, 2013; Engster and Hamington, 2015).

The view that care should have a social and political element stands in some contrast to the earlier work of feminist care ethicist Nel Noddings, whose foundational work in the area of care ethics positioned care as intuitive, responsive and intrinsically feminine. In *Caring: A Feminine Approach to Ethics and Moral Education* (2013), Noddings focused her philosophical approach on the voice of the mother whose perspective, she argued, was largely absent from wider discourses around morality and ethics. Up to this point, as Noddings pointed out, ethical theory had 'been discussed largely in the language of the father: in principles and propositions, in terms such as justification, fairness and justice' (2013: 1). However, while the repositioning of debates around morality and ethics into the terrain of the family was very influential to the development of care ethics, Noddings was also criticised for the unproblematised correlations she made between natural caring, femininity and motherhood. This led Noddings, at a later point, to concede that while she 'wanted to acknowledge the roots of caring in women's experience' the term 'feminine' is problematic for the evaluation of care ethics (2013: xiii). Following Held's approach, Noddings advocated the use of the term 'relational' as a better way of describing the shift away from autonomy and the focus on interdependence that care ethicists sought to advocate. Certainly, as care ethics has developed since the 1980s, it has gained further influence with the concepts of relationality and interdependence as a central tenet to new thinking in this area.

One of Noddings' critics was the care ethicist and political theorist Joan Tronto, who, in her book *Moral Boundaries: a Political Argument for an Ethic of Care* ([1993] 2009), proposed a vision 'for the good society' that shifted the focus away from a naturalised concept of the feminine and repositioned the 'moral arguments' around care firmly within 'a *political* context' ([1993] 2009: 3, original emphasis). For Tronto, care is not simply about the moral decisions that emerge within one-to-one personal relationships; rather, she positions it as having a political dimension. Drawing attention to the inequalities of caring labour both at home and beyond, Tronto conceptualises care as being fundamental to social relations, and argues that '[f]or a society to be judged as a morally admirable society, it must, among other things, adequately provide for care of its members and its territory' ([1993] 2009: 126). However, as we have seen, while care is arguably a central 'aspect of human life' (Tronto, [1993] 2009: 157), it is also perpetually devalued. This leads to social injustice in the distribution of caring labour, as Tronto writes: 'Because our society does not notice the importance of care and the moral quality of its practice, we devalue the work and contributions of women and other disempowered groups who care in this society' ([1993] 2009: 157).

The devaluation of caring work ultimately also conceals the problems of care from the very social policies that try to resolve how societies might respond to the current care deficits. Furthermore, the societal tendency to view the labour of care as the domain of only certain types of workers 'means that caring needs are being met through a process that distorts reality and renders care invisible' (Tronto, [1993] 2009: 174) and this ultimately makes it difficult to intervene in some of the problems of care we encounter today. Tronto's account of the invisibility of care also points to neoliberalism's preoccupation with autonomy and freedom and its failure to account for the elements of interdependence that are necessary for a society to thrive and flourish.

In the debates that are developed in the following chapters, the invisibility and the visibility of care emerges as a thematic source of much discussion, particularly in relation to what James Thompson describes as the 'aesthetics of care' that becomes visible and present within certain performance practices and in some medical or social contexts (2015; Chapter 13 this volume). Central to any understanding of an 'aesthetics of care' within performance is the question of spectatorship and the possibility of communicable caring experience. This is debated throughout the edited collection, and contributors consider whether performance can make caring processes more visible, how this might reveal new ways of *thinking* and *doing* care and, critically, whether an engagement with theories of care might lead to the development of more careful and more caring performance practices. The performances of care explored in this edited collection consider the possibility for more careful and more caring social engagements, while generating modes of critique of the uncaring elements of performance processes and of care itself. Taken together, the debates in this edited collection lay the ground for new modes of being together and a growing understanding of how certain performance practices can promote and aspire to a more caring and just society.

The exposition of the edited collection

To help readers navigate this edited collection, we have broken it into four sections. Part I, 'Performing interrelatedness', commences with Chapter 1 by Maurice Hamington who, drawing on theorisation in performance philosophy and care ethics, repositions the relationship between the giver and receiver of care as an encounter of improvisation and rehearsal. By theorising care as 'improvisational moral performance', Hamington argues that the act of caring emerges from the rehearsal and acquisition of 'cognitive and bodily skills' that establish the ground work for a responsible mode of caring on 'behalf of the needs of others'. James Thompson also considers care as a performative, aesthetic encounter in Chapter 2, which originally appeared in *Research in Drama Education: The Journal of Applied Theatre and Performance* in 2015 and is reproduced here with the kind permission of the journal. The ideas explored in Thompson's chapter have been formative to the development of this edited collection and are cited widely within it. Thompson positions 'community-engaged arts work within the framework of care' and invites us to also think about the care performed by medical staff and nurses as both artful and aesthetic. Arguing that 'our tender relations with others' should be understood as 'central to the rationale of many political and art-making projects', Thompson recognises the importance of performance practices that are not based not on autonomy and self-realisation but that acknowledge, value and enhance the relationships of interdependency upon which it depends. In Chapter 3, I consider how the performance of tenderness and mutual care in Fevered Sleep's dance-based performance *Men & Girls Dance* creates moments of resistance to gender-normative stereotyping, inviting audiences 'to imagine a context in which the performance of care in some way replaces, or at the very least challenges, the discourse of anxiety and risk that can frame and predetermine relationships between men and girls'.

The possibility of dance becoming a mode of care is further examined in the first chapter of Part II, 'Care-filled performance', where in Chapter 4 Sara Houston explores a series of dance works by Israeli choreographer Yasmeen Godder. Through the generation of a community dance project with people with Parkinson's disease, Houston argues, Godder established a care-oriented practice that ultimately led to the development of new chorographical innovations 'rooted in relationality, attentiveness and caring'. This relationship between participation and professional practice is a thematic that is also examined by Dave Calvert in Chapter 5, which considers the tensions between participatory performance and directorial innovation in two performance projects where actors with learning disabilities are directed by non-disabled directors. Through an analysis of *Disabled Theater* by Theater HORA and Jérôme Bel and *Contained* by Mind the Gap theatre company, Calvert discusses how 'the dynamics of dependency, equality, interdependence and care' can be embodied or occluded within performance. Concluding Part II is Chapter 6 by New Zealand-based artist researchers Julieanna Preston and Jen Archer-Martin. In their discussion of *bit-u-men-at-work,* a site-specific live art performance created and performed by Preston in 2015, Preston and Archer consider the performance of road care. Positioning this performance as an exploration of the 'durational labour of repairing the cracked, pitted asphalt pavement with bitumen', Preston's and Archer's discussion expands our understanding of the 'affective and gestural qualities of material caring labour' and its relationship to the performance of 'non-human' caring practices.

The problematic of overlooked or deficient care forms the focus of Part III, 'Care deficits'. In Chapter 7, Caoimhe McAvinchey positions Clean Break Theatre as an organisation that not only provides care for women 'who have fallen beyond the reach of state systems of welfare' but that also 'critiques the intersectional oppressions that shape the lives of many women who experience the criminal justice system'. Drawing on the many different strands of the organisation's work, McAvinchey argues that for Clean Break, care becomes 'something that is both structurally planned for *and* responsive' (original emphasis). The possibility for care to enhance social relations and civic engagements also emerges in Chapter 8, where Kathleen Gallagher and Rachel Turner-King examine some key moments in a 'multi-sited, ethnographic research study' that took place across multiple locations in different continents between 2014–18. Reflecting on some of their findings from the UK strand of the project, they discuss their collaboration with the Belgrade Theatre's Canley Youth Theatre and Coventry Youth Services and examine how this research project used performance and oral history practices to explore the lived experience of austerity and cuts in the area. An arts project with young people also forms the focus of Chapter 9, where Ella Parry-Davies considers the relational art-making and care-orientated practices that developed between Lebanese community artist Dima el Mabsout and a group of Syrian refugee children who live on the streets in the Hamra area of West Beirut, selling flowers to survive. Mabsout invited the children to begin to take photographs of their flower-selling labours and, through her examination of this arts-based intervention, Parry-Davies considers Mabsout's emerging arts practice as being rooted in a performance of care that 'evidences the conditions of precarity' the children exist within, while also performing 'relational infrastructures of care that seek to work against this'.

Part IV, 'Care as performance', begins with Chapter 10 by Sylvan Baker and Maggie Inchley, exploring how caring performance practices can become a form of resistance to the precarity of care experienced by young people who are being looked after by the state. In their discussion of *The Verbatim Formula*, Inchley and Baker consider how they use verbatim theatre techniques to intervene in the 'care-less' processes of state care that often leave young people feeling objectified within bureaucratic processes that are antithetical to caring practice. Verbatim theatre methodologies, they argue, 'honour the experiences of care-experienced young people' enabling 'opportunities for self-narration'. Chapter 11 by Matt Jennings, Pat Deeny and Karl Tizzard-Kleister examines an interdisciplinary teaching project developed at Ulster University where drama techniques were adopted to provide 'nurses with a systematic approach to improving the performance of care' across a wide spectrum of different nursing practices. Chapter 12 by visual artist and researcher Jayne Lloyd examines an arts-based project she led at a care home where many of the residents were suffering from dementia. Through her exploration of the performative, aesthetic quality of everyday domestic labour, Lloyd argues that 'the performance of everyday practices in art sessions can provide a space for […] attentiveness', generating openings to more reciprocal caring encounters. Finally, Chapter 13 by James Thompson further considers the possibility for responsible and 'care-filled practice'. Drawing on several contrasting examples of performance practice, Thompson examines the reliance on relationships of dependency and reciprocity within performance making, calling for a practice that forefronts 'inter-human forms of care' and that can lead ultimately to the generation of a 'mutually reliant, less selfish, destructive form of sociality'.

In our contemporary moment, when carelessness and neglect appear to be the dominant mode of political and social action, we hope this edited collection will make a contribution to debates about the importance of arts practice in building and sustaining more equitable, just and caring societies.

Notes

1 Founded in 2015, Phosphoros is a theatre company based in London that makes theatre with actors who are refugees or who are in the process of seeking asylum. For more information see www.phosphorostheatre.com (accessed 07/02/19).

2 Asylum seekers under the age of eighteen are legally entitled to more care than other asylum seekers in the UK because they are children and are therefore considered vulnerable.

3 I am thinking here of the reporting of UKIP MEP Geoffrey Bloom's accusations that many child refugees arriving at Calais were in fact grown men. Bloom and other right-wing politicians called for X-ray dental checks to prove these young people were under the age of eighteen (see Stromme, 2016). For a more detailed account of how negative representation of child refugees emerged in the media, see McLaughlin (2017).

4 For an account of the crisis confronting adult social care in the UK, see Parliamentary and Health Service Ombudsman (2011).

PART I

PERFORMING INTERRELATEDNESS

Care ethics and improvisation: can performance care?

Maurice Hamington

Acting is a gateway to living more. (Zamir, 2014: 17)

The only hope we have of building societies that are peaceful and prosperous for all is to train the members of these societies to respond creatively, rather than fearfully, to the challenge of tradition versus progress, and to see all of the other members of different communities that make up this larger political society as engaged in variations on the same project. (Nicholls, 2012: 5)

This chapter suggests that reimagining the relationship between caregiver and cared for as one of improvisational moral performance can provide the means to not only understand the emergent dynamics and phenomena of care but also reorient our approach to teaching ethics and cultivating ethical behaviour. To accomplish this reimagining, I suggest that care is aligned with 'performance philosophy', a term that I use to denote the use of a framework of reflection that privileges performance and that valorises the aesthetics of what emerges from intentional experiences in the phenomenal world.[1] Although most humans have the capacity to emotionally, cognitively and physically care, we seldom attend to our caring capacities and develop them to their potential. A *caring improvisation* is a moment when we draw upon a set of rehearsed cognitive and bodily skills of enquiry and action to responsively perform care on behalf of the needs of others. Perhaps it seems odd to claim that improvisation is rehearsed, but many elements are indeed practised albeit not in rote or deterministic ways. The learned habit of improvisation is still a habit. All care is ultimately improvisational because we respond to the other in the moment including their needs and circumstances. The label 'caring improvisation' is an effort to focus attention on the seemingly paradoxical combination of skilful and extemporaneous elements of care that emerge in relationship.

How is the term 'performance' defined in this chapter? As Shannon Jackson describes, 'performance' is a highly contested term: 'For some philosophers, performance is an intentional realm of purposive action; for others, it is an unintentional realm of spontaneous or habitual enactment' (2004: 14). In this chapter, caring is described as existing within the tension of Jackson's two poles. Performance, then, as it is used here is any purposeful action taken in front of an audience, even when that audience is only the person taking the action.[2] The analysis offered below is intended to enrich and inform the daily performances of care. Nicholas Ridout describes performance 'as an opportunity to experience an encounter with someone else' (2009: 8). Most of our interpersonal encounters come without a script. The performative and aesthetic aspects of care ethics have received little attention. I contend that care ethics has much to gain from performance philosophy and a focus on improvisation. Although I am endeavouring to comment on everyday uses of care performances, this chapter often draws from stage performance as a source of insight.

Care ethics was born of women's experience and feminist theory in the 1980s as a relational approach to morality that eschewed formulas, abstractions, generalisations and absolutes in favour of valuing particularity, context and emotion. Care ethics reframes the fundamental condition of humanity from one of atomistic agents to that of interconnected beings situated in webs of relationships. Early formulations of care ethics focused on dyadic personal relationships but theorists quickly moved to addressing social and political practices and policies of care. Today, care ethics enjoys intellectual attention across a spectrum of disciplines in both theoretical and applied analysis. The growing adoption of care ethics has resulted in a number of attempts to adapt it to traditional conceptions of ethics. For example, in Stephanie Collins' thorough examination of care ethics, she endeavours to make care palatable to analytic philosophers and claims that care ethics can be captured in abstractions (2015: 3). Of course, the mere fact that we can write about care ethics means that there is a certain amount of abstraction and theorising. However, approaching care ethics from the standpoint of performance and improvisation is to contend that there are elements not entirely reducible to cognitive abstraction. Caring improvisation offers an emphasis on the surprising and untamed aspects of the caring relationship that must be adapted to.

The chapter begins by introducing the reader to the notion of care as embodied performance. This characterisation of care as performance situates care ethics as distinct from traditional moral approaches that tend toward reinforcing cognitive hierarchies within mind–body dualisms. Although embodied care (Hamington, 2004) stands within the intellectual stream of feminist care ethics literature, it emphasises the visceral in a holistic approach to morality. In the second section of the chapter, the significance of improvisational caring is established by challenging the current concept of the moral domain to include methods and practices rather than simply cognitive concepts. The next section of the chapter contends that improvisation can provide a structural framework for caring interactions that are extemporaneous by nature. Accordingly, normativity, or the right thing to do, is understood as emergent within relational experience. Care ethics is offered as providing both a method and a theory here rather than an abstract and a priori moral system. Within an improvisation model, normativity emerges from the performance. The fourth section of the chapter engages performance philosophy and in particular the idea that 'performance thinks' to suggest that performance also 'cares' in creating singular human connections not easily obtainable through cognitive processes. The epistemic and ontological aspects of care are emphasised in this section.

The conclusion of the chapter argues that within the framework of performance philosophy, care ethics reaches its radical potential as a critical theory. As an aesthetic approach care ethics can challenge the hegemony of normative theory as it simultaneously confronts non-caring political policies and practices. In particular, it challenges the primacy of a priori moral structures. In other words, as one who cares, if I recognise that I am improvising, even if I am doing so with great skill, I cannot be complacent or smug in moral knowledge as is the case for the epistemological and ethical certainty found in Western philosophy. Improvisational care implies a more egalitarian approach to the caring relationship just as it suggests humility and mutual respect. Caring improvisation is a means of describing caring practice, broadly construed to include action, reflection and rehearsal. Accordingly, the notion of attention training or rehearsing for *disponsibilité* is explored. Because improvisation is deeply relational and responsive, it requires intentional openness.

Embodied care

> Care is like the air we breathe – we cannot live and survive without it, but it is often invisible and unacknowledged except when it is lacking. (Mayseless, 2016: 3)

Within the dominant forms of modern Western moral theorising, bodies and ethical philosophy generally do not mix. René Descartes went so far as to declare that bodily sensation cannot be trusted, and the only way for a person to know that they exist is through their mind. Despite widespread critique, the Cartesian framework persists. Christianity's notion of the 'sins of the flesh' is symptomatic of a morality that eschews embodiment because it is a source of moral detriment. Sexual revolution notwithstanding, the idea of corporeal sensation leading us astray of ethical ideals also endures. For their part, contemporary philosophers generally favour elaborate normative systems that answer the question 'what is the right thing to do?' in a cognitive exercise that resembles a decision science. Bodies need not participate.

Perhaps surprisingly, the literature of care ethics rarely addresses corporeality as well.[3] Although 'care' is an all too common term, care ethicists use the idea of care in a particular, albeit not unified, manner. What care ethicists agree upon is that care is founded on a relational ontology, which is to say that humans are fundamentally social and relational. This claim is significant because traditional approaches assume atomistic individuals who transact with one another rather than humans who exist and assume their identity from a relational web of people. For example, rights, duties and virtues are often theorised as tied to discrete agents without regard to other human entanglements. Furthermore, care ethics is profoundly contextual. To care is to take into account the rich circumstances of the one cared for. In this manner, care is often tied to moral epistemology because effective care requires particular knowledge of the one in need. Finally, care is effective when there is responsive action. Caring is not enacted unless an actual reaction to explicit and/or implicit needs occurs. The insights of care ethics have attracted worldwide scholarly attention that traverses disciplinary boundaries, nevertheless, embodiment is seldom integrated into the discussion.

Another salient characteristic of care in the contemporary literature is the notion of responsiveness (Noddings, 2010a: 180–204). In the effort to avoid any hint of relativism, most ethical theories do not value responsiveness. However, care ethicists embrace the particularism of responding to the context and needs of individuals. Care is a response to a particular need. Klaartje Klaver and Andries Baart claim that responding with care can be described as 'attending' – presence, listening and understanding (2011: 689–90). We can experientially affirm this phenomenon when we recall how good it feels to be genuinely and deeply listened to. Ends and means are collapsed in the process for preparing for the caring response (i.e. listening, attending), which is itself an act of caring. As Virginia Held describes, 'An ethic of care focuses on attentiveness, trust, responsiveness to need, narrative nuance, and cultivating caring relations' (2006: 15). Similarly, Marian Barnes emphasises care that observes and acts accordingly: 'Being attentive to needs and taking responsibility for making sure that these needs are met in order to enable people to flourish' (2012: 5). In her original work on care, Nel Noddings went so far as to refer to the necessity of attention within care ethics as 'engrossment' (2013). We can understand how important the notion of attention and responsiveness is to care from our own experiences of caring. We do not attribute rich experiences of care to interactions where we are treated superficially or stereotypically. Caring, like improvisation, requires those involved to be abundantly present and to respond accordingly. What goes largely unstated is that all of this attending occurs through the body.

In 2004, I described care as '*an approach to personal and social morality that shifts ethical considerations to context, relationships, and affective knowledge in a manner that can only be fully understood if its embodied dimension is recognized. Care is committed to the flourishing and growth of individuals; yet acknowledges our interconnectedness and interdependence*' (Hamington, 2004: 3, original emphasis). What is not addressed in this definition is temporality and the improvisational character of caring performances, which is the subject of the rest of this chapter. Embodied care resonates with James Thompson's contention that there is an aesthetics of care – a 'sensory ethical practice' (2015: 437). At the most experiential level, all care is received and delivered through the body. Our bodies are the epistemological and imaginative basis for care. We first grasp care through the senses in the satisfaction of needs. As we grow and develop to intellectualise care, the source of understanding remains the body. Many of our metaphors, including those for sympathetically appreciating others, are grounded in schemas of the body: the mapping of the unknown on to bodily experience; i.e. claims that people have moral 'strength' or the person was being a 'pain' (Johnson, 1987). I understand the value of feeding, protecting or comforting someone because I have been fed, protected and comforted. I can conjecture about elaborate social systems that augment care, such as health care or welfare, but ultimately the success or failure of these imagined systems rests with the experience of individual bodies in relation with other bodies. Our bodies not only retain muscle memory, they provide originary metaphors for understanding experience including the experience of others.

To summarise, caring is a holistic and integrated investment of thought, sensation and emotion. Because it lacks the prescriptive a priori baggage of other moral approaches, care ethics is particularly well suited to engage performance philosophy and improvisational theatre in particular. In encounter, the moral domain is confronted and possibly changed by the experience.

Trusting ourselves to redefine the moral domain

Depending upon one's reading of history, our theoretical structures have been in the grip of modernism for several centuries (Aylesworth, 2015). Modernism's manifestation in contemporary theorising is characterised by a quest for certainty, categorical delineation, clarity and control. These are not unusual or unworthy goals given the precariousness of the human condition. We all seek the comfort of certitude and precision. However, the intellectual pendulum has perhaps swung too far in favour of theories that rely too heavily upon abstraction and rule. One such manifestation is in ethical theory, where the reliance on authoritative texts, formulae and ideas has produced moral approaches so far removed from the human experience that we often have to engage in intellectual gymnastics to make sense of them for our complex existence (see, for example, Bauman, 1993; Caputo, 1993). For instance, prohibitions against killing are almost universal and yet a variety of exceptions are often made including for self-defence or war. However, even in battle, not all killing is sanctioned. Although perfectly serviceable in existing moral systems, such prohibitions and their machinations read more like guidelines for adjudication of particular acts rather than anything that addresses the underlying conditions for morality. In legal cases 'mitigating circumstances' are taken into account, however they still serve as assessment techniques rather than proactive moral approaches to ameliorate harm and need. One can easily characterise much of the modernist analytic theorising around ethics as a kind of decision science or game rather than serving the complexity of human moral reality to build a moral environment. I am not claiming that ethical exceptions are wrong or not well intentioned, but they do seem to indicate that human experience is sometimes uncomfortably forced to fit abstract analytic systems.

An active question in philosophy and moral psychology addresses the nature of the 'moral domain'. Typically, the moral domain is understood as including a rational and objective analysis to adjudicate the rightness or wrongness of particular actions. For example, Elliot Turiel defines the moral domain as 'prescriptive judgments of justice, rights, and welfare pertaining to how people ought to relate to each other' (1983: 3). In 'Mapping the Moral Domain', Jesse Graham *et al.* (2011) endeavour to broaden the standard understanding. The authors take an inclusive approach going beyond normative questions of justice, to address spirituality and non-Western characteristics of morality. Based on moral foundations theory, the authors create a questionnaire to gather data on scales of 'harm/care, fairness/reciprocity, in-group/loyalty, authority/respect, and purity/sanctity', labelled the 'Moral Foundations Questionnaire'. They conclude:

> People disagree about the size and content of the moral domain – that is, about what 'morality' means. Researchers therefore need theories that encompass the true breadth of human morality, and they need measurement tools that can detect a broad array of moral concerns. In this article, we presented Moral Foundations Theory as a way of thinking about morality that goes beyond harm and fairness (with inspiration from Shweder *et al.*, 1997). And we presented the Moral Foundations Questionnaire as a reliable, valid, and easy-to-use tool for exploring this expanded moral domain. The MFQ, and its progeny, will be useful for extending, critiquing, and otherwise improving psychology's map of the moral domain. (Graham *et al.*, 2011: 17–18)

This is a useful and informative project that is admirable in many ways, including its recognition of multiple modes of thinking about what moral domain means. However, the concept of 'moral domain' utilised here continues to suggest a container with 'size and content': making morality a thing, separate from humanity yet accessible to us. In this chapter, I am arguing that care, as understood in care ethics theory, is embodied and thus *embedded* in our improvised performances of interaction. Accordingly, the radical implication is that moral normativity is not a domain of items or categories but intimately tied to our relational being that is dynamic and unfolds in each interaction. Performance matters.

In some respects, caring improvisation is about trust. In regard to ethics, Western moral philosophy has indicated that largely, humans cannot be trusted. They are too self-interested to handle moral situations and need some outside help, whether that help is a rubric or a rule or a sanctioned authority. Care ethics is entangled in issues of establishing trust. The care-giver engages in varying degrees of risk in order to care: risk of time, effort and emotional energy. Caring enquiry – the listening and questioning required for the understanding necessary to truly care for another being – is predicated on creating a climate for the exchange of information. Can we learn and train to trust ourselves, our bodies and one another to respond in our moral performances?

Improvisation and emergent normativity

> Solving of problems together; the ability to allow the acting problem to evolve the scene; a moment in the lives of people without needing a plot or story line for the communication; an art form; transformation; brings forth details and relationships as organic whole; living process. (Spolin, 1963: 383–4)

In this section, I concentrate on improvisation as a method of interaction, the performance of which provides a model for caring. The suggestion here is that skilful improvisation is a moral methodology, a way of creatively interacting and responding with openness, enquiry and imagination, such that the right thing to do emerges from engagement with others. This 'emergent normativity' is improvised but not happenstance. Caring action flows from our experience, training and rehearsal and unfolds in the relational circumstance. Within this framing, trust in our performances becomes a source for subverting traditional configurations of moral authority. This chapter asks, what if we trusted our humanity in that moment of confronting the other as much or more than the authority of the socially constructed moral rules (content or domain) we have been taught? What if improvisation was at the heart of a robust relational ethic? This exploration is aligned with what Thompson has described as an 'aesthetic turn in care studies' (2015: 432) to find in improvised performances of care a richness and dynamism that extends beyond modernist approaches that favour the analytic.

The interest here is not merely the passive observation of the trained actor but the integration of improvisation skills and thinking into the lives of caring human beings. Perhaps just as significant as the interplay of bodies, improvisation has a creative function. As Naphtaly Shem-Tov describes, improvisation is the heart of creativity: 'There is no creative process if there are only known procedures' (2015: 36). Something new and unique is generated in each improvisation. In this sense, the improvisation performance 'thinks': offering novel phenomena for audience consideration. The improvisation spectacle exists at the nexus of intention and unintention; the known and the imagined.

It is striking how many definitions of improvisation are expansive beyond merely describing stage performance. We can see Spolin's definition above offers both stage and non-stage elements. John Hodgson and Ernest Richards claim that improvisation is a form of cognition: 'Improvisation is a means of training people to think. It aims at the inculcation of clear mental habits and training of the expression of these thoughts in a concise and orderly way. Because it places people in a human situation involving other people, it calls for fairly quick thinking and at times for different levels of thought at one and the same time' (1966: 22–3). Anthony Frost and Ralph Yarrow offer a skill-based characterisation of improvisation: 'The skill of using bodies, space, imagination, objects and all human resources to generate or to reformulate a coherent physical expression of an idea, a situation and a character (even, perhaps, a text); to do this spontaneously, in response to the immediate stimuli of one's environment, without pre-conceptions' (2016: xv). In *Theatrical Improvisation, Consciousness, and Cognition* (2013), Clayton Drinko explores several of the important schools of improvisation and how their theories mesh with developments in neuro-science and philosophy. He notes how Spolin thought her students could bring their improvisation skills into their everyday lives. Drinko concurs with Spolin, suggesting that improvisation may 'open up people to stronger identity formation, more empathy, and changes and changes in conscious-ness where time, memory, and space can all be altered [...] improv and the mind is a topic about empathetic social interactions as much as it is theatre' (2013: 9). This is a crucial notion for our purposes. Although improvisa-tion by professional actors offers an outstanding model, the concern of this chapter is an inclusive notion of improvisation: adopting the skills and dis-position of improvisation in our everyday lives to serve human flourishing, which is often called 'care'. Improvisation describes the reality of the care experience: robust care is always a form of extemporaneous action. There must be the performance of enquiry, imagination and risk.

The taxonomies of improvisation characteristics are many and varied. One possible description of improvisation is that it entails underlying inten-tion, playfulness, risk, responsiveness, action and communication. These six elements are used to describe the foundation for serviceable care including its epistemology, ethics and psychology. 'Underlying intention' indicates that improvisation is not pure spontaneity, but rather it is driven by a relational commitment toward a goal such as entertainment, dramatic preparation or, as in the present context, care. Improvisation uses the actor's skill in service of a goal as caring applies the caregiver's proficiency in responding to need. 'Playfulness' describes the creative and innovative aspect of improvisa-tion. Caring often involves problem solving and playfulness represents the requisite novelty of thought. Improvisation entails 'risk' as one commits to the character and circumstances created. Caring relationships also involve risk because one does not always know the physical and emotional labour that caring will require. The one cared for must also risk to admit vulner-ability and share information if the care is to be valuable. 'Responsiveness' is an essential part of improvisation and care. It is in responsiveness where performance catalyses knowledge creation. Without depth of contextual-ised knowledge, care is superficial and possibly misguided. Improvisation also includes expressive 'action'. Care without action is simply disposition, which lacks ethical import. Felt concern is 'nice' but unless it manifests into responsive caring enactment, it has accomplished very little. Finally, improvisation communicates and is expressive. Similarly, care conveys both explicit and tacit information between the caregiver and the one cared for. Improvisation implies a high degree of awareness in the moment rather than 'going through the motions'. Caring improvisation is an engaged activity of personal effort and investment. Taken altogether, the improvisation framework can be utilised to understand care ethics as a set of skills that can be actualised when called upon.

Given the desire to understand care ethics in terms of improvisation, it is not surprising that care is described here as a responsive function of both mind and body, or perhaps more appropriately, head, heart and hand. Our bodies provide the fodder for imaginatively and creatively understanding others. Our corporeality, including our senses and comportment, is the grounding of metaphor and the basis of empathy. As Roberto Ciulli describes:

> With the mind, everything does go much more quickly, but the path from the mind to the heart, to experience to life, that is the difficult process. Acting renders this process possible, it is precisely this path which improvisation opens up. For what one has understood only at the level of the understanding is of no use in life. Through acting I can reach the point where I myself determine how I behave towards myself and others and where I take the decisions. That is more than understanding, it is performing actions. And that is why I believe that acting in the theatre in this way is one of the most important methods of practising for life. (Quoted in Bartula and Schroer, 2003: 55)

In the quotation above, Ciulli claims a high degree of agency for the improviser: 'I myself determine how I behave towards myself and others.' Embodied care shares this notion in something that can be referred to as 'emergent normativity'.

To care is not only to improvise what to do, it is to determine the moral parameters that unfold in the given situation. As such, the caregiver is humble before the one cared for and their context. The lack of a priori systems in care ethics should not be seen as a negation of normativity altogether. Care offers a moral approach or moral trajectory without the need for strict abstract prescriptive detail: I can care for you but I best determine what form that care takes once I know your circumstances and expressed needs. Similarly, an actor may know they will engage in improvisation but not know the make-up of that improvisation until the parameters are revealed. As performers who engage in improvisation must trust themselves in the moment of the performance, improvisational care suggests that one cannot simply bring a predefined moral domain to the performance. Care provides an open-ended telos or notion of the good in caring but the nature of that good is always responsive, adaptive, reacting. Such an approach should not be confused with relativism. Responsiveness in service of human flourishing is the measuring stick of care. Circumstances cannot lead me to determine that beating someone is for their own good or that opposing same-sex marriage contributes to the caring and flourishing of individuals. If care ethics is not relativistic, neither is it purely abstract or formulaic. Caring is the disposition and trajectory that guides moral interaction but never in a deterministic manner. There is always an element of improvisation in responding to the needs of others in a meaningful way. Robust and individualised care is always emergent. Performance philosophy elevates the moment and experience of performance as if it were an entity or a creative phenomenon beyond and somewhat autonomous from the sum of its parts.

If performance 'thinks', can it also care?

> To act, to think, to speak 'without delay', such urgency requires the skills of an improviser, a performative, intellectual, and rhetorical agility that does not await the arrival of a thought that in all of its fullness can be attached to a methodology that would only then launch a thought process that carries its origin along with it like a lead weight. (Peters, 2009: 154)

Performance philosophy provides a lens of analysis (as well as an 'anti-analysis' – a way of being and appreciating that is not merely more analysis) that can highlight the similarities between robust acts of care and improvisation.

Laura Cull succinctly describes performance philosophy 'as an emerging field of research concerned with the myriad potential conceptualisations and enactments of the relationship between philosophy and performance, including drama' (2013: 499). More specifically, Cull finds performance philosophy in conflict with the traditional hierarchy of intellectual understanding regarding philosophy and performance:

> Precisely by erasing 'the &' between Performance and Philosophy that prompts a renewed attention to their relation particularly insofar as it allows for the possibility of seeing performance as philosophy: as equally capable, as traditional forms of philosophy, of doing philosophical work; and more radically still, perhaps, as the site of new kinds of thinking that present a challenge to Philosophy's sense of itself as *The* discipline licensed to determine what counts as thought. (2015: 2)

In her subsequent work, Cull argues that performance 'thinks'. What Cull means by this is that performance not only creates something but 'it is *performance itself* that is doing the philosophy' (2015: 8, original emphasis). Tony Fisher helps explicate the idea of performance thinking and teaching by describing performance as an 'event of thought' (2015: 178) every bit as valuable and meaningful as philosophy. Cull and Fisher critique the modernist intellectual hierarchy (an extension of the Cartesian mind–body hierarchical dualism) of performance over philosophy. Accordingly, philosophy is the authority and performance is an object of theoretical application. Fisher recognises that more than an intriguing new intellectual field, performance philosophy may proffer a revolution in how we regard the relationship between experience and theory, including how we view ethics. His claims are nothing short of postmodern in character: performance philosophy is 'irreducible to the particular' and a 'hypothesis of the *revolt* of thought: a revolt that brings thinking back from its transcendental and normative pretensions, and its flirtation with power, to its properly democratic dimension, as the thought of the one and the "anyone"' (Fisher, 2015: 182, original emphasis). Care ethics often seems misplaced and uncomfortable within the parameters of traditional moral theory. Performance philosophy offers care ethics a radical intellectual framework that matches the postmodern approach to normativity suggested here.

In exploring the notion of whether performance can care, the work of Nicholas Ridout is particularly instructive. In a clever play on words, Ridout opens *Theatre and Ethics* with the simple question 'How shall I act?' (2009: 1). This is not just a question of dramatic performance but it restates the classic question of Western moral philosophy. Ridout concludes with an aporia: 'Theatre's greatest ethical potential may be found precisely at the moment when theatre abandons ethics' (2009: 70). On the intellectual journey that Ridout curates, he establishes that performance spawns both sympathy (2009: 34), an ability to feel with others, but the critical distance of reflexivity (2009: 36). Drawing from Levinas, Ridout suggests that explicit ethical content is not needed for a performance to be moral (2009: 69). It is in deeply engaging with the relationships within a performance that morality emerges. By extension, performance does not require the overt ethical content of a philosophical treatise to offer rich moral insight. Similarly, although the number of books about care ethics has burgeoned, there is an aesthetic quality to care that defies explicit articulation. It may be that performance captures care in ways that words cannot.

Particularly pertinent to the discussion of improvisational care are the notions of immanence and ontological participation. Cull draws from the work of Deleuze in developing her notion of attention training (2011: 82). Although traditional philosophy has emphasised transcendence in the primacy of theory, the idea that performance thinks refers to an unmediated experience of reality. Similarly, caring improvisation is responsive in the moment without the mediation of a prescribed moral outcome. Cull makes the broad claim:

> One implication of this affirmation of immanence, in Deleuze at least, is a resistance to any ontological separation of thought and being (or subject and object), which in turn, proffers the possibility of a direct (rather than always-already mediated) encounter with the real. More broadly then, an immanent perspective also suggests that there is no ontological basis for a separation or hierarchy between the nature of body and mind, self and others, human and nonhuman, words and things, theory and practice and so forth. (2011: 82)

Our embodied connections that are the basis for care require the ability to traverse the alterity of other minds/bodies reinforced by this immanent approach. As Cull describes, Deleuzean immanence resides in tension. Although there is no separation, our existence participates in difference (2011: 82). Such a notion is essential to care. To responsively care is to find connection *but across difference.* The attention, enquiry and engrossment of care must confront the difference of the other to create the activity of caring. Perfect alterity and perfect identity are two poles that do not exist. Having ultimate knowledge of the other would render care unnecessary (or at least incredibly easy). If the other was an unknowable other or ineffable, then care is impossible. Because as an immanent phenomenon, performance thinks, by extension, it also cares through confronting others in the moment. Because care and knowledge are such intimate companions, it is difficult to discuss one without the other.

The 'thinking' or the knowledge generated by relational performance is the foundation of caring. Knowledge and caring go hand in hand as has been described by many authors (Dalmiya, 2002; Puig de la Bellacasa, 2012; Code, 2015). Care ethics reintegrates emotion in the form of motivational displacement or empathy with its basis in enquiry. Given Cull's notion of performance thinking, María Puig de la Bellacasa offers a particularly apt notion of 'thinking with care' that she describes as 'a style of connected thinking and writing that troubles the predictable academic isolation of consecrated authors by gathering and explicitly valorising the collective webs one thinks with' (2012: 202). Although Puig de la Bellacasa does not use the term 'emergent normativity', she problematises traditional understandings of normativity by describing care as a singularity, much like performance, it offers something unique: 'Care is a good word to exhibit the singularity of the non-normative ethics carried here. Not only because caring is always specific – a mode of caring is not necessarily translatable elsewhere – but because it cannot be reduced to a moral disposition, nor to an epistemic stance, a set of applied labours, not even to affect' (2012: 211).

To reiterate, caring improvisation is a set of mental and physical habits activated when circumstances of perceived need call for it. In leaving the definition of performance philosophy undetermined, Cull offers that it might be the enactment of the immanent, an embodied attitude or act of pluralism open to continuous revisioning, or a practice of openness (2014: 33). It is the latter idea that we conclude with.

Conclusion: caring improvisation and rehearsing for disponibilité

> It is rehearsing *itself* that must be rehearsed; the very act of rehearsing – as
> a life-long task – bespeaks a decisive commitment far more significant that
> the choices made while rehearsing or performing. Without 'contracting' the

> habit of rehearsing, the 'contemplation' necessary for the habitual to become transformative and 'make a difference'. (Peters, 2017: 147, original emphasis)

In this final section, I suggest that a notion of 'caring improvisation' frames a moral activity of life-long skill development through humble openness to the other. Our bodies and minds have the capacity to care, but the habits must be honed to care with proficiency. Accordingly, the contention here is that despite its extemporaneous appearance, one can indeed rehearse for improvisational care. For example, when I take public transport, I never know what experience will manifest from the close proximity to others. I have variously experienced individuals yelling, weeping quietly, requesting money, engaging in pleasant conversation, etc. I cannot prepare myself to be caring for every expressed need that arises from engaging another human being. However, I can prepare or rehearse an architecture of caring skills including physical, emotional and intellectual habits that not only help me navigate the performance of care but also influence who I am and how I subsequently address others.

First, a note on terminology. I use the terms 'rehearse' and 'practice' interchangeably; however, some theorists (Peters, 2017: 145–7) have ascribed particular parameters to these terms. The important distinction to be made is between preparing for a performance that is a rote replication of what was practised and preparing for a performance that will improvise within the context. Peters describes: 'At its most radical (if that's the right word) practice can create a practice that is self-aware enough and agile enough to outwit the habitual' (2016). It is this form of agile practice that I am referring to when I describe rehearsing for caring improvisation. An authentically caring performance is one that is capable of adapting to the circumstances with deft enquiry and responsive action.

Cull, in the process of defining what makes performance philosophy distinct from conventional philosophy, emphasises both attention and collaboration – two ideas that are also crucial to care (2015: 12–15). Attention participates in how performance thinks but it entails an openness to novelty: 'Attention is not about a decision to think harder, look harder about X; rather attention occurs when an unexpectedly forces us to think anew' (Cull, 2015: 14). Here, she is emphasising the fluidity and openness of attention rather than a routinised focus. Important for my argument regarding preparing for improvisational care is Cull's subsequent discussion of 'attention training'. Drawing upon the work of Deleuze, Allan Kaprow and Henri Bergson, Cull offers attention training as a mindful way of being in the world through 'exercises that affirm our ontological participation in immanence' (2011: 91). Without explicit reference, Cull is offering a kind of preparation for caring improvisation through embodied and intellectual habit development. Although perhaps not with the same theoretical foundation as Cull, Jacques Lecoq developed a similar understanding of the significance of attention training in his performance practice.

Lecoq is an important figure in modern Western theatre having founded what is now known as the School of International Theatre in Paris. His teaching emphasised physicality and movement. Among his important acting themes was *disponibilité*, which he described as 'a state of discovery, of openness, of freedom to receive' (2000: 38). Although the term does not translate precisely into English, Jennie Gilrain indicates that Lecoq uses the term *disponibilité* to mean 'available, open, present, listening, sensitive, pliable, flexible, and ready' (2016: 130). Simon Murray suggests that what Lecoq asks for in terms of *disponibilité* may not appear that much different than other dramaturgical approaches, but Lecoq emphasises a whole-body openness and readiness rather than simply a cognitive disposition (Murray, 2004: 70). Co-founder of the Pig Iron Theatre Company, Gabriel Quinn Bauriedel describes how Lecoq sought personal integrity around the notion of *disponibilité* and challenged those around him to embody this openness:

> Lecoq charged his students and, indeed, himself to stay disponible. First and foremost, this was a deep belief about theatre; that its innate power comes from its ability to pose questions rather than answering them, and to activate an audience's imagination. But it was also a way of living, a way of absorbing the world and staying available to the contemporary moment […] To be disponible was to move, to be curious, and to be alive. It was the opposite of stuck, fixed, inert, dead. (2016: 358)

Bauriedel's last few sentences are particularly pertinent. Caring improvisation implies a nimble ethics that is humble and open to experience. *Disponibilité* is not a passive stance but one that is assertively engaged with enquiry from a position of active openness. To effectively care, one must paradoxically be both respectful and truly hear the other (thus humble) and simultaneously vigorously involve oneself with the other (thus proactive). Noddings describes the declaration 'I am here for you' (2002: 26) as indicative of a caring disposition, which resonates with how *disponibilité* is described. However, Noddings adds that there must be consistency in the claim. The implication is that 'I am here for you now and in the future'. To care is to establish something of an enduring relationship. It is more than a one-time performance or improvisation of care. Accordingly, care suggests that a series of improvisations will occur in a similar trajectory, creating a relationship of trust and *disponibilité*.

Whether it be training for attention or for *disponibilité*, rehearsing for improvisational care suggests a more embodied and holistic approach to moral education that shifts the normative authority away from a priori structures to a method or practice that integrates the self with the immanent. Greater empathy and understanding and, of course, more care, are in the offering if we take our relational performances seriously. Ultimately, life is an improvisation and as Caputo declares, 'one is rather more on one's own than one likes to think, than ethics would have us think' (1993: 4). We can offer others unskilled, unreflective moral performances or we can do better by developing our *disponibilité* and caring responses. As skilled performers, we can learn to trust ourselves to see the emergent caring norms of a situation and respond accordingly.

Notes

1 The boundaries of what constitutes performance philosophy are contested. According to the Performance Philosophy website: 'What counts as Performance Philosophy must be ceaselessly subject to redefinition in and as the work of performance philosophers. Performance Philosophy could be: the application of philosophy to the analysis of performance; the philosophy of performance and/or the performance of philosophy; the study of how philosophers and philosophical ideas have been staged in performance or how ideas and images of performance have figured in philosophy; the theoretical or practical exploration of philosophy as performance and/or as performative; and likewise, experiments emerging from the idea that performance is a kind of philosophy or thinking or theorising in itself. But it could also be much more besides' (see https://performancephilosophy. ning.com/page/about, accessed 28/02/18).
2 One might argue that actions taken alone do not normally qualify as performances. However, even when we are alone there is an audience. Humans have the ability to be both the *subject*, or agent of action, as well as the *object* of our own perception and reflection. We are always our own actor and audience. In discussing the ethical work of Adam Smith, Nicholas Ridout describes, 'each of us carries within us an "impartial spectator"' (2009: 35).
3 There are a few examples of embodiment being addressed in the care literature including Hamington (2004) and Kittay (2013). For example, Eva Kittay interprets this statement of caring presence as having a distinctly embodied form: 'I will posit that the body to whom one gives care is itself a place, and moreover that it constitutes a here for the caregiver' (2013: 206).

2

Towards an aesthetics of care

James Thompson

> [B]y focusing on care, we focus on the process by which life is sustained; we focus on human actors acting. (Robinson, 1999: 31)

In 2012, my colleague Antoine Muvunyi, a drama worker from eastern Democratic Republic of the Congo (DRC), lived in Manchester with my family and me for over six months. He survived an incident in which seven of his co-workers and friends had been killed and spent his time in the UK having surgery and physiotherapy on his injured elbow. The chapter that follows, and the orientation it proposes, makes sense only in light of caring for and observing the care for Antoine. It is an enquiry into the possible shape of *an aesthetics of care*, drawn from the collision of professional practice, personal politics and domestic circumstances that inevitably occurred when a Congolese drama worker, with whom I had conducted theatre workshops in the DRC, ended up sharing my house. The political, ethical and ultimately intimate challenge this made forced me to rethink the boundaries of my practice. There is no claim in this writing that the experience was in any way easy, heroic or exemplary. It was in different ways and at different times inspiring, moving and challenging for my family and myself. But ultimately it taught me very directly that if I failed in this call to take care of a colleague, then the ethics – and as I will go on to argue here aesthetics – of my professional work was worth very little.

I had worked with Antoine and his colleagues on teacher training, girls' education and community theatre programmes for over five years. This work was based in the particularly conflict-affected South Kivu province of eastern DRC and was a partnership between Children in Crisis, a non-governmental organisation (NGO) based in London, and a Congolese organisation called Eben-Ezer Ministry International (EMI). In a broader school building and teacher development programme, sponsored by Comic Relief among others, my responsibility had been to train local community animators in interactive and participatory theatre techniques so that they could subsequently create performances on the subject of girls' education and women's rights. EMI believed that by encouraging communities not to discriminate against girls in access to schooling and challenging the common assumptions about early marriage, the overall mission to improve educational attainment in the area was more likely to be successful. The programme was developed across the inaccessible and poorly served High Plateau region of the province, and my visits had involved working with Antoine on the theatre training courses, watching performances and offering support to a local young people's arts organisation that was a key supporter of the work.

The project frequently met the obstacles faced by any initiative working in a conflict zone, and particularly in the unpredictable region of eastern DRC. This came to a head in October 2011, when a vehicle with the overall project manager, several teacher trainers and other passengers was attacked by a militia group on its way to a training course. Those members of the team that were identified as belonging to the Banyamulenge ethnic group were selected from the travellers and killed by either gun or machete. Antoine was shot in the arm, but luckily escaped with his life. The driver, project director and two teacher trainers from EMI were killed, along with the young sister of the organisation's cook, the elder father-in-law of the driver and another associate. My reunion with Antoine in a military hospital when I visited for the funerals, and an elaborate sequence of events too complex to narrate here, led to him arriving in Manchester for surgery and rehabilitation at the end of 2011. The first month and during the initial operation, he was accompanied by the director of EMI, but then he remained for a further five months of post-operative physiotherapy and another operation on the mobility of his fingers. He arrived with no movement in his right arm and the long-term prospect of losing it altogether and left with increasing movement in his reconstructed elbow and some tentative articulation in the fingers of his hand. We accompanied him through the orthopaedic and plastics operation, the post-operative frailty, the agonising physiotherapy and slow recuperation. His endurance, good humour and flashes of mourning for his colleagues then became a stable part of a family routine of work, hospital visits, cooking/eating, occasional wound dressing and restful afternoons of indulging a mutual passion for watching football.

While care was distributed around many people during these six months, the two main health workers – the plastic surgeon and the specialist physiotherapist – became key points of inspiration behind the argument that will be made here. My family, friends in the local community, members of a local church and the team at the hospital all became a network of care around Antoine. The way this care was exercised by these different constituent groups suggested very directly that care is enmeshed in questions of ethics – as will be outlined below. However, it was the proximity I had to the relationship of care between the professional physiotherapist and her patient that was the primary spur to the argument that is sketched here. Antoine required at first daily exercise on the joints in his shoulder, elbow, wrist and individual fingers. This was extraordinarily painful and needed a clarity of purpose, mutual respect, intimacy and quality of touch that I found breath-taking. The relationship that developed and the tireless, joint-by-joint work was intense and demanded a kind of eyeball-to-eyeball trust between patient and carer. My wife and I found ourselves using the same word as we struggled to capture the quality of this relationship: independently of each other, we referred to it as *beautiful*. We, thus, both used aesthetic criteria to judge the exceptional in this example of care. We were drawn to some quality in the touch, the attentiveness and the focus of the relationship that demanded to be appreciated using a language more usually associated with artistry.

At the end of this chapter, I will return to how the notion of the *art of care* appears in nursing studies in order, tentatively, to suggest that the argument is directed at a social care audience as well as a more familiar arts practitioner and researcher community. These concluding remarks will also suggest that the fact that the treatment of Antoine was done outside normal processes of institutional care (paradoxically for *free* in a *private* hospital) indicates some possible issues with the contemporary dynamics of quality health and social care practice in relation to the case that I am making for an aesthetic turn in care studies. The point to emphasise, however, is that the experience of hosting my colleague Antoine started a process of researching how ethical challenges and aesthetic questions might be usefully considered in light of this area of practice and research. The remainder of this chapter is, therefore, my first attempt to explore the significance of a new focus on care: what relevance an aesthetics centred around this term might have for my more familiar research and practice territory of applied theatre, community-based performance and participatory arts. The argument of this chapter is that this might provide a different way of thinking about the work, but also a new orientation to the practice and the political ambition of that practice.

While we all experience care and many have been called to care, both the institutional and private practices of care tend to be marginalised, gendered and devalued. Similarly the public world of campaigns for justice and rights – for example, a girl's right to education – are too frequently assumed to be detached from a world of caring, which is downgraded as either a personal matter or a concern for under-funded public bodies. The argument here seeks to overcome a tendency in the literature that I discuss later to bifurcate a world of public justice and private care, with a case suggesting the productive connection of these supposed separate spheres. Intimate care, I believe, can be connected to an affective solidarity and felt sense of justice, and ultimately might be foundational to the ethics and aesthetics of a theatre and arts practice that seeks to engage with communities. The remainder of the chapter aims to make this case. First, it will outline the field of feminist ethics called *ethics of care*, to illustrate the claim that care ethics is vital for understanding any claims to justice. The chapter will end with an outline of what an aesthetics of care may look like in the preparation, execution and exhibition of projects, and finally return to the process of caring for Antoine.

In looking to base community-engaged arts work within the framework of care, I hope to expand its radical potential rather than reduce it. Rather than dismiss the incident of a colleague drama worker living in my house as the unfortunate intervention of the professional into my personal life, I seek to challenge the very categories and suggest the 'professional' cannot be sustained ethically without a commitment to the potential for it to blur dynamically with the personal. This work, therefore, forms part of what Bourriaud called 'an angelic programme' (2002: 36), where the intimate and interpersonal, rather than be ignored, are acknowledged as an important source of our politics. This is not something to be elided or overcome, but should be accepted and perhaps welcomed. While there will be a critique of Bourriaud's relational aesthetics in the work that follows, I am accepting his perspective that making art could be a 'proposal to live in a shared world' (2002: 22). This, in turn, suggests a rethinking of some existing community-based theatre practices.

Ethics of care

We have all experienced care, perhaps of varying quality, in order to grow and enter adulthood. Of course since this early experience, many adults might also have taken on caregiving roles supporting others, whether children and other family or friends, or patients and clients, and similarly they might have been cared for in major ways because of complex illnesses or in less substantial ways through the minor challenges many face throughout life. While *care* appears to need an adjective to endow it with value – so we receive good care, thoughtful care and so on – it often has positive value in its verbal form without adverb support. So 'I care' or 'she cared for her son' suggest positive attributes whether done for duty, love or payment. Care thus hovers between a descriptive category with no inherent moral quality, to a normative one that implies it is a proscription of the positive values found within caring per se. The claim here is that this descriptive/normative ambiguity enables care to be considered as a source for questions of ethics, but in choosing to use it in this way, we locate these debates in a particular relational zone of human interaction with which we are all at least somewhat familiar.

So care is important because it is 'part of everyone's life' (Philips, 2007: 169) but also because it simultaneously raises issues of value and practice. Care suggests, according to Judith Philips, a range of meanings including 'affection, love, duty, well-being, responsibility and reciprocity', which are then demonstrated through 'touch, action, emotion and bodily expression' (2007: 1). This combination of values and practices has become central to the field emerging from feminist ethics called the 'ethics of care'

(Robinson, 1999; Hamington, 2004; Held, 2006; Slote, 2007), which in its earliest form, exemplified by foundational work from Carol Gilligan (1982) and Nel Noddings (2013), sought to challenge conceptions of ethics based on justice and rights, with an ethics based on the values central to the way humans care for each other. While focused on close relationships between people, the claim is that what might have been relegated to a private realm and therefore assumed not to be a concern for public ethics is in fact an important area of ethical concern. The private space, it was argued, is a crucial site of ethical behavior, and the public realm needs to include attention to the importance of the caring relations between people. Rather than situate ethics solely within a vision of the individual rational actor operating in public, care ethics analysed the connections between people, so that 'a caring person will cultivate mutuality in the interdependencies of personal, political, economic, and global contexts' (Held, 2006: 53).

The 'ethics of care' frequently sets itself against an 'ethics of justice', offering a different basis from which to debate and question issues of positive action and a search for a more equitable society. An ethics of justice became shorthand in the care literature for different moral philosophies of the European Enlightenment which in themselves have different traditions and orientations. While early writers in care ethics, particularly in the work of Noddings and Gilligan, tended to essentialise differences between justice and care in gendered terms – so care is associated with 'mothering' and justice belongs to a public 'masculine' world – more recent work, notably that of Jean Tronto ([1993] 2009), Marian Barnes (2006) and Maurice Hamington and Dorothy Miller (2006), creates a more nuanced account of care as a habit that is learnt and practised in different ways and to different effects across varied settings, and these in turn inevitably blur distinctions between the private and public. While ethics of care challenges the vision of the autonomous actor as the sole source of ethics and questions the idea that it is through the defence of individual autonomy that the best source of protection and promulgation of a just society is found, in more recent writing justice and care become imbricated rather than oppositional (notable in the work of Hamington, 2004; and Tronto, 2013). The key point for the argument here is that care ethics draws attention to our reciprocal relations with others, or reliance on others, as a source of ethical enquiry. It does not reject justice, but instead calls into question 'the individualist, atomistic ontology, the liberal-impartial view of persons as "generalized" rather than "concrete", and the concomitant reliance on abstract moral principles' (Robinson, 1999: 25).

While I am wary of the danger of essentialising caring as a particular practice of women, Michael Slote's critique of the 'traditional masculine thinking in terms of justice, autonomy, and rights' (2007: 2) does point out that the preference for morality drawn from the rational, has historically been a validation of a very particular rational *man*. The ethics of care sees autonomy as partly illusionary, fostering the myth that 'society is composed of free, equal, and independent individuals who can choose to associate with one another or not' (Held, 2006: 14). Instead, care ethics values real attachments between individuals and groups, where there is a felt responsibility for the other and concomitant commitment to aid that other. These close relationships become the source of a morality that starts from valuing certain dispositions to the other, whether it be love, affection or trust, and then viewing positive caring relations as a source for concepts of justice that might be relevant beyond the interpersonal. Care ethics thus deliberately refuses a boundary between private realm and public, to argue that 'the values of trust, solidarity, mutual concern, and empathetic responsiveness' (Held, 2006: 15) can be the source of ethical behaviour between groups and within wider society. As Robinson argues, care ethics should not be viewed as a parochial concern: it is 'relevant not only to small-scale or existing personal attachments but to all levels of social relations and, thus, to international or global relations' (1999: 2). More recent writing on care ethics (Barnes 2006; Myers 2013; Tronto 2013) has thus tried to emphasise the way care ethics can contribute to debates that are more assertively tied to questions of social policy and no longer 'start at home' to paraphrase the title of Noddings' second major book (2002). Put more simply by Slote, this is the belief that 'someone who cares deeply or genuinely about someone else is open and receptive to the reality – the thoughts, desires, fears, etc. – of the other human being' (2007: 12). Care ethics, then, suggests we can learn about seeking justice and a practice that urges a fairer world from relationships where we are called to care for or have experienced the care of some other: where our interdependence and reciprocal needs are highlighted.

It is best, therefore, not to see the ethics of care as somehow opposed to an ethics of justice, but as a mode of enquiry that seeks to draw attention to interdependent human relations as a platform from which to enunciate broader conceptions of justice. The political aspirations for a fairer world should draw on the realisation that we are mutually reliant and that a better world cannot come about without a closer awareness of our reciprocal attachment to others. This is, in many ways, an extension of the post-Second World War Levinasian challenge to the preoccupation of ethics with the self and a reorientation of our attention to the 'face of the other' (Levinas, 1969) and similarly Simon Critchley's account of our lack of autonomy as a source of drawing universal claims from the interpersonal (2007). This shift is well summarised by Nicholas Ridout as an ethical position that 'encourages the spectator to stop seeing performance as an exploration of his or her own subjectivity and, instead, to take it as an opportunity to experience an encounter with someone else' (2009: 8). Writers on care ethics have extended this by adding a focus on the processes by which these inter-human connections might be realised. So, the activity of caring and being cared for need to develop from an 'engrossment' (Noddings, 2013: 9) or 'attentiveness' (Tronto, 2013: 34) that can translate to a sensitivity to those communities who are unattended or excluded. As Joan Tronto has so ably analysed, this is not inevitable (as Levinas' 'call of the face' might suggest) but needs to be considered in relation to a contemporary world where care has moved 'out of the household' to being a crucial issue within public policy (2013: 6). The ethics of care, therefore, should also be understood as a critique of a society where the habit of caring for others is devalued, placed at the whim of the market and radically under-resourced. The domination of an individualised ethic of self realisation, where a person is deemed free when able to act unencumbered by debilitating social constraint, has, I would argue, resulted in a society where neglect of others is both inevitable and also seen as positive. 'Striding out on your own' as an autonomous rational choice, becomes valued to a greater degree than deep awareness of our interdependence. This is not to say that caring responsibilities are distributed fairly, and Tronto's work in particular indicates the inequalities of care that arise as part of the 'professionalization of nurturant care' (2013: 2). Care ethics recognises and includes a critique of both the quality and quantity of care and is best understood as a proposal: the focus on care reveals a normative plea for a better and more caring world. It is a direct commentary on what might be called an ethics of neglect, which has resulted in a *careless society*: one in which there is a lack of solidarity between individuals (see Amin, 2012), where being apathetic and unmotivated is championed against caring about issues and causes, and one where disregard for the wider environment has meant our world is discarded rather than sustained. *Carefree* as a social good has meant that *careless* (in all senses) has become a defining value. This is not to argue against a desire to break free from stifling interpersonal constraints, but to posit that that desire in itself can be understood as a critique of the quality and attentiveness of care and should not be used to dismiss the benefits of mutual reliance per se.

It is important to note that an argument for care is not meant to be a naive demand that we all get on a little better or a nostalgic hark back to a more communal past. I have already noted in the work of Tronto that a focus on care is very much a commentary on contemporary care institutions, the quality of care services and the retreat from commitment to public support for high-quality and fairly distributed support. It absolutely focuses on a critique of how care beyond the home 'creates a new class of people, mostly women and people of color, who are increasingly left behind by economic growth in the bottom rungs of society' (Tronto, 2013: 2). Carelessness is a comment on the absurdity of cuts to social care in the local authorities in the UK that, in the name of 'personalisation', has led to one announcing that support will be offered at the level of 'just enough' (Salford City Council, 2012: 30). However, this critique has a longer history. Another way of describing what I am calling here the *careless* society is through the notion of a 'contract of mutual indifference', outlined by political scientist Norman Geras in his work on 'political philosophy after the holocaust' (1998). His argument in brief is that the crimes of the Holocaust were in part enabled by the willingness of people to be indifferent to the suffering of their neighbours; to have turned away when they were most in need. Indifference to the other is, therefore, a disposition accused of sustaining immense cruelty, barbarism and ultimately genocide. Geras' account shows that while indifference was common under the Nazi regime, there were examples where people undertook exceptional acts of 'other-regarding effort' (1998: 36) and these, in a form of prefigurative politics, were a 'possible harbinger of an alternative world' (1998: 44). An 'imperative of mutual care' is, therefore, not separate from an 'agenda of progressive change' but has to 'inform any worthwhile politics of justice or equality' (Geras, 1998: 75). For Geras, our imperative to help others is part of our right not be harmed, and a struggle against the obscenities of the Holocaust insists that we have an obligation to aid or care – indeed 'the queen of all virtues' should be not remaining 'a bystander in the face of preventable and remedial suffering' (1998: 48). The care ethics expounded here, therefore, might be premised on the intimate moment of support exercised between two people, but it is insisting on a vision of politics that asserts a contract of mutual regard that extends far wider and demands a more fundamental realignment of human relations than one might at first assume. It is an argument for what Ash Amin has called an 'attentive society' (2012: 33), where 'caring in different ways and for many things becomes central to identity and institutional practice' (2012: 34).

Aesthetics of care

This then returns me to the question of *an aesthetics of care*. If, as I have already argued, a care-based ethics helps raise questions of justice and 'other regarding effort', how might art making be judged from this perspective? The starting point is the notion of relations and the simplistic statement that art making takes place in a series of relational acts, some more explicit and intentional than others. Where an ethics of care focuses upon the values inherent, exhibited or perhaps desired within these human interdependencies, the aesthetics of care seeks to focus upon how the sensory and affective are realised in human relations fostered in art projects. The French art theorist Nicolas Bourriaud is a useful point of departure here in his work on *relational aesthetics*. Bourriaud defines a relational aesthetic as a 'set of artistic practices which take as their theoretical and practical point of departure the whole of human relations and their social context, rather than an independent and private space' (2002: 113), and his book announced from the perspective of the late 1990s French visual art scene how 'for some years now, there has been an upsurge of convivial, user-friendly artistic projects, festive, collective and participatory, exploring the varied potential in the relationship to the other' (2002: 61). Bourriaud's work appears to attach an implicit value to this upsurge, with the 'angelic programme' I mentioned at the top of the chapter being instigated in order 'to patiently restitch the relational fabric' (2002: 36) and 'turn the beholder into the neighbour' (2002: 43). However, ultimately he is more concerned with the formal aspects of this trajectory than the potential that new relational practices have for announcing or creating a fairer world. Inventing new neighbourly relations today, he asserts, is disconnected from programmes that seek to foster 'happier tomorrows' (2002: 45). As the writing above on the ethics of care would suggest, and the contract of mutual regard urged by Geras, the values that can be materialised in the convivial should in fact be the ground on which happier tomorrows are built. The power of the concept of relational aesthetics is weakened by the fact it does not suggest why relations with others might be endorsed or what type of relations we might aspire to develop. If the socially critical inference in the notion of relational aesthetics is to have greater explicit ethical weight, and to move from a moderately interesting description of a form to a movement with more normative clout, it needs to be refigured. And the argument here is that thinking in terms of an aesthetics of care might provide this reorientation.

An 'aesthetics of care' is then about a set of values realised in a relational process that emphasise engagements between individuals or groups over time. It is one that might consist of small creative encounters or large-scale exhibitions, but it is always one that notices inter-human relations in both the creation and the display of art projects. It is an aesthetics that is unafraid to lay bare what Shannon Jackson calls the 'supporting infrastructures of […] living beings' (2011: 39), but importantly this is an aesthetics that could both present those mutually beneficial structures and foster them. It would not pretend to a distinction between a process and an outcome because both might stimulate affective solidarity between people – perhaps participant to participant or performer to audience. There is a sense that this aesthetics would value intimacy, but it would not be at the expense of what Nato Thompson refers to as 'explicitly local, long-term, and community-based' engagement (2012: 31). While care might be exhibited fleetingly, it is more likely that care aesthetics would be realised in more enduring, crafted encounters between people. Seeking to overcome widespread social indifference implies commitment to deep and extended processes.

At the beginning of the chapter, it was noted that the ethics of care is a reference to both a set of values and a practice. This is repeated in this proposal for an aesthetics of care, so that it suggests both a demonstration of mutual regard, but simultaneously it instigates a process that is seeking to create or secure it. Amin asserts that there is a process of cultivation in his project for overcoming the disregard experienced in a society of strangers (2012). It is a 'craft that requires continual attentiveness and care, such that empathy – for objects, projects, nature, the commons – can spread as a public sentiment that also serves to regulate feelings among strangers' (Amin, 2012: 7). Attentiveness (a term also found in Tronto, 2013: 34) is both at the heart of the creative process and the outcome of it. An aesthetics of care is, therefore, a sensory ethical practice, that, following Robinson, involves 'not only learning how to be attentive and patient, how to listen and respond, but also how to rethink our own attitudes about difference and exclusion' (1999: 164).

The difficulty in nurturing an ethics of care through an aesthetic process should of course be acknowledged. Kester, in talking about participatory modes of art making, explains it as a 'temporally extensive form of social interaction in which models of expression, enunciation, and reception are continuously modified and reciprocally responsive' (2011: 112). It is a form of crafted caring where learning to create, respond and be in close dialogue with others is vital for the quality of the experience: but it is a 'temporally extensive form' because it needs to be 'continuously modified' (Kester, 2011: 112) as it is practised. In order to outline something of the shape of that form, the remainder of this chapter will divide care aesthetics into *preparation*, *execution* and *exhibition*, where each of these moments might be minutely connected but they are also likely to be dispersed over a long period. First, preparation would involve an openness and honesty of intention, the selection of artists or participants and questions of the location of a project. Decisions about accessibility (whether in terms of the appropriateness of the space for people with disabilities, the location in terms of costs of travel or the timing for people with different commitments) are not mundane organisational matters, but crucial ethical propositions. In being taken in reference to the ethics of care, they will imbue the project with an affective sense of the importance of mutual respect and regard. Jackson's 'supporting infrastructures' are not the hidden mechanism of creative endeavour but a valued component of the aesthetics. *Preparation* is, therefore, paradoxically part of the *exhibition* within this mode of artistic project: it can demonstrate and model a form of mutual regard. There is a sensory quality in the relationships to which a project that *prepares* in this way aspires.

The notion of *execution* focuses on the process of collaborative working on artistic projects that forge inter-human relationships. The emerging connections between individuals coalescing in this process have an aesthetics – a shape, feel, sensation and affect. This does not exist within one particular person or object of the work, but appears in-between those involved, so that there is a sensory quality of the process and outcome that cannot be disaggregated from the collective effort. This connects to Richard Sennett's work on the history and practice of cooperation (2012). Sennett's conviction that a practice of working together, and his central example of the Hull House settlement in Chicago, demonstrates that a shared commitment to building caring relations turns 'people outward in shared, symbolic acts' and these in turn have a potential place in countering a society that is figured 'brutally simple: us-against-them coupled with you-are-on-your-own' (2012: 280). For theatre, this form of cooperation might involve a challenge to the quality and texture of a rehearsal or devising experience so that the reciprocity of gradual creation is valued over and above the discipline of the single-minded voyage towards the first night. Those intimate negotiations are the aesthetics of the project, and not merely an unremarkable preparatory period. Borrowing from David Gauntlett's work on craft, there is a suggestion that within a creative process the power is realised 'in gentle and quiet ways, with no need for grand celebratory announcements' (2011: 66). This is not meant as a dismissal of the art of public theatre making as part of the search for a more 'care-full' aesthetics, but it does suggest that 'actively seeking out opportunities to be creative together' (Gauntlett, 2011: 67) might be a good starting point where *the show is not always the thing*. I would argue that there is a boldness and important aesthetic quality in work that 'seeks no external recognition' (Gauntlett, 2011: 66) because it implies that aesthetic value is found in co-created moments and not only in public display. The execution of a project figured around an aesthetic of care, therefore, relies on building mutual activities of sharing, support, co-working and relational solidarity within a framework of artistry or creative endeavour. Aesthetic value is located in-between people in moments of collaborative creation, conjoined effort and intimate exchange: these are new virtuosities of care that do not rely on the singular display of self-honed skill.

While the preeminent place of the show or display is questioned here, the idea of *exhibition* can still be part of an aesthetics of care. Public acts clearly present relational opportunities – and are an important moment of 'regard' both in connection to the notion of 'mutual regard' from Geras and what I would argue is somewhat callous disregard championed in certain art theoretical accounts where a desire for audience 'discomfort' (see Bishop, 2012: 26) is prioritised. At a minimum, therefore, performances might need to move from a suspicion of the audience, to one where the range of life experiences of the spectators is not assumed. This means that an exhibition, whether music, theatre or visual art, might display respect for the different possible capacities of the audience and also a recognition of the different expectations and purposes for attendance. The presupposed need for shock and disruption that is articulated, for example in the work of Claire Bishop (2012), is replaced by an awareness that an audience of parents, family or neighbourhood members each brings different concerns and desires into a space that needs to be acknowledged. A display of singular creative expertise or virtuosity is countered with an evocation of an aesthetic experience in the encounter between those present. Caring for an audience means thinking hard about their experience and needs. This is not to say they should witness insipid unchallenging presentations, but an event should model a caring insight into the different conditions of engagement. The affective, sensory dynamic becomes located in the mutual interaction that is only possible because of the relations that are created by the event. An exhibition in the mode of an aesthetics of care would involve an invitation, a dialogue and an opportunity for reciprocity, with an aesthetics built in the sensations stimulated in the particular moment, specific to the differences of each audience or spectator and not located in the assumed preordained power of the art work itself. The aesthetics of care is realised in affective connection between those participating in the whole event of the performance or show – in the sensations of mutual regard and respect.

An aesthetics of care can be demonstrated in the astonishing sense of connection between different people involved in making art together – whether as audiences of pre-rehearsed shows or collaborators in participatory community projects. Applied or community-based performance is about exactly this proposition, but too often it has assumed to locate its value in the individualised self-esteem or personal capacities generated through the process, or displayed on stage. An aesthetics of care, whether in the event, the preparation or execution of a project, models and exhibits the fairer and more mutually sympathetic world that is sought. The care and attentiveness between participants in the enactment of their work, and between that show and those invited to witness it, is a display of care distributed between each component part of the event. This in turn forces those people planning or devising these types of initiatives not to distinguish between the private moments of a project and more public displays. The shape and feel of the relationships at the heart of the project are its aesthetics – whether presented in front of hundreds or in a small circle in a rehearsal room. In experiencing this type of care, the aim is to cultivate the understanding that regard for others is central to making the world a better place – where remaining the bystander is an affront to shared feelings of mutual concern.

Postscript

In the field of nursing studies, Paul Wainwright (2000) and Louise de Raeve (1998) have analysed the work of Barbara Carper on aesthetic knowledge in nursing training (1978) to question whether there can be a notion of the *art of nursing*. While the conclusions are varied, they understand that the skill exhibited in a moment of care can be understood as a thing of beauty or grace (de Raeve, 1998: 405). Without explicitly calling it an aesthetics of care, I understand their discussion as an attempt to grapple with the care aesthetics exhibited in nursing practice. Although the argument in this chapter has sought to elaborate an aesthetics of care in relation to deliberate projects of art making, the reference to nursing here points to the fact that an aesthetics of care might be encountered beyond the creative arts. This in turn leads me back to the experience with my colleague Antoine. There is a tension in the argument here, in that Antoine's care was done outside the official system of care that would normally be encountered in the UK. The time he was given, the ability to get his appointments, operations and post-operative support were all done informally for free by a private hospital after intervention with some colleagues of mine at the university. Extended care was permitted within an institution but outside the standard and more familiar constraints of institutional social practice. The questions of quality care and how it is delivered within the severely limited resources of a National Health Service and welfare state is the nexus around which debates on social care currently concentrate (see, for example, Barnes, 2006; Hamington and Miller, 2006). The 'engrossment' in care promoted by Noddings is fanciful if a carer, working with a zero-hours contract, is not paid for travel between clients and has a maximum visit time of fifteen minutes to engage with an elderly person. Or she or he is working in a high-pressure, overstretched ward in a cosmopolitan UK city hospital. The *beauty* identified in Antoine's relationship with his physiotherapist would have been starkly absent from these regimes. The search for an aesthetics of care, therefore, must also be seen as a critique of the current politics of the care industry, and its relevance needs to be tested in contemporary health and social care contexts. I would hope that ultimately the notion of an aesthetics of care could be orientated as much to institutional care practices as it might be to community-based theatre. The tension between a personal and political call to care and a statutory, highly regulated care industry (a tension that is particularly well articulated in the work of Illich, 2001; and Cayley, 2005) needs to be part of a vision of a care aesthetic and is, I hope, part of future research in this area.

In conclusion, I have argued that care has an ethics, but attention to its feel for all parties is crucial for the quality it delivers and the justice it proposes. The sensation of reciprocity and inter-reliance acutely demonstrated in the profoundly moving acts of caring that I experienced and witnessed in a short period of my family's life with Antoine made me realise how our tender relations with others were central to the rationale of many political and art-making projects in which I have been involved. The proposal is that remembering the shape and sensation of mutual care, is a direct invitation to imbue that feeling, that aesthetics of care, in all places where we believe our work is seeking to negotiate positive change. And now the next challenge is to seek out those projects where that fullness is witnessed, and practices of joyous affective solidarity hint that a society of horrendous and cruel disregard can be countered.

Performing tenderness: fluidity and reciprocity in the performance of caring in Fevered Sleep's *Men & Girls Dance*

Amanda Stuart Fisher

Writing about what could be interpreted as a starting point for *Men & Girls Dance* in the 'newspaper' accompanying the production, David Harradine, one of Fevered Sleep's co-artistic directors, describes a moment at a local village bonfire, where he found himself watching a group of boys 'chasing each other round in the rain and mud' (Harradine, quoted in Fevered Sleep, 2017). As he stood watching the boys playing, he describes a growing sense of uneasiness as he realised that he too was being observed by the other adults present, who were positioning him as 'a solitary man, alone at the village bonfire, watching someone else's children playing' (Harradine, quoted in Fevered Sleep, 2017). The sensation of being watched and judged evoked an anxiety for Harradine both about the narratives that were being read into his presence at this event and his observation of the boy's playing, providing a poignant insight into the often unspoken social taboos that attach themselves to men's encounters with children. Harradine's account of this moment of self-conscious observation draws attention to a broader social unease indicative of the 'risk anxiety' (Jackson and Scott, 1999) that often permeates our perceptions of adult interactions with children in general and male adult relationships with children in particular. As sociologists Stevi Jackson and Sue Scott suggest, childhood today is increasingly viewed as a site of anxiety and risk, characterised both by children's risky behaviours and (adult) *risk anxiety*. Childhood, they argue, 'is increasingly being constructed as a precious realm under siege from those who would rob children of their childhood, and as being subverted from within by children who refuse to remain childlike' (Jackson and Scott, 1999: 86). The risk anxiety associated with children is often sexualised, '[crystallising] around the threat of sexual violence from strangers', yet this threat is 'rarely made explicit to children' (Jackson and Scott, 1999: 101) and so the anxiety remains in the minds of adults as something unsaid and unsayable. As Jackson and Scott explain: 'Adults project their sexual scripts and anxieties on to children in ways which are relatively inaccessible because they are bounded by what cannot be said. This makes it extremely difficult to communicate to children the precise nature of the danger they are being warned about' (1999: 101). Furthermore, the conception of childhood as a period of innocence is, as childhood studies researcher Emma Renold points out, a highly gendered process, where innocence is also often eroticised and subjected to processes of 'feminisation' (2005: 24). As Renold argues, 'From depictions of sexualised images of prepubertal girls in the Victorian era [...], to the Lolita-like commodification of little girls as sexual consumers and performers in contemporary society [...], it is the girl-child, not the boy-child, whose innocence is eroticised' (2005: 23).

The issue of gender, girlhood and adult sexualised risk anxiety, while not explicitly addressed in *Men & Girls Dance*, emerges poignantly in this production as a social and cultural topography. Described as 'exquisitely beautiful' (Gardner, 2016), 'joyful' and as a 'celebration of the relationships on stage' (Love, 2016), *Men & Girls Dance* 'reclaims the rights of adults and children to be together, to play together and to dance together' (Fevered Sleep, 2017). While the production certainly celebrates adults and children being and dancing together, *Men & Girls Dance* arguably achieves much more than this and performs a mode of caring that both challenges and extends our understanding of both our preconceptions of encounters between men and girls and how we think about strength, vulnerability and the power structures of care in performance. Through its improvisational structure and choreography, *Men & Girls Dance* critiques many of the gender-normative assumptions that often become projected on to encounters between men and girls and replaces the adult risk anxiety associated with this with care-filled interactions that generate moments of togetherness, marked out by a mode of tender and reciprocal caring. In so doing, performed care emerges in this production as a mode of resistance, opening up new understandings about structures of caregiving and care receiving in performance and rethinking the ethical demands of working within contexts of vulnerability and risk.

One of the key ways that *Men & Girls Dance* reconsiders the dynamics of the encounter between men and girls is by offering a critique of the bifurcated, gendered categories of difference that tend to predetermine we how position masculinity and femininity in relation to men and girls. Rather than emphasising differences, *Men & Girls Dance* explores how masculinity and girlhood might be understood as being enfolded within the same world and constructed through the same discourses. My thinking in this area is influenced by the research of the cultural theorist Rebecca Coleman, who, in her book *The Becoming of Bodies: Girls, Images, Experience* (2009), examines the 'becoming' of girls bodies through an engagement with Deleuze's concept of the 'fold'. By understanding both men and girls as being enfolded within the same discourses, I suggest that *Men & Girls Dance* interrogates the limitations of the highly gendered discourses that construct our understanding of both girlhood and manhood, opening up new possibilities for thinking about how men and girls might be together.

Drawing on Coleman's account of 'enfolding', I argue that in *Men & Girls Dance* both the girls and men who participate must navigate the often unspoken taboos that become inscribed into the discourses of both masculinity and girlhood and the sexualised risk anxiety associated with this. Incorporating feminist theory, visual culture and theorisation of girlhood, Coleman problematises the concept of girls as passive spectators, rejecting the idea that girls automatically become subjugated to the negative images of women that appear in media and teen magazines. Instead, she positions girls as being enfolded within the same world as the mediatised images of women in magazines, arguing that the experience of girls should be understood as operating *in relation* to these images. Rather than viewing 'images and bodies [...] as spatially separate and capable of having effects on each other: "bad" images = "bad" bodies', Coleman argues for an 'ontology of becoming', where 'bodies and images are processes which are inextricably entwined and which become through each other' (2009: 17, 3).

Importing Coleman's theorisation of the becoming of girls bodies into my reading of *Men & Girls Dance* is productive because it draws attention to how performance projects like this can both resist and exist within the gendered structures that determine the way we think about men and girls. The heteronormative and gendered discourses that become inscribed into men's relationships with girls tend to posit masculinity as synonymous with a predatory sexuality and with action and aggression, while girlhood is viewed as being in some way equated with passivity, latent sexuality and the risk of corrupted innocence. However, through the performance of a tender togetherness, as I will argue in this chapter, *Men & Girls Dance* breaks down these divisions and instead generates moments of mutual caring and openness. By troubling and critiquing the bifurcated normative structures of gender that separate men and girls, adults and children, masculinity and femininity, the process of performed togetherness in *Men & Girls Dance* also invites us to rethink how the gendering of caring structures impacts on our understanding of care and how caring encounters can be rethought by positioning men and girls as enfolded and implicated in the same discourses of risk, threat and vulnerability.

Dancing with the media monster: performed caring as resistance

My initial encounter with *Men & Girls Dance* was as an audience member for the London edition of the performance that took place on 21 April 2017 at the Place Theatre. Prior to this, *Men & Girls Dance* had been performed at various other venues around the UK including Brighton, Nottingham, Salford, Huddersfield and Folkestone. Funded by Arts Council Strategic

Touring funds, every *Men & Girls Dance* performance is created through a residency within each of the different locations to which the company tours. In each setting, the company works with a group of 'adult, male professional contemporary dancers' who remain connected with the project throughout and a different group of local girls from the community 'who dance for fun' (Fevered Sleep, 2017). The performances that emerge are therefore specific to each area, are semi-improvised and co-created with the dancers who participate in the residency. By structuring the creation of each performance around a residency, Fevered Sleep are able to foster closer and more meaningful, participatory collaborations with each new community to which the show tours.

The atmosphere at the Place Theatre on the evening of 21 April certainly reflected this community-based participatory approach. A community reach that extended beyond the confines of the theatre was signalled initially by the presence of various writing materials laid out in the bar area, inviting audience members to write down their responses to the ideas the performance evoked. This invitation was eagerly taken up, enabling the audience to write themselves *into* the performance process and to leave a map tracing the thoughts and feelings of the spectators after each performance. It is an approach that was reproduced elsewhere on the tour, in what Fevered Sleep described as 'talking places', community-oriented discursive spaces that, as the project evaluation report indicates, sought to establish a 'safe space for the public to discuss the project's themes, unique to each tour residency' (Morris *et al.*, 2017: 4). In this sense, both on stage and off, this production 'was intentionally devised to create conversation – with the Talking Place and newspaper being key elements' (Morris *et al.*, 2017: 12). The *Men & Girls Dance* newspaper was created for each of the residencies and was used to extend the conversations raised by the performance and in the local talking places. It was distributed widely within the local community, in places such as schools, libraries, pubs and doctors' surgeries by 'community catalysts', individuals from the local community who were commissioned by Fevered Sleep to act as ambassadors for the project. The material in the newspaper reflects on the issues the performance explores, drawing on a wide range of different perspectives, including people associated with Fevered Sleep, the dancers themselves, members of the public who have seen the show and those who have been involved in the talking places. It also includes contributions from people interested in the themes explored in the performance, these were garnered through an 'open call' to those who live or work in each of the areas to which the performance toured.

These reflections extend and draw attention to the debates that surround the social taboo that the very concept of men dancing with young girls elicits, while also drawing out some complex and emotional responses the project provokes in those participating or watching it. The London newspaper, for example, included an extract from a safeguarding policy from an independent school advising against any form of physical contact between teachers and children, while also including reflections from audience members who saw the show. One reflection, for example, says 'I'm actually really saddened that we live in a society where it's very difficult for men and girls to be together in that way' (Fevered Sleep, 2017). Whereas, another states that, 'It's hard to talk to people about this performance, because a relationship of tenderness and equality between men and girls is not something that has a presence in our society. It's hard to describe something that doesn't otherwise exist' (Fevered Sleep, 2017). Through both the structure of the project and the performances themselves, Fevered Sleep establishes dialogue and relationships of trust and engagement with local communities, the performers, the company and with audiences.

Taking my seat at the Place, with my partner and our two daughters, aged nine and twelve, I soon found myself engaging with some of the discourses of risk, girlhood, adolescence and masculinity that frame *Men & Girls Dance.* On the stage, the back wall was covered in newspaper print that had been stuck on to it. Nine girls aged between eight and eleven and four male dancers were engrossed with the task of sticking more newspapers together on the floor to form a large sheet of paper. The stage itself was strewn with stacks of crumpled newspapers, conveying an amalgamation of news stories and social commentary that had been crumpled up and tossed away. Asked for their first impressions, my eldest daughter said that she felt the setting to be 'symbolic', the newspapers, she felt, represented the stereotype 'that women are supposed to be skinny', while my youngest reported that the men 'look kind' because they were 'helping the children and playing at being a dinosaur' (Field notes, 21 April 2017). These reactions are indicative of the age gap between these two girls and their positioning within the transitional phases of adolescence. Indeed, my youngest daughter who, at nine years old, is at the very threshold of adolescence, did not, I suspect, initially see 'girls' on the stage but rather 'children'. Correlatively, my oldest daughter, aged twelve, immediately not only noted the gender of the children, but also started to piece together some of the symbolic connections proposed by the scenography in relation to the media's role in determining how men and girls might interact.

The age of the groups of girl dancers recruited for each of the residencies ranges between eight and eleven years, which means that the majority of the girls performing in the production are on the threshold of their early adolescent years. This transitionary period of development, which is fluid and individual and incorporates both physical and psychological changes, is not easily defined by age alone. Psychoanalyst, Margot Waddell describes adolescence as a 'process of becoming, one that begins with puberty and ends [...] sometime during the twenties' (2018: xv). In these transitionary years of 'becoming', adolescents negotiate a letting-go of childhood, while simultaneously projecting themselves into a conception of an adult self. As Waddell argues, it is a difficult period of time, a 'developmentally challenging borderland time between childhood and adulthood' (2018: 31). The process of moving through this transitionary period is also framed by normative structures and values that become inscribed into cultural and social attitudes towards childhood, gender and the other elements of the adolescent's emerging identity. Cultural theorist Catherine Driscoll distinguishes adolescence from the biological process of puberty and positions girlhood – or feminine adolescence, as she describes it – as a social and historical construct, determined by the dominant discourses of the age. Describing adolescence as a gendered terrain, Driscoll points out that, historically at least, women have tended to be viewed as possessing attributes that are also associated with the adolescent, such as malleability, fluidity and spontaneity, leading her to argue that '[t]wentieth-century adolescence is thus characterized by feminized attributes […] even when the adolescents are men' (2002: 54). Girlhood itself tends to signify a transitionary process that always remains incomplete and incompleteable because 'girlhood' denotes a process of becoming, the quest for an identity that ultimately erases any sense of girlhood as soon it reaches the desired goal: womanhood. This stands in contrast to how discourses of boyhood are constructed. Describing boyhood as 'a chaotic dynamism', for example, psychoanalyst Ken Corbett (2009) suggests that the transition from boy to man tends to be socially and psychologically viewed as a process in which masculinity is categorised and developed. The term 'boyhood', he argues, 'strives to capture and categorise the gender pattern called masculinity and more precisely the development of masculinity' (2009: 3). As I will go on to discuss later in this chapter, masculinity tends to be associated not with feelings, incompleteness and fluidity but with the presence of the masculine body and purposeful action.

The precarious, transitionary terrain that the girls in Fevered Sleep are negotiating as they approach adolescence is therefore one not simply defined by a biological process, but is discursively constructed and framed by normative structures of gender. It is perhaps therefore not surprising, that at the start of *Men & Girls Dance*, my twelve-year-old daughter immediately made connections between the newspaper print and stereotypical images of femininity and women. In doing so, she was not only addressing the way women are stereotyped in the images that proliferate in the media, but also reflecting on what these stereotypes reveal about society's expectations of how women are expected to behave in relation to men. The action of sticking the newspapers together served to draw attention to the way that both men and girls are implicated and 'enfolded' within the social discourses that structure both girlhood and masculinity and how these structures predetermine how the co-presence of men and girls is to be construed.

Fevered Sleep's approach, however, refuses to position either the girls or the men as victims of these somewhat oppressive, heteronormative structures. Instead, the performance creates motifs of interdependence and cooperation that collectively operate to resist and counter these normative discourses. In these opening moments of the performance, we observed some of this interrelational togetherness beginning to emerge as the two groups of dancers became absorbed in the action of the sticking the newspapers together on the stage. The gesture of sticking together newspaper seemed also to symbolically highlight how relationality between men and girls often comes to be narrated by the tabloid press and the media. The performance of this task also revealed an emergent, mutually held sense of openness and trust developing between the men and girls; this relational caring binded them together in a relationship that became more and more visible throughout the piece. However, the question of who is designated as caregivers or care receivers here becomes a difficult one to answer, as the power dynamics between the two groups of dancers remain in constant flux, shifting and changing as the performance progresses. In this sense, *Men & Girls Dance* does not reproduce representations of care as such, but through the co-presence and the performed encounters between the two groups of dancers, a mode of fluid caring begins to emerge, not bound to a specific caregiver or care receiver; rather, it becomes itself through structures of interdependence, fluidity and reciprocity that are mutually developed and fostered throughout.

As we shall see, this sense of a fluid reciprocal mode of caring between the dancers owes much to the methodological structures adopted during the creative process that are reflected on and documented in the *Men & Girls Dance* newspapers and in a video on the project posted on the company on the *Men & Girls Dance* micro-website. While some of the performed encounters of caring are rooted in certain choreographical choices, the tenderness and trust evident in the relationships between the men and the girls exceeds choreography and instead points to the participatory and improvisational strategies adopted during the construction of the piece. As Orla Markey, one of the young performers explains: 'It's not choreographic routine, it's like some of it is improvisation' (Markey, quoted in Fevered Sleep, 2018). The project documentation reveals how both groups of dancers were encouraged not to simply follow particular choreographical steps but instead were invited to open themselves up to each other to explore the limitations and possibilities of dancing with one another. In this sense, as Fevered Sleep co-artistic director Sam Butler points out, 'as an audience member you are seeing a unique experience' because in each performance, the playfulness of the action is differently improvised (Butler, quoted in Fevered Sleep, 2018). In this sense, the creative process required the dancers to not only engage with their bodies but also their selfhood and feelings, and it was the dancer's perceptions, joyfulness and sense of vulnerability that became central to the development of each performance. Care emerges in *Men & Girls Dance*, then, not as a representation of a caring encounter but as a form of embodied knowledge whereby the dancers come to know each other through an emerging and embodied understanding of caregiving and care receiving.

To further explore this embodied understanding for the other, I draw on the theorisation of Maurice Hamington, a philosopher of care and contributor to this edited collection, who argues that constitutively care, by its very nature, can only be understood by 'attending to its embodied dimension' (Hamington, 2004: 4). Positioning care as '*an approach to personal and social morality that shifts ethical considerations to contexts, relationships, and affective knowledge*' (2004: 3, original emphasis), he argues that care for the other has an ontological basis, grounded in human existence: '[c]are is a way of being in the world', he writes, 'that the habits and behaviours of our body facilitate' (2004: 2). Drawing on Hamington's theorisation of care leads me to suggest that it is through the development of trust, interdependent relationships and openness in *Men & Girls Dance* that caring knowledge is able to develop between the two groups of dancers. Hamington develops the term 'caring knowledge' to describe an understanding of the self–other relationship that emerges through bodily co-presence within the caring encounter. As he argues, knowledge that is acquired through the body can often address that which cannot be iterated or verbally described and, as he also indicates, 'the body has the ability to capture the subtleties of emotion communicated outside of explicit language' (2004: 4).

In *Men & Girls Dance*, this unspoken caring knowledge is acquired and performed in various different ways throughout but becomes most visible within the moments of semi-improvised performed playfulness. In the performance I saw at the Place, one such moment of playfulness emerged in the first half of the performance in a game I will call 'newspaper monster' tag, which commences when the newspapers have been stuck together on the floor and a large-sheet collaged newsprint has been formed. At this point, two male dancers take centre stage and, with a slight gesture, invite the girls to come and join them. Gradually the girls moved to the centre and four of them began to playfully cover the heads of the two male dancers with newspaper. Once the dancers' heads were completely covered, a third male dancer appeared from beneath the newspaper at the back of the stage, where he had been concealed before the start of the show. He emerged completely covered in paper and slowly performed a dance as he moved forward down the stage. This led two of the girls to unwrap him, rip off the newspaper and reveal the man beneath. He in turn then unwrapped the heads of the other male dancers and everyone then gathered together around the giant sheet of newspaper collage created at the start of the performance that is then lifted up high into the air. Unseen by the audience, one of the male dancers had slipped beneath it, only to suddenly re-emerge as a 'newspaper monster' who rushed towards the girls, roaring at them ferociously. They responded and encouraged the chasing further, smiling, screaming and running until a wild game of tag ensues. The girls who had been caught by the monster, laughing, ripped the newspaper off him to reveal the dancer beneath. The paper that had been ripped off is then wrapped around the head of a fifth man, making a large, monstrous newspaper head. He then danced with his giant head until finally it was removed by two of the girls and thrown to the back of the stage. This 'newspaper monster' sequence was punctuated with much laughter and enjoyment from the dancers and consequently the audience. The newspaper, in this moment, became something the dancers were at different times enfolded within and that also bound and encumbered their movement. It was a playful encounter and it was clear that the girls and the 'monster' were enjoying the game they were playing with each other. My youngest daughter was also laughing; she too enjoyed the fun she was witnessing.

What is so interesting about this newspaper monster tag game is that it both performed and, to some degree, deconstructed the gender dynamics of care. In her account of the way that care work is devalued by society, care ethicist Joan Tronto argues against the idea that caring should be positioned as being an innately feminine activity, rooted in the dyadic, mother–child caring encounter, arguing that care is 'devalued conceptually through a connection with privacy, with emotion, and with the needy' ([1993] 2009: 117). By making care a 'private activity', she suggests, it is seen as belonging only to a realm of women who 'are expected to care for those in their household' ([1993] 2009: 119). At the time of writing, it is twenty-five years since Tronto's book was first published in 1993 and, arguably, there is now a wider recognition of the importance of de-gendering care, particularly in relation to childcare and care within the family. However, despite this, there is still evidence to suggest that cultural, economic and social barriers continue to make it difficult for men to participate equally in childcaring duties (see Sodha, 2018) and, as a consequence, caring for children remains socially constructed as an emotional labour that tends to be undertaken by women. This gendering of caring arguably contributes to the social acceptability of women being in close proximity with girls, but not men. While the gendering of care positions emotional labour and feeling work as intrinsically feminine, correlative discourses around masculinity, as Raewyn W. Connell argues, tend to centre around action rather than feeling and what the masculine body can and cannot do. As Connell argues:

> True masculinity is always thought to proceed from men's bodies – to be inherent in a male body or to express something about a male body. Either the body drives and directs action (e.g. men are naturally more aggressive than women; rape results from uncontrollable lust or an innate urge to violence) or the body sets limits to action (e.g. men naturally do not take care of infants, homosexuality is unnatural and therefore confirmed to a perverse minority). (2005: 45)

Connell's account of the structure of masculinity reveals how the regulatory discourses around gender and caring actively work against the possibility of men being seen as suitable nurturers and carers for children. By positioning care as an innately feminine attribute, as opposed to a rational action, discourses of gender and care prevent caring labour from being viewed as belonging to the realm of 'masculinity', thereby relegating this kind of activity to women and girls.

In the performance of the newspaper monster tag, it is these gendered discourses of masculinity and care, I suggest, that become symbolically evoked by the newsprint text that covers and conceals the male dancer. Simultaneously, however, the performance of the male dancer within this game does not seek to foreclose the dancer's own masculinity. On the contrary, the performance remains very much in line with Connell's account of masculinity's focus on body and action, and it is the action of the game that emerges as a mode of care in this instance, while remaining rooted in a conceptualisation of masculinity that is physical and action orientated. Significantly, the form of care performed here is not a mode of emotional labour, rather it is a physical and visceral caring that takes account of the vulnerability of the girls in the space while also inviting them to take risks with their own co-presence with the newspaper monster and explore the limits and boundaries of this very physical game. It is a moment that is created from a certain degree of spontaneity and improvisation, and its success depends on the quality of the caring knowledge that has been acquired by both groups of dancers throughout the creative process itself.

Caring knowledge is also performed through the structure of the game itself, which is determined by reciprocity and interdependence; after all, it is the girls who invite the monster to chase them and the male dancers respond with just the right amount of ferocity and physical play. However, in other moments of *Men & Girls Dance*, care is performed with altogether different dynamics. In the following section of this chapter, I will consider how touch and attentiveness operates in *Men & Girls Dance*, which I suggest is another example of how caring knowledge emerges as a performed mode of caring for the other.

Performing tenderness: care as attentiveness

> Her hand, touch, warmth, soft skin. Creases at the wrist. Old nail polish. Freckles on her arms and face [...] The heat of her back on my face as I listen to the creak of her body [...] I am drawn back to the audience. 'What are you thinking? Why am I so sad? Why won't you let this just be what it is – safe, simple, a demonstration of listening and watching with care? Is it my fault that you can't, is there something weird about how I do it? I look at each of the eyes looking at me. Some turn away, some smile, reassuring, awkward, family, friends scanning across them. I feel hot, the skin on my face feels like it's been hit and the bruise is coming through, tight skin and tender. I might cry. (Robert Clark, quoted in Fevered Sleep, 2017)

In his personal account of performing in *Men & Girls Dance*, dancer Robert Clark describes the feelings of vulnerability and anxiety he experienced when performing an exchange of close observation and description with one of the girl dancers. This is one of the most poignant examples of performed embodied caring that emerges in *Men & Girls Dance* and takes place through a series of close observations by the girls of the men and by the men of the girls. Emerging at various moments throughout the performance, these are tender exchanges of reciprocity and trust, where the dancers carefully attend to one another, observing and describing what they see, hear and feel. The first of these micro-observations in the version of *Men & Girls Dance* I saw at the Place commenced with two of the girls standing centre stage with a microphone, describing one of the men dancing. Speaking into a microphone they carefully described the dancer they observed and any action or slight gesture that he made. This action of observation and description was then repeated but with one of the men observing one of the girls, closely describing what he saw and heard and using touch to describe what he could feel, placing his hand on her arm, for example. Later in the performance this motif was repeated and three girls observed and described three of the male dancers. This time they used touch to describe the feel of the other person, describing the feel of his skin, for example, and placing an ear on his back to describe the sound of his breath.

The descriptions produced through these moments of close observation were factual but also intimate, performing a mode of care that emerged as an attentiveness towards the other. This care was framed by an embodied knowledge of the other person but also by a sense of mutual openness and a recognition of a shared sense of vulnerability. The form of care performed in this context, possessed an almost meditative quality, drawing attention not only to the self–other relationship at hand, but also to a sense of shared humanness and an interrelatedness that connects us with other people. In these exchanges of observation and description, personal boundaries and consent were respected and carefully negotiated. The moments of touch, for example, focused only on arms and backs and were carefully and sensitively carried out. The language adopted to describe what was observed then became semi-ritualised, following a predetermined pattern that added to its meditative quality and always starting with 'I see', 'I hear' or 'I feel':

> I can feel the hairs on his arms
> I can see his blue eyes blinking
> I can see his slightly red cheeks
> I can see him looking at me
> I can hear him breathing
> I can hear his pulse through his wrist. (Fevered Sleep, 2017)[1]

The positionality of the observer and observed explored in these moments remains interchangeable and when the male dancer described the girl in front of him he too made use of the semi-ritualised form of address and used touch to describe what he saw and felt: 'A strand of hair across her face [holding her hand] I feel the weight of her hand. I hear her laugh, I see a green mark on her wrist [placing his head on her back] I can hear her breath' (Field notes, 21 April 2017).[2] As audience members, this process of observation and description was profoundly moving. There was a poignancy that seemed to derive from a tender and embodied attentiveness that emerged in the performance, fluidly flowing between the men and the girls. In this context, the performed care became mutual and reciprocated and in these gentle moments of exchange, the caring encounter felt to be held equally by both groups of dancers. The actions of observing and being observed, elicited a vulnerability from both the men and the girls as through the process of describing or being described they became implicated within an intimate address that was established on a mutual process of an opening up to the other. It was also a moment that, in some way, responded and returned to the feelings of self-consciousness and anxiety experienced by Harradine at the village bonfire, as described above. This was highlighted by the male dancer who in the process of describing the girl in front of him says, 'I can see her looking at me'. Then looking at the audience, he extended this further, acknowledging that he too was being observed, saying, 'I can see you looking at me'. By reimagining and reflecting on the act of observing and describing in this way, the production repositioned these moments of observation and description as an exchange of tenderness where care entered the performance space and reconfigured the potentiality of a relational engagement between men and girls. These gentle moments of attentive caring emerged as an invitation to audiences to recognise caring afresh, shifting the characterisations of tenderness and togetherness away from the regulatory gendered discourses that usually frame it.

In this way, these performances of attentive touch and intimate encounter both reflect on and invert some of the social taboos that are inscribed both in the way we think about care and how we think about gender, feelings and acts of tenderness. Writing in 1935, in his book *The Origins of Love and Hate*, the psychiatrist Ian Suttie adopts the term 'the "taboo" on tenderness'([1935] 2005) to describe how certain feelings acquire a taboo status because they are perceived as being highly gendered. In his essay, Suttie argues that for men, feelings of tenderness must be repressed because tenderness is constructed as something socially and psychologically unacceptable within normative masculinity, despite it being – in Suttie's terms – 'the very *stuff* of sociability' ([1935] 2005: 80, original emphasis). Drawing on Freud's account of the love of an infant towards his or her mother, which Freud characterises as an object-related desire, Suttie argues that tenderness has become understood as 'a derivative of sexuality' ([1935] 2005: 80) and feelings of tenderness, for men at least, acquire a social taboo status when not encountered in relation to sexuality. This leads Suttie to suggest that men must then seek out moments of homosociality, such as scenes of brotherhood or affectionate relationships with pet animals in order to sublimate these repressed feelings of tenderness.

Of course, our understanding of sexuality, gender and psychoanalysis has changed significantly since Suttie was writing in the early part of the twentieth century. However, I am inclined to agree with cultural theorist Gavin Miller, who argues that despite these changes, Suttie's 'argument still holds true, *mutatis mutandis*' (2007: 669). Arguably today, the capacity for men to exhibit forms of tenderness to children, but particularly to adolescent girls, is often undermined by discourses of risk and anxiety that sexualise such gestures. Through the tender and poignant performances of care and proximity in *Men & Girls Dance*, audiences are invited to uncouple tenderness from sexuality and to look beyond the gendered discourses that ultimately restrict conceptions of girlhood and masculinity and which ultimately exclude men from the possibility of these kinds of caring encounters. As discussed above, the risk anxiety that so often becomes inscribed into men's interactions with girls tends to remain unspoken and, while this is not explicitly addressed by the performance, the taboo of men's co-presence with adolescent girls becomes present in the performance as a spoken fear, hovering at the edges of the stage, within the minds of both the audience and the male dancers, who, as we discover from the *Men & Girls Dance* newspaper, are concerned about how the audience will judge them. The evaluation report for the project also indicates that the very ideas explored within it were initially met with 'suspicion and resistance' from some of the communities in which the residencies took place (Morris *et al.*, 2017: 21). In this sense, rather than banishing the 'monsters that lurk in our suspicious minds', as the theatre critic Lyn Gardner suggests in her review of the show (2016), *Men & Girls Dance*, I suggest, stages an engagement with these suspicions and anxieties and, by generating moments of mutual and reciprocal caring, resists them.

The repeated performance of the motif of observation and description between the men and girls, therefore, not only resists the discourses of risk anxiety that get inscribed into encounters of tenderness between men and girls, but it also generates new ways of thinking about the way caring can be conceptualised and embodied. Through the mutually held moments of attentiveness between the men and girls, relationships of trust and openness are foregrounded, revealing how performance can generate a caring togetherness and a performed sociability, which implicates a group of individuals in a fluid exchange of responsiveness and mutual support.

Performing trust and togetherness: care as an embodied aesthetic

These moments of *caring togetherness* do not emerge arbitrarily, rather they are structured into the fabric of the rehearsal process and the choreographical structure of the piece itself. As the documentation of the project in the *Men & Girls Dance* newspaper reveals, in rehearsal, both groups of dancers were directed to set aside pre-learned approaches to dance and performance and were instead invited to explore the experience of 'being themselves' and their responses to dancing with one another. Fevered Sleep's co-artistic director, Sam Butler, explains that this instruction often came as 'a surprise', particularly for the girls who approached the process thinking they were 'going to be doing some very snazzy choreography and maybe some lovely leaps and lifts and turns and maybe some splits' (Butler, quoted in Fevered Sleep, 2017). On the contrary, through the processual, participatory development of the piece, a sense of respectful being-together was fostered, allowing a shared sense of care and trust to develop. As Harradine argues, these relationships needed safety and care to be nurtured and emerged out of a rehearsal process that was 'completely about trust and respect and care and tenderness and playfulness and love' (Harradine, quoted in Fevered Sleep, 2017).

Harradine's reference to the importance of 'trust' here draws attention to the central positioning of the embodied concepts of dependency and trust in theories of care where 'trust' is positioned as constitutively bound to relationalilty, because it requires some form of dialectical engagement with one or more selves. Care ethicist Virginia Held, for example, positions trust as 'a value inherent in an ethic of care', arguing that 'good caring relations require and are characterised by it' (2006: 56). Yet for Held, 'trust' does not simply describe the caring encounter itself, rather it determines an intention. She argues that, 'To trust is not simply to predict what someone will do; it is most needed when what others will do is uncertain. It is an understanding that another person or persons will have trustworthy intentions, rather than intentions to take advantage of one. For there to be trust between persons, such understanding must be mutual' (2006: 57).

This sense of a mutuality of trust is particularly significant in the context of performance because it suggests that the physical interactions within a performance and the rehearsal process that generated it both have an ethical dimension. Certainly, it would seem important that the development of trusting relationships during the creative process ultimately fosters productive forms of risk-taking in which performers feel supported and cared for. This interconnectedness between caring and trust informs the Danish philosopher Knud Ejler Løgstrup's account of the ethical demand, where he addresses not the intention behind trusting relationships but the obligation evoked when others *place their trust in us*. For Løgstrup, this obligation is part of an unspoken ethical demand that emerges when we encounter another person's trust. Trust here becomes a process of self-surrender, leading Løgstrup to argue that '[t]hrough the trust which a person either shows or asks of another person he or she surrenders something of his or her life to that person' (1997: 17). The encounter with a relationship of trust then becomes a mode of opening up to the other, a process that compels us to take care of the one who has trustingly placed themselves into our hands. This action of opening up to another also evokes caring, in Løgstrup's terms it 'implies the demand that we take care of the life which has been placed in our hands' (1997: 53).

The ethical demand to take care of the other in *Men & Girls Dance*, is arguably encountered by both groups of dancers who must, at various points in the process, open themselves up to the other, placing their trust in another's hands. Trust and care then becomes a fluid encounter that flows between the dancers, underpinning both the creative process and the performance itself, implicating each of the dancers in an ethical relationship of responsibility to each other. In her account of drama education, Helen Nicholson describes trust as a 'slippery concept' that 'is generally understood [as involving a] correspondence between belief and expectation, commitment to a person or situation, responsibility for oneself, co-operative behaviour and care for others' (2002: 82). Connecting trust with responsibility and a care for the other, Nicholson draws attention to the complexity of trusting relationships, arguing that these 'can be painful and difficult, as well as pleasurable, liberating and rewarding' (2002: 87). In each of these accounts, trust and care emerge as being intimately connected; certainly both concepts could be understood to be mutually sustaining and convoked by the situation in which they are demanded.

In *Men & Girls Dance*, the performances of trust and care are also closely associated with an attentiveness that is carefully constructed and that implicates both the men and the girls in a careful togetherness that is co-created and mutually held. In this sense, *Men & Girls Dance* reveals how performance can begin to disrupt some of the traditional bifurcated structures of care, where caring becomes a mode of transaction between a caregiver and care receiver. Through a performed attentiveness and mutual trust, care is no longer bound only to the loci of a caregiver; instead it emerges within a set of complex relationships that become highly fluid. Deriving etymologically from a Latin term meaning 'to give heed to', the concept of 'attentiveness' embraces both a sense of care and thoughtfulness but also the idea of attention and focus (as in 'to attend to someone or something'). To be 'attentive' to another person then signifies both a regard for the other but also a sense responsiveness and the act of paying close attention. For care ethicist Joan Tronto, attentiveness is understood as being 'the first moral aspect of caring', denoting a process of 'simply recognising the needs of those around us' ([1993] 2009: 127).[3] Drawing on the philosopher Simone Weil's theorisation of attention and will, Tronto – like Weil – aligns attention with a sense of passivity, placing it firmly in opposition to will. In this sense, for Tronto and Weil, 'attentiveness' discloses an opening up to the other, an act of self-surrender – rather than something that prescribes a specific moral action as such. For Weil, attention emerges from a faithfulness or a commitment to a situation and is an almost meditative, sacred opening up and surrendering of oneself to an encounter with the other. While Tronto does not adopt Weil's sense of a religiosity of attention, she argues that Weil's vision of 'passivity' and 'the absence of will' aids our understanding of the relationship between attentiveness and care, for 'in order to recognise and be attentive to others', she argues, '[o]ne needs, in a sense, to suspend one's own goals, ambitions, plans of life, and concerns' ([1993] 2009: 128).

In *Men & Girls Dance*, we get a glimpse of this setting aside of the goal-orientated will. For here, both the men and the girls engage in a process of self-surrender and opening up to the other, where personal vulnerability and anxiety are allowed to co-exist and become implicated within in the relationships of trust that emerge between the two groups of dancers and are staged aesthetically in the choreography itself. In this way, caring is performed not simply as a process of caregiving or care receiving; rather, care is reimagined as an embodied aesthetic that is reciprocal and that generates what could best be described as a community of care, a community that places an ethical demand on the performers who form it.

Conclusion: tenderness and care as a way of knowing the other

This vision of caring emerging as something communally held, fluid and unbound by predetermined roles of caregiver and care receiver disrupts conceptions of caring relationships as being structured around a transactional exchange between the giver and receiver of care. Through the performance of a fluidity of care, any sense of a caregiver or care receiver or a 'them' or an 'us', becomes disrupted and care is performed not as a transaction but as a qualitative engagement between a group of performers. In the exchanges and mutually held moments of caring modelled in *Men & Girls Dance*, there emerges a mutual tenderness that flows between the performers, a fluid caring that, like the ethical demand, has an infinitely demanding quality. It is not an action that can be completed and concluded, rather it has an epistemological character; it is a way of knowing rather than *a type of knowledge*, determining how the dancers operate together and take responsibility for one another within the space of the performance.

As the piece develops, this sense of a mutual care becomes more robust, allowing the dancers to take greater risks with one another producing some exhilarating and beautiful moments of togetherness. This occurred most strongly for me in the final section of the performance. Here, the men and girls danced together using increasingly complex, choreographical and aesthetic structures. No longer observing and describing each other as being separate and at a distance from one another, the men took the girls in their arms and lifted them high, creating some beautiful and exciting lifts sequences. These lifts were risky but were also bold and dynamic as the smallness of the girls' bodies was juxtaposed with the strength of the men's bodies – a contrast that became woven into the choreography itself. Yet these lifts did not conceal the labour of their creation, these were not ballet-type lifts that were executed with little or no visible effort; instead the choreography allowed us to witness the complicity and trust between the girls and the men that facilitated these moments of elevation. These were actions that were constructed through a process of co-created and reciprocated engagement, for while it was the men's strength that lifted the girls, the girls sustained each lift with the careful positioning of their bodies and poise. There were also moments when the choreography was designed to show the girls supporting or taking the weight of the men. In this sense, this choreography becomes established upon relationships of interdependence and a mutually held caring that is founded and fostered through the methodological development of the piece. As audience members, we witness not only the aesthetics of these moments, but a glimpse of what becomes possible through the pursuance of a process rooted in caring exchanges and mutually held attentiveness.

Men & Girls Dance invites audiences to look beyond the specifics of each performance and think differently about the moments of togetherness between men and girls more broadly. The mutuality and affective quality of these caring exchanges unsettles some of the preconceived considerations around strength and weakness, vulnerability and power that tend to become so inextricably gendered and inscribed with the discourses of risk and anxiety that circulate around moments of proximity between men and girls. In this sense, by taking such risks with the very conceit and development of the *Men & Girls Dance* project, Fevered Sleep invites audiences to look beyond social taboos and to imagine a context in which the performance of care in some way replaces, or at the very least challenges, the discourse of anxiety and risk that can frame and predetermine relationships between men and girls.

The existentially demanding process of moving *beyond* risk anxiety is summed up well by Nathan Goodman, one of the performers in the piece, who in the Fevered Sleep video describes the challenges of being involved in a creative process that required him not only to be present as a dancer but as a 'human'. He says, 'There was no hiding [...]; if you're quiet, they know you're quiet. It wasn't just about being a dancer, it was also about being human and opening up to them, for them to open up to you, so then that whole connection could work' (Goodman, quoted in Fevered Sleep, 2017). By embedding care, relationality and reciprocity within the choreographic structure of *Men & Girls Dance*, the production demanded a different form of engagement from the dancers who participated in it. Rather than simply following choreographical sequences, the design of the creative process invited the dancers to explore the dynamics and nuances of caring for one another, collectively recognising moments of individual and shared vulnerability, trust and risk. Arguably, to make this mode of mutual opening possible, both groups of dancers had to commit themselves to an attentiveness to one another. Drawing on Joan Tronto's theorisation of attentiveness, as discussed above, I suggest the dancers had to 'suspend' their individual 'goals and ambitions' and to commit to a form of collective togetherness where they would be able to 'recognise and be attentive to others' (Tronto, [1993] 2009: 128). By responding to the risk anxiety that circulates around interactions and moments of co-proximity between men and girls not with fear and avoidance but with care, tenderness and openness, *Men & Girls Dance* also begins to critique some of the gendered and oppressive discourses of masculinity and adolescence that so efficiently serve and prop up the taboos that establish and ossify bifurcations such as masculinity and femininity, men and girls, them and us. Placing caring encounters centrally within the choreography of the performance structurally positions both the male and girl dancers and their lived experience of girlhood and masculinity as being in some way enfolded within the same world. The lived experiences of both groups of dancers, to borrow from Rebecca Coleman, become '*folded though* [their] *bodies* in particular ways' (2009: 214, original emphasis) and are implicitly explored and examined by the relationships and structures of dependency and trust that develop from and are sustained by the performance process itself.

In this sense, I suggest, *Men & Girls Dance* invites us to consider how performances of care can initiate new ways of thinking about interrelationality and can be harnessed to illuminate and navigate the perilous range of anxieties that close down and prejudge how certain relationships are to be construed or imagined. In this context, performance and care can be understood as operating together as mutually transforming elements. Care places certain demands upon performance, opening up new ways of understanding the relationships of dependency and mutual support that make performing possible. Correlatively, performance provokes us to think afresh about the structure of the caring encounter itself and to recognise the power dynamics and structural inequalities that frame certain kinds of caring encounters with other people. Performing care can trouble the taboos and preconceptions that frame how we think about the gendering of caring, by challenging us to think differently about the embodied concepts of strength, power and vulnerability. Rather than concealing the risk of vulnerability, the mutually held caring in *Men & Girls Dance* reveals how it is possible to generate a performance approach that recognises and celebrates the risks of opening up to another, inviting us to look beyond the taboo of tenderness and to rethink what might be gained by acknowledging, exploring and understanding how the many interrelated connections between men and girls operate and how best to understand this experience of being folded within the world together.

Notes

1 This is an example of some of the descriptions of the men observed by the girls in the London performances and transcribed in the *Men & Girls* newspaper (Fevered Sleep, 2017).
2 Transcribed by the author from the performance at the Place Theatre, London, 2017.
3 Joan Tronto argues that there are 'four ethical elements of care', she names these as: 'attentiveness, responsibility, competence, and responsiveness' ([1993] 2009: 127).

PART II

CARE-FILLED PERFORMANCE

Caring beyond illness: an examination of Godder's socially engaged art and participatory dance for Parkinson's work

Sara Houston

A tall, balding man in shorts falls. He falls little by little, slowly. As his knees bend, he leans his body into the arms of a slight, young woman, who stands feet apart, arms gathered around his back. As he trusts her with more and more of his weight, she guides him down, down all the way to the floor. Cradling his head so he does not bang it, she whispers something to him. She stays kneeling by his curled-up body. (Field notes, *Stabat Mater*, Bassano del Grappa, 2016)

The above description is an extract from my field notes of a performance at B Motion 2016, the contemporary dance festival in Bassano del Grappa, Italy. Four choreographers were selected each to make a dance work around the Medieval lament *Stabat Mater dolorosa* (The Mother was standing full of sorrow). The particular work I describe above was devised by the contemporary expressionist choreographer, Yasmeen Godder.

Stabat Mater (2016) was the second of two works made by Godder that year. *Common Emotions* premiered in Freiburg, Germany in May, and the short, improvised work *Stabat Mater* in August at B Motion. Both works depart from previous processes Godder has used in dance making and performance: these works, being made with the dancers as leaders during the performance, unusually involved audience participation. *Common Emotions* could be considered as the 'mother' work to *Stabat Mater*, in that one movement motif – the one described above – was taken from the former work and implemented as the main and only motif in the latter. In 2017, Godder renamed *Stabat Mater*, calling it *Simple Action* and toured the work internationally, allowing for a variety of different spaces to be used for the event. In this chapter, which was largely written before *Simple Action*, I explore the new approach adopted by Godder in 2016 when developing *Stabat Mater*.

Through my reading of this piece, I argue that Godder positions the caring encounters at the heart of the creative process, drawing on the practice of care to redefine dance performance, generating a choreographic practice that is determined by an aesthetics of care. The chapter discusses this idea by exploring a specific symbiotic relationship between a community dance programme – Godder's dance for Parkinson's programme[1] – and the professional concert production of *Stabat Mater*.

While the focus of this chapter is a study of Godder's work, the productive dialogue between care and choreography emerging from *Stabat Mater* arguably has implications for dance practice more broadly, particularly for dance initiatives developed with participants who have chronic health conditions. Furthermore, I argue that by placing care centrally within dance practice, dance artists are challenged to reimagine their artistic relationship with non-trained participants and ultimately redefine their own artistic processes and dance works. Correlatively, this approach also challenges community dancers with Parkinson's to step out of their role as care receivers to position them firmly as co-creators who have some agency over their bodies and creativity.

Community dance developed in the West through the work of practitioners, such as Rudolf Laban in the 1930s. Participatory in approach, it 'involves a set of attitudes or precepts' with 'the belief that artistic practices can have an effect on the social world' (Kuppers and Robertson, 2007: 2). Diverse in its forms of dancing, it welcomes everybody, including people who are advanced in age or who have degenerative conditions, as in the case of those with Parkinson's. Collaborative by design, community dance focuses on the participant experience, making it predominantly process orientated rather than for performance (Amans, 2008). In community dance, some work is developed, for instance, with people who are marginalised or excluded in society; for example, in rehabilitation programmes for young offenders, in projects with child sex workers, in work with adults with learning disability and with those who have dementia. Dancing in these contexts, artists argue, highlights a way of resisting injustice within social situations where discrimination and exclusion is apparent (Mills, 2016). In this chapter, I intervene within these debates, proposing a dialogue between socially engaged dance work and theories of care, as developed by care ethicist Joan Tronto ([1993] 2009) and explored in the choreography of Yasmeen Godder. I propose that this dialogue enables the development of an approach to community dance that not only foregrounds inclusion and the validation and visibility of marginal people, such as those with Parkinson's, but importantly also lays the groundwork for the emergence of an aesthetics of participatory community dance, one that is rooted in relationality, attentiveness and caring.

People with Parkinson's are often vulnerable and marginalised. Symptoms are multifarious and debilitating, with the person often in need of another's care as the disease gets more severe. A neurodegenerative disease, Parkinson's is characterised by three main symptoms: slowness of movement, rigidity and tremor. The first two contribute to a dangerous deterioration in balance and postural stability. But Parkinson's is more than a disease with motor implications. Movement challenges are accompanied by other non-motor symptoms, such as diminished voices and handwriting, cognitive slowness, apathy and depression. Mainly affecting people over the age of fifty, it is the second most common neurodegenerative disorder after Alzheimer's, with one in five hundred receiving a diagnosis in the UK (Parkinson's UK, 2014). Symptoms of Parkinson's affect people in different ways, but it is common for many individuals to become increasingly isolated, often tied with a lowering of self-esteem. Mobility and the use of public transport often become problematic because of a lack of balance, loss of flexibility and freezing (which is characterised by a sudden and involuntary inability to move). Simultaneously, people living with Parkinson's also report experiencing friends abandoning their long-held friendship, so social networks decrease in size and become unable to support the individual. Apathy is also a symptom of Parkinson's and that contributes to leading a less active life. Depression is much more common in those with Parkinson's than in the general population, which again may lead to less social participation.

Research on therapeutic support for people living with Parkinson's has strongly advocated dance as an activity that helps temporarily relieve some motor symptoms (Hackney and Earhart, 2009, 2010; Batson, 2010; Heiberger *et al.*, 2011; Houston and McGill, 2013; Westheimer *et al.*, 2015), as well as helping to foster improved social networks (Foster *et al.*, 2013; Houston and McGill, 2015). Dance programmes for people with Parkinson's have been set up around the world in response to grassroots demand and a growing interest from dance artists to work in this area. Specialist training for dance artists – mainly those who are already established community dance teachers – is currently provided by a number of influential organisations around the world, such as Dance for PD® (USA), the Dance for Parkinson's Partnership UK and Dance for Parkinson's (Australia), which has meant that this sort of provision has escalated globally. However, what has not been so widely explored is the effect these engagements with community dance have had on the dance artist and on dance as an art form, and correlatively neither has the notion of care for people living with Parkinson's become part of dance discourse. Through my examination of Godder's performance work with people with Parkinson's and the focus on care, I examine how new structures of reciprocity and exchange emerge in this kind of socially engaged dance work, providing new ways of imagining dance both as a mode of care for the other and as an evolving choreographic form that enables us to rethink care in the context of the support of people living with Parkinson's.

Stabat Mater: *a performance of care*

First, I would like to start with an examination of *Stabat Mater*, a scored (improvised with instructions) performance, led by the Yasmeen Godder Company and that, I argue, should be understood as a performance of care.

Godder's interpretation of *Stabat Mater* was first set in the nave of a small chapel in the North Italian city of Bassano del Grappa. The chapel features patterned squares of cold marble and an ornate apse decorated with large, white-bodied angels, with painted walls soaring upwards to a high ceiling depicting biblical scenes. Prior to the beginning of the performance chairs are set in a pattern that follows the architecture of each individual space where the work is performed (sometimes a square, sometimes a rectangle, even a hexagon). In the chapel in Bassano, the chairs face the centre of the nave and this is where the audience and company dancers sit. At first in silence, one dancer stands up and walks over to a random audience member. Offering their hand, they talk quietly, inviting them to come into the space with them: 'Hello my name is […], I would like to offer you, if it's ok, to give me your weight, and slowly we will go down towards the floor. You can really lean on me.' In accepting that offer, the audience member, now participant, falls slowly to the floor in the dancer's arms. Slowly releasing their weight, giving it all to their partner, the participant relinquishes control over their body. Falling slowly, both figures reach the ground, the supportive partner taking care over their charge's head on the marble floor. Once on the floor, the participant is invited to stay there for as long as they want before going back to their seat. Their partner stays for a while too, sitting or kneeling by the other's body.

Slowly, the other dancers from Godder's company stand and make the same offer to other audience members. At the same time, the music begins. Performed by composer and sound artist Tomer Damsky on a shruti box, it is the old medieval lament of *Stabat Mater*, but the timing of the music is stretched. Each syllable of each word is drawn out so that nothing familiar remains of it, but the intense emotion: it conveys the searing, grieving lament through the drone and an achingly raw, sung solo chant.

The dance work develops by allowing participants to invite other audience members into the space to hold them in their arms and take them down to the floor. There is no obligation to take part. Men hold women, women hold other women, children hold men, men hold men, older and younger bodies fall, keep falling and lying on the ground. Although the movement instructions remain the same, the work itself shifts and develops as audience-participants are gently encouraged to adopt more challenging levels of participation and actions, all of which are framed by a responsibility of caring for each other.

The responsibility for care seems high. If the faller is dropped, there is potential for their head to strike the hard, marble floor or for their legs or back to get twisted. Even if the fall is physically safe, there is still potential embarrassment for both parties if one overbalances and falls on top of the other or skirts rise too far to maintain dignity. The risk is not low and yet everyone takes time to lower to the floor, taking time to think through what they need to do in order to take care and to think through the steps required to lower someone safely and with dignity to the floor. The instruction 'to give weight' also allows for different interpretations of going down to the floor, permitting fallers different ways of conceiving 'giving weight'. Timing is established by the music, which, through the drone, carries all participants on a repetitive wave, lingering within each note, bending into dissonance and consonance, and by the freedom of the score where each couple has the flexibility of taking as long as they want. Additionally, because each couple's moment of falling is special in that it is uniquely theirs to make, each couple needs to attend to each other in a very focused, even intimate and careful manner. They do not perform falling to the audience. This moment is just for them, a private moment that if one is in the audience, one is privileged to watch, and it is not uncommon to see an audience member weep from the emotion created. In creating this private moment, each couple develops a collaborative caring journey together that is structured through a shared understanding of a relationship of trust that is safe and dignified. The private endeavour is an important way of thinking about *Stabat Mater* as performing, what theatre scholar James Thompson calls 'an aesthetics of care' (2015). The quality of these participatory moments resonates with Thompson's account of aesthetic quality that 'seeks no external recognition' and that possess a 'boldness' because the 'aesthetic value' of the project 'is found in co-created moments and not only in public display' (2015: 438). Projects such as this, as Thompson argues, tend to be configured 'around an aesthetics of care' and rely 'on building mutual activities of sharing, support, co-working and relational solidarity within a framework of artistry or creative endeavour' (2015: 438).

In *Stabat Mater*, there is a vulnerability in falling and holding that produces a performance of a 'conjoined effort' and 'intimate exchange' that discloses a real attempt, in each moment of falling, to embody the sense of trust, responsibility and dignity evoked in this risky undertaking.

As a participant in this performance, lying on the floor, looking up at the ceiling, listening to the incantation, I feel like it allows a space for contemplation, where I am invited to make my own room and to let in the sound of the grieving mother, standing, embracing and falling with her dead son. Holding someone else is more of a responsibility – I hope I won't drop them – it feels a serious, yet pleasurable task to offer someone my embrace. Observing others, I notice a beauty in the piece's simplicity. It is a moving tribute to the Pieta, inscribed in the images around us and alluded to within the musical score. It also seems to offer contemporary reflection on a relation between two people, made all the more genuine by the use of unassuming, untrained audience members. The falls enacted around the room all start with an embrace. The participants must place their trust in the strangers holding them while they let go and each participant and dancer is charged with a responsibility for the person who has entrusted them with the care of their body and dignity. In this way, Godder invites an experiential engagement with both giving and receiving care, while also using this participatory structure to create potent images of the performance of caring itself.

The performances of care in Godder's *Stabat Mater* emerge in several different ways: there is the action of physically caring for another while that person is falling, the care taken when leading an audience-participant into the performing space so that he or she may fall (with their consent), the care of the embrace of the arms around the body, the careful taking of the body down gently to the floor, the staying with and caring for that person while they lie down and the choreographical care taken when re-enacting the ritual in the same way. To further understand how these different caring actions are conceptualised and embodied, it is useful to reflect on Joan Tronto's ([1993] 2009) account of care being made up of four elements, which include: noticing the need for care, taking up the responsibility of doing it, the work of caring and how the care is received. Within an artistic context, these four elements form part of what Thompson terms 'preparation, execution and exhibition' (2015: 437), which encompasses the preparation and decision making undertaken prior to the commencement of a community arts project, the process of working through art with others and then showing that work to others in some form. Each element can be thought about in terms of the care needed at each stage to foster connection and relationships between participants and artists.

The elements of preparation, execution and exhibition are also all evident in Godder's work, with care central at each stage. Godder made the decision to place care for others, notably, strangers (some old, some young, some possibly with chronic disease or ill health) as a central thematic to *Stabat Mater* at the beginning of the choreographic process when she started preparing for the project and noticed the need for care within the participatory moment itself – when the offer to fall is made within the execution of the performance. The offer to enter the performance space is approached with respect for the hesitant audience member. The stretched-out hand offered to an audience member is open. The person it is directed to need not accept it, yet if they do, they are led by the hand gently into a clear area. The explanation is done in a whisper so only the audience member can hear. This emphasises the privacy of the fall, despite being surrounded by people, and underlines the specialness of the fleeting yet intimate relationship between catcher and faller. This offer with awareness or 'listening', as philosopher Maurice Hamington suggests (2004: 6), is accompanied by a responsibility to perform the encounter of that care. While the dancers initially take on the role of caregiver, this is then passed on to audience-participants who enter the space and then become the caregivers to other audience members who also join. The piece itself choreographically generates an exchange of care. There is even a feeling of reciprocity where roles change, even reverse, where the cared for give back to the carers or to others who have yet to experience falling within the piece.

Thompson argues that arts initiatives are ethical when care is taken to invest in creating relationships between the people involved. It is this thematic of relationality, responsibility and the exchange of care that emerges in *Stabat Mater* that I suggest is most strongly resonant of what Thompson refers to when he uses the term an 'aesthetics of care' to describe an adherence to 'a set of values realised in a relational process that emphasise engagements between individuals or groups over time' (2015: 437).

Likewise, there is also a connection to be made here with Tronto's ([1993] 2009) account of what she describes as the four basic ethical elements of care, which are attentiveness, responsibility, competence and responsiveness. In order to better understand the performance of care in *Stabat Mater*, I shall examine how three of these elements – attentiveness, responsibility and responsiveness – become activated within this participatory context. First, I shall explore responsibility: Tronto describes responsibility of care as a moral decision to say 'I will', because of the specific context in which I am living; not through obligation, but through a moral sense that this may be a good act. She gives the example of the responsibility displayed by some Europeans during the Second World War, who helped Jewish neighbours and strangers to escape Nazi persecution (Tronto, 2015: 132, 209). They did not do this out of duty, but out of a sense of responsibility to their fellow human beings. During *Stabat Mater*, the responsibility during the performance emerges first from the audience-participants, who after experiencing a fall take up the option of continuing with the care act – in other words, taking responsibility for holding someone in their arms as a catcher – and second from the performance act itself where the vulnerability of the individual falling exposes the risk involved. No one is told how to catch someone falling, rather the company dancers perform this and embody the implicit responsibility involved from the beginning of the work. By relying on a form of embodied and remembered know-how, the catcher-audience member has to conduct not just a feat of memory – Where did she hold her hands? At what moment did she bend her knee to help take weight? – but also a feat of embodied imagination. As Hamington argues, our own knowledge about how to care can be embodied and transferred to new situations and to strangers through a 'caring imagination' (2004: 4). In stepping into the performing space, the (now) catcher-audience member draws on his or her own embodied knowledge of care in order to help navigate and support the journey of the next faller. Using his or her imagination and through experimentation, the catcher-audience member finds the best and most supportive way of guiding the person in their arms. This also becomes an ethical act because the catcher-audience member uses empathy and his or her bodily understanding of caring to cross into the unknown territory of catching and to keep the stranger secure and held with attention and care.

The decision to step forth and become a participant in *Stabat Mater* is not without risk in relation to the act of falling itself but also in terms of the care needed to support someone else who falls. While some audience-participants struggle to hold their charges, they are immediately supported by attentive members of Godder's company who quickly step in. No one drops anyone's head on the marble floor. In these shared performances of mutual support and care, Tronto's ethical element of responsibility emerges as an embodied way of knowing and caring for others. The shared sense of responsibility that emerges between the professional dancers and the audience-participants only becomes possible because of the embodied caring knowledge that develops between both groups. This knowledge is enhanced and extended further through performances of attentiveness, an element of performance that manifests Tronto's second ethical element of care.

The performed attentiveness in *Stabat Mater* creates a situation where the catchers' bodies become alert and able to respond to minute changes of body weight in the faller and where the company dancers are able to respond to occasional drastic changes in the catcher's stance in relation to the faller's weight. In this way, attentiveness is performed through sensing, through sight, through feeling the pressure of another's body, as well as through knowledge of a body's mechanics. Attentiveness in this context, in other words, is channelled through, or resides in the body, yet as shown above, it is also imaginative. The need to sense when the situation becomes too dangerous involves not just bodily embodied knowledge, but also bodily imagination in order to change the course of action. 'What if?' is a question that the catcher's body continually asks in order for the couple to stay safe (What if I put my hands here? What if his head goes back? What if I lunge to the side? What if I go slower?). 'What if?' is a question for the imagination and, following Hamington (2004), is an ethical question of care because it demands that the catcher thinks of the faller's welfare in relation to the catcher's own present and future actions. The response to the other is framed through an imaginative response to care for his or her bodily welfare.

Responsiveness is the third ethical element of care I want to explore here. Although in essence, it focuses on the manner in which the care receiver responds to the caregiver, in Tronto's account of it ([1993] 2009), she concentrates on reminding the reader of the ethical implication of caring for someone vulnerable, where power resides in the caregiver, rather than care receiver. She states: 'The moral precept of responsiveness requires that we remain alert to the possibilities of abuse that arise with vulnerability' ([1993] 2009: 135). Responsiveness calls the carer constantly to evaluate his or her understanding of the needs of the care receiver. Tronto argues that because caring challenges the idea that we are all self-reliant and autonomous beings, one needs to 'consider the other's position as that other expresses it. Thus, one is engaged from the standpoint of the other, but not simply by presuming that the other is exactly like the self' (Tronto, [1993] 2009: 136). Tronto's account of responsiveness in caring acknowledges the unequal power structures between the carer and the care receiver, as well as the need for a physically close relationship. It draws attention to the vulnerability of the care received and highlights the otherness implicit in the different physical, mental and environmental situation of the care receiver compared to the caregiver. As I will now move on to discuss, *Stabat Mater* provides a useful manifestation of how vulnerability and care operate together as Tronto's account of care usefully illustrates.

Tronto's argument about the 'ethical vulnerability of caring' draws attention to the power a carer has over the care receiver. To think critically about this in the context of *Stabat Mater*, it is useful to examine Dana Mills' (2016) proposal that dance may cultivate a situation where it provides equality for all participants. However, first it is important to note the fertile ground on which dance, as a medium of connection and communication, may have the potential to create a difference for those who feel vulnerable or marginalised. Mills argues that dance is a mode of communication that may give a voice to those who are silenced by other modes of communication and signification. By way of an example, she considers the black miners in apartheid South Africa who invented the gumboot dance to communicate when they were not allowed to speak. Mills argues that this provides a potent example of how dances open up a 'greater equality in our own political discourse' through participation (2016: 122). She argues that 'Dance moves human beings beyond boundaries – of their own bodies, constantly reinterpreted and reconfigured as spaces; and of their shared worlds, challenging the limits of who they may speak with and who perceives them as equal interlocutors' (2016: 122).

Mills also examines some groups of marginalised people who use their bodies to bring a feeling of connection to others, such as Palestinian Dabke dancers and the female 'One Billion Rising' marchers protesting against domestic abuse.[2] She proposes the notion that by dancing, people may circumnavigate their own boundaries and challenges and find connections with others, an idea that is also explored by other scholars (see, for example, Jackson and Shapiro-Phim, 2008; Rowe, 2010; Houston, 2015). I argue that thinking about the possibility of forming interconnections with others through dance enables us to understand some of the relational moments in *Stabat Mater*. These relational moments – connections between participants – are highlighted at the moment of the fall, when overcoming the challenge to fall and to hold, as well as through the offer of a positive space to take a risk to fall. Yet the idea of equality that Mills also promotes is less evident within Godder's piece, particularly when framed through the element of responsiveness. In *Stabat Mater*, responsiveness is indicated in the minute shifts of body weight of the faller into the carer. As the piece has developed, it has been possible to notice that as the faller trusts more, more weight is given to the person supporting them. The partnership in terms of supporting weight becomes more unequal as the pair get closer to the floor. The faller entrusts where and how they fall to the carer. The carer then starts to take more responsibility for the faller whose vulnerability increases as the fall progresses and at the point the carer realises that this person is not falling like the last person he or she embraced. The carer has to take each individual faller as a unique case as they present themselves to him or her and experience the uniqueness of that fall with the care receiver. Moreover, as the faller sinks into the floor, the audience may witness the body at its most visibly vulnerable, which is heightened by the staging and the positioning of the faller's prone body displayed on the hard marble floor after the fall. The audience also witnesses the crumpled clothing, the socks that the person chose, the dirt on their shoes, dishevelled hair and yet arguably these fallers appear strangely beautiful. I would suggest that in the moment of the fall, the audience witnesses the human being, rather than the performer. In the vulnerable state as the cared for, the audience-participant is seen in all his or her imperfections most human.

Godder's *Stabat Mater* is not just a performance of care based on the actions and relations within the show, the choreographic approach adopted in this performance is rooted in Godder's participatory dance work with people with Parkinson's. As I shall now go on to discuss, it was Godder's experiential engagement with Parkinson's dancers that led to the caring encounter being explored and placed so centrally within *Stabat Mater*. In order to contextualise Godder's engagement in dance for Parkinson's, I need to situate myself, as a dance scholar, within this context. From 2010–15, I led two mixed-methods research studies evaluating the effect and experience of people living with Parkinson's who came once a week to a dance class led by the English National Ballet (Houston and McGill, 2013, 2015; McGill *et al.*, 2014; McGill *et al.*, 2018). The programme had the art of ballet at its centre. The focus of the project was not to try to heal people through dancing, although the evaluation strongly pointed to the programme's therapeutic benefits on physical, social, emotional and cognitive levels (Houston, 2015; Houston and McGill, 2015). Rather the project aimed to engage with a group of people not normally within the company's core audience (as spectators or participants) and to introduce them to ballet and the repertory of the company.

As I expanded the research nationally and internationally to absorb the contexts and theoretical dimensions of the field of dance for Parkinson's, I became aware that art making and art doing were ultimately the primary aims for most of the initiatives that had emerged around the world and, furthermore, many dance artists rejected the idea that their work was dance therapy (Houston, 2014). Many of these dancers were influenced by Dance for PD, a dance programme for people with Parkinson's originally set up in 2001 by the Mark Morris Dance Group mentioned above. Like the English National Ballet programme it influenced, Dance for PD is a model of incorporating company repertory and music within an artistic environment, with the imaginative inflections of poetic imagery, language and movement and a focus on work created by Morris, the teachers and people who live with Parkinson's. One of the artistic initiatives that had a slightly different emphasis was the dance for Parkinson's programme in Freiburg, Germany. Held in the *Museum für Neue Kunst* and initiated by Theatre Freiburg, it was led by dance artists Monica Gillette, Mia Habib and Gary Joplin. What attracted me to this programme was that Gillette, in particular, was eager to explore what dance could offer in terms of thinking physically about movement challenges and what dancers with Parkinson's could offer to the inquisitive dance artist.

In 2015, Gillette helped set up the collaborative German and Israeli project Störung/Hafra'ah.[3] In conjunction with Theatre Freiburg and the University of Freiburg, it brought together dance artists in Europe and

Israel, postgraduate scientists from several universities in the two countries and people with Parkinson's who danced. I was invited to become a mentor for the postgraduates and a contributor to the Freiburg meetings. The project aimed to explore Parkinson's and movement by disrupting the habits of all those participating in the project. It encouraged project members to research and dance differently to habitual experiences in order to not only potentially learn new ways of exploring movement, but also to think from another's perspective. All the different group members were treated as equals, with everyone participating in the movement sessions and discussions as important contributors.

Godder and her company took part in the project, hosting and leading dance sessions for people with Parkinson's and the Israeli scientists in Jaffa, where the company was based. They also contributed by participating in various symposia hosted in Freiburg and Tel Aviv. The sessions Godder hosted were led by various members of her company and her artistic partners and were based around the expertise of each leader, incorporating movement practices, such as release technique, improvisation, capoeira and folk dance. Despite not having had any experience of community dance work with people with movement disorder before, Godder embraced the project as a challenge and despite Störung/Hafra'ah ending in 2016, Godder continued to offer twice-weekly dance sessions to local people living with Parkinson's in the region of Tel Aviv.

Often framed as research workshops, the sessions with the Parkinson's dancers and scientists became a catalyst for the development of Godder's other performance work, leading her to work differently with her company members. For Godder, the experience of working with people living with Parkinson's became impactful not only for the aesthetics of the choreography she was interested in but also how she worked with her company, leading her to say:

> The Störung/Hafra'ah project really influenced how I see my dance making by simply opening the door of my studio to different people and communities and dancing together in a common space. This kind of unexpected intimate meeting in the studio – through the body, through different methodologies of movement and improvisation – created a drive for me to bring this exact thing onto the stage and propose it in real time in a performative environment. (2016a)

From my observation of the project and the development of *Stabat Mater*, it would seem that what shifted in Godder's approach to her own company work was not simply the meeting of these different groups of people but rather her own developing engagement in the often unspoken dialogues of care that framed the Störung/Hafra'ah work. Ostensibly focusing on movement disorder, the Störung/Hafra'ah initiative gave members a platform to work together through movement exploration, discussion and experimentation with different research methodologies, and this allowed for new thinking, not only in terms of research, but also in terms of how the company relates to and involves each other. An illustration of new thinking and new approaches to artistic collaboration and experimentation can be seen in the meeting of different bodies and movement strategies that inspired Godder's choreographic developments in *Common Emotion* and then in *Stabat Mater*. In both of these works, an offer was made to audience members to participate and contribute meaningfully to the development of the performance while it was happening. The participatory experience in the studio was not one that was separate from Godder's performance and creative work. Rather, the importance of interdependence, the demands for attentiveness, responsibility, competence and responsiveness in Störung/Hafra'ah began to determine Godder's thinking and how she approached the choreography of *Stabat Mater*.

The participatory experience in the studio also had other impacts, as Godder recalls: 'I think the strongest impact this project has had on my research process has been more on a conceptual level of what a company is' (2015a). Dance companies commonly tend to be conceived as around a hierarchical structure with the artistic director and executive director taking the lead. Moreover, dance companies also tend to make work for audiences, without generating much interaction with them. What Störung/Hafra'ah introduced into Godder's work was a change in relations between the audience, artists and director and this required company members to reflect on their own interdependence. Godder drew on this challenge to further redefine the relationship between members of her company, as well as between the dancers and audiences. The goal of making art was still there, but audiences took on an importance that became intertwined with making art.

Godder comments that the Parkinson's work 'really shifted something in the way I think about a process' (2015a). So, for Godder, both structure and artistic process were influenced by the Parkinson's engagement and in several ways. Importantly, the experience of opening the door to people with a movement disorder triggered what Godder (2016b) calls a 'cross-pollination' of people, ways of dancing, ways of leading and relating. She notes that, 'it created new relationships and dynamics. Learning this from each other' (2015b). Godder describes this cross-pollination of people as a process of coming together for a common project 'where we met each other and ourselves in different ways, offered a rich renewal in the studio for creation' (2015a). For Godder, Störung/Hafra'ah had fulfilled its objectives in that it had allowed her the opportunity to reassess her approaches to movement and choreography and to what it meant to be a contemporary dance company working within, and contributing to, a community. I would also argue that it is the recognition of the need for caring relationships and caring practices when working with individuals different from oneself that has elicited new approaches to making dance. Godder (2015b) describes this as 'a small revolution inside the workings of my company and myself in how I worked with my collaborators'. She views the revolution as shifting 'the artistic process, interpersonal relationships and hierarchy and how to create classes' (2015b), and it is evident that the Parkinson's work challenged Godder's tendency towards autocracy and seeing the choreographer as the creator who keeps a firm hold on what is produced and how.

In opening the company studio to others to use alongside company dancers, Godder also developed a sharing of space and ideas. The Parkinson's dance sessions brought about a more facilitative, consensual way of working, where learning became more of a two-way process between the non-professional and professional dancers and because of that, input from each individual grew to be valued. So much so, that in 2018, Godder set up the Moving Communities conference (2018) to celebrate the learning from Störung/Hafra'ah, inviting people with Parkinson's to co-lead a movement workshop for delegates. There is a connection here with Tronto's account of care's capacity to contribute towards the practice of being democratic citizens. Tronto proposes that: 'The qualities of attentiveness, of responsibility, of competence, or responsiveness, need not be restricted to the immediate objects of our care, but can also inform our practices as citizens. They direct us to a politics in which there is, at the center, a public discussion of needs, and an honest appraisal of the intersection of needs and interests' ([1993] 2009: 167–8). For Tronto, and I would argue for Godder, caring hones the qualities of attentiveness, responsibility and responsiveness as well as the skills of competence. Many people living with Parkinson's are vulnerable, vulnerable to the effects of physical and mental degeneration, as well as vulnerable to social stigma and loss of dignity (Solimeo, 2009; Houston, 2015). Dancing, however, arguably creates a safe environment in which to take physical (and social) risks and to be supported through a network of people who understand (Houston and McGill, 2015; Westheimer *et al.*, 2015). Moreover, it creates an environment in which people with Parkinson's may suggest and create movement ideas themselves. As a productive, positive and collaborative activity, I would suggest that dancing can also aid in building communal strength, inclusivity and richness. Nachum Almog, a Parkinson's dancer who participated in Störung/Hafra'ah articulated this well when he said, 'I started feeling a lot more light and refreshed on a daily basis. Participating in the project made me want to move more than before. I feel more vital. I started thinking about new projects I'd like to initiate in the spirit of this project' (2016).

By engaging with dancers who move differently and who sometimes have a high degree of vulnerability, Godder and her company developed ways of working that were caring and embraced people. This meant finding ways of working that initiated a great generosity of feeling and enthusiasm. It put the humanity back into the creation process, in other words. However, I also contend that Godder's decision to take part in Störung/Hafra'ah enhanced our understanding of how dance can be attentive and caring in and of itself. While the attentiveness that Godder initially displayed was simply a first action of opening her studio doors to people with Parkinson's, rather than keeping it within the closed circle of contemporary dance aficionados and virtuosos, this simple gesture led to a fundamental development in her choreographical process and the structure of her company. As Maurice Hamington states, 'we must come to know one another, preferably in direct ways, to appreciate difference and create common cause' (2004: 147). In this sense, for Godder, literal acts of opening her studio door (situated in the mixed Arab and Jewish town of Jaffa) to people with Parkinson's, led to the symbolic championing of diversity and inclusion within dance practice and dance making. This ultimately leads, I suggest, to an emerging embodied awareness of the other.

Working together as partners in dance also importantly challenges the primacy of the trained, non-disabled body over the disabled, non-trained participant within professional performance, as well as in the community setting. By altering her working practices and opening her study to people living with Parkinson's, Godder created an expanded vision to moving, both by people with Parkinson's and also by her company. One Parkinson's dancer who participated in the project wrote: 'I learnt how to start dealing with the disease' (Shalom, 2016), and one of the company dancers commented: 'The meeting with the scientists and Parkinson's dancers forced me to incorporate a new and different way of thinking, change my habits and the very way I express myself as an artist and a human being' (Enosh, 2016). Workshops set up as part of the project were diverse in what they offered, and this alone allowed people with Parkinson's and Godder's company to explore differences and a variety of dance forms, such as folk dance, and movement practices, such as capoeira, which may not have been familiar dancing styles for many people in the workshop. Described as a 'toolbox' by Godder,[4] the varied forms and practices led to different systems of moving, as well as the development of distinctive philosophies and techniques. As a toolbox, the participants with Parkinson's and the professional dance artists collectively had a wider palette of approaches from which to draw to supplement or overturn physical or mental habits and times of movement challenge. Uri Shafir, one of Godder's dancers and a choreographer of his own work, stated: 'I've discovered new ways I engage with the present in my work. I changed the way I perform and opened my mind to a new experience of being in the moment' (2016). Some of the leaders of each workshop, who were members of Godder's company, also had the first-time experience of needing to adapt movement phrases and tasks for some of the participants, which necessitated thinking differently about their approach to movement. Working specifically with those who move differently, as people with Parkinson's do, challenges the assumptions and attitudes to what movement is considered 'good' or 'correct' in the dance class: the aesthetic moral order alters. Within the workshop context and this inclusive environment, Godder and her company experienced a shift in how they thought about the creation of movement for performance and the aesthetics of performance itself: how movement was created, its aesthetic, who does it. These ideas began to emerge as the company began to develop a new sense of care for each other and the participants they were working with.

Conclusion

Working with people with Parkinson's and the care this necessitated also changed Godder's choreographic approach by leading her to develop more trusting relationships with her dancers and with the work itself. The invitation to become audience-participants in *Stabat Mater* requires individuals to react and be present in 'real time', rather than to rely on rehearsal processes. This means that no one is entirely sure what is going to happen on stage each night. In trusting to the humanity of the artistic process and the caring structures nurtured through the community sessions and rehearsal process, Godder took a big risk artistically, one that required her to also adopt a position of vulnerability. The outcome is a style of work that is rooted in care; that is nurtured, developed and changed by participant involvement. In being openly generous in offering the audience a place to participate in their own style, Godder incorporates a community dance ethos into her artistic work. She also folds back into the performance her own need to trust from a place of vulnerability; just as she asks the audience-participants to trust their carers to catch their fall, so she opens the performance process up and trusts the audience-participants to present in their own ways.

What *Stabat Mater* and Störung/Hafra'ah underline is the interdependence and care at the heart of Godder's Parkinson's and performance projects. More than this, what is revealed from these projects is how the demands of caring for others who are vulnerable and physically challenged became a fundamental creative force in Godder's practice, leading to the development of new aesthetics and new ways of positioning professional dancers and community participants together. Responsiveness to caregiving and care receiving becomes a two-way process here, opening out the generosity of that initial attentiveness to trust and vulnerability on all sides. In this way with Parkinson's dancers, artistic practice as caring may be thought of slightly differently to caregiving in the sense of looking after someone ill or frail. Although this is not to deny the power of influence the choreographer still holds, artistic practice as described above may give all participants a feeling of agency and creative ownership within the process at the same time as putting everyone in a position of vulnerability, as well as trust. Interdependence and reciprocity then become a key feature of Godder's participatory, socially engaged art work and art practice.

The implications for community dance and performance work in the light of these innovations are interesting. Godder demonstrates how community dance practice does not have to exist as something shut off from professional performance work. It may be allowed to bleed into and arguably ultimately shape artistic decisions. She is not the first to use non-trained performers.[5] Godder's work, however, is nurtured within community dance exploration and in this way is different to many other choreographers' works using community dancers. Crossing over into dance for Parkinson's work, she has instituted a three-way discussion between participants, company dancers and choreographer, where learning is mutual and where care for the integration of different people, bodies, ways of moving has become an important theme and process within artistic creation and production. A more aligned example with similar values would be Fevered Sleep's *Men & Girls Dance* project (2013), discussed in Chapter 3, where the thrust of the work is mutual collaboration and play between a group of girls who dance for fun and the professional male dancers.

The initiatives taken by Godder also have implications for the development of specialist provision for people with long-term health conditions who would like to dance. Although the notion of care is at the heart of the practice, *Stabat Mater* illustrates how dance in this context does not have to be focused around healing or around a direct engagement with medical treatment; it also moves beyond some forms of applied theatre and community dance where participants make art and show what they can do. Godder's choreographic work demonstrates how socially engaged dance can offer a symbiotic relationship between participant community dancers and with artists who are open to investigate their own practice through a performance of care. This caring about the wider social remit of artistic work may alter the aesthetics of dance works. It may also alter ways of working where care for people in the process of making art becomes as important as producing a critically successful end product.

Notes

1 See http://yasmeengodder.com/Parkinson/contemporary-dance-for-people-living-with-parkinson-s-disease (accessed 05/12/17).
2 The One Billion Rising movement became a worldwide protest movement in the early 2000s. Learnt dances were used as the content of flash mobs and marches to highlight the fact that one billion women globally are violently abused by partners and others.
3 The title is often written Störung/הערפה, which can be translated as 'disorder' from the German and Hebrew (Hafra'ah, 2017).
4 See http://yasmeengodder.com/works/common-emmotions (accessed 05/12/17).
5 Jérôme Bel is another high-profile choreographer who includes non-trained dancers in his work, for example. *Gala* (2015), by way of illustration, featured mostly community dancers and highlighted their individual approaches to dancing, although the work was tightly conceived and directed by Bel. See Chapter 5 by Dave Calvert in this volume for a critical response to Bel's work.

Convivial theatre: care and debility in collaborations between non-disabled and learning disabled theatre makers

Dave Calvert

Over the last century, while the labels used to identify learning disability have frequently been reviewed, intellectual impairment itself has remained resolutely wedded to the concept of care. In the UK, for example, the 1913 Mental Deficiency Act, which legislated for the coercive institutionalisation of people with learning disabilities in asylums, was built on the Royal Commission for the Care and Control of the Feeble Minded, which had presented its report to Parliament in 1908. At the other end of the twentieth century, the collapse of the asylum system in the UK in the 1970s led to the Thatcher government's policy of community care, as set out in the Mental Health Act of 1983 and refined in the NHS and Community Care Act 1990.

Academic attention in America has also been preoccupied with care, as Patrick McDonagh suggests: 'For years, the only available histories of idiocy and related concepts were works such as Leo Kanner's *A History of the Care and Study of the Mentally Retarded* [...] and Peter Tyor and Leland Bell's *Caring for the Retarded in America*' (2008: 10). This centrality of care reflects the medicalisation of the learning disabled field in the nineteenth century, which superseded a period of interventions by educationalists who had sought to develop teaching methods that would liberate the developmental potential of people with learning disabilities; the medical model, by contrast, emphasised individual deficiency over capability and defined learning disability as an unimprovable condition requiring lifelong care, especially medical care. The medical model remained dominant until challenged at the end of the twentieth century by the social model, which reimagined disability as the product of an inaccessible social environment rather than individual difference. Agendas of care also began to widen at this point, from the institutional regimes of medical care, linked (as in the 1908 Royal Commission) with control, to personalised care with the educational aims of offering support and nurturing potential. Theatre with learning disabled actors, which emerged alongside community care in the 1980s, continues to cater for the dependencies of learning disabled actors, while also seeking to develop accessible training and aesthetic forms that liberate capacity and engage with the actors as artistic collaborators.

Ellen Feder and Eva Kittay have recognised that dependents, as well as their caregivers, are excluded from the public sphere by 'models of social and political life' which, under a liberal worldview, are 'fixated on interactions between autonomous equal agents' (2002: 2). They have accordingly argued for 'the need to reintegrate care into a paradigm of just moral and political arrangements, but one that acknowledges those dependencies that call for care and support' (2002: 3). Kittay's own radical assertion of the social value and necessity of care is grounded in reflections on her personal relationship with her profoundly disabled daughter Sesha and her observation that 'the inclusion of people with mental retardation may well be liberalism's limit case' (2002: 258). In developing her 'dependency critique of equality' (Kittay, 1999: 4), Kittay acknowledges that she starts from 'the case of a dependent who is unable to reciprocate' but does so 'not because [she] assume[s] it to be the most typical case, but because it is the case most in need of consideration if one is asking about the social responsibility to the caregiver' (1999: xiii).

In examining this especially heightened example of dependency, however, Kittay (1999) is clear in adding two key caveats: that the relationship with Sesha is still a reciprocal and mutually caring one in which Kittay is also dependent on her daughter; and that all people in a complex society are dependent, even though some forms of dependence may not be apparent. Through exploring the dynamics of care and dependency invoked by learning disability, therefore, Kittay proposes that '[r]ather than denying our interdependence, my aim is to find a knife sharp enough to cut through the fiction of our independence' (1999: xiii).

In this chapter, I will pick up these concerns to consider how the dynamics of dependency, equality, interdependence and care play out in two performances in which ensembles of actors with learning disabilities collaborate with non-disabled directors: *Disabled Theater*, produced by Theater HORA and directed by Jérôme Bel; and *Contained*, produced by Mind the Gap theatre company and directed by Alan Lyddiard. Through a cross-reading of the two performances, I will argue that new ways of reading *Disabled Theater* can be opened up by acknowledging the hidden mutual dependencies and 'attitude of care' (Kittay, 2002: 259) that are made more explicit in *Contained*. To extend the analysis of these performances as political theatre whose dynamics of care contest the foundations of liberal, and neoliberal, principles, I will connect Kittay's project with Jasbir K. Puar's 'push for a broader politics of debility that destabilizes the seamless production of abled-bodies in relation to disability' (2009: 166). Adopting Puar's concept of 'conviviality' (2009: 168), I introduce the term 'convivial theatre' to identify performances in which the politics and reciprocal dynamics of care are operative and palpable.

Disabled Theater

Disabled Theater, first produced in 2012, is a touring production by Theater HORA, a Swiss company of learning disabled actors established in 1993 by non-disabled director Michael Elber. For this production, the company invited the celebrated French choreographer Jérôme Bel to direct, and the resulting performance is often perceived as belonging primarily to Bel's repertoire rather than Theater HORA's. Gerald Siegmund (2017) proposes that Bel's collected work constitutes an ongoing critical interrogation of dance itself, a discursive project in which Bel sets the parameters for a theatrical examination of the dancing body as culturally produced. Everything that happens within these parameters therefore participates in 'the discourse "Jérôme Bel"' (Siegmund, 2017: 12).

Siegmund accordingly suggests that *Disabled Theater* attends to several recurring concerns within Bel's discursive project:

> First, it analyses the features of a theater or dance production by reducing, isolating and displaying its constituent elements […] Second, it cleverly […] investigates and, above all, celebrates the role cultural codes and sign systems […] play in producing subjects […] Third, […] it broaches the issue of the power relations at work in the theater and its apparatus. (2015: 14)

While maintaining these long-standing concerns, *Disabled Theater* also belongs to a particular phase of Bel's work, in which he extends the discourse 'by allowing amateurs or untrained dancers to take the stage' (Siegmund, 2017: 226). Although he frequently works with non-dancers during this phase, *Disabled Theater* is Bel's first experience of working with professional learning disabled actors.

Critical considerations of the production have often focused on the aesthetic and political significance of learning disability, producing tensions between competing claims that Bel's discursive project either grants agency to the learning disabled actors or exploits them. In outlining these tensions below, I propose that the discourse shaped by Bel fails to take account of the discursive dimensions of learning disability itself, undermining the political efficacy of his project. My subsequent analysis, which argues that such tensions can be alleviated through closer attention to the dynamics of care, is based on experiencing the show in two formats: a video recording of a performance at the Schauspielhaus Zürich in March 2014 and two live performances at La Commune, Paris in October 2017 as part of Festival D'Automne's Jérôme Bel season.

The staging for *Disabled Theater* is pared back and functional, with a single row of eleven empty chairs, one for each of the learning disabled actors, forming a shallow arc across the stage, each with a bottle of water placed beside it. This minimal setting establishes the actors as the focal point of the show, which is structured around six tasks that they are asked to perform individually: to spend one minute on stage before the audience; to state their name, age and occupation; to identify their disability; to dance to a piece of music of their own choosing; to give their opinion of the show and to take a bow.

Downstage left, a technical desk is set up for the operation of sound, which is run in semi-darkness by the non-disabled 'translator', a role undertaken variously by freelance performers Simone Truong and Chris Weinheimer, employed solely for this production. The translator introduces each task for the audience, in French, German or English as appropriate, and then again for the actors in their native Swiss-German, as well as translating the actors' individual speeches. Beyond its practical function in international touring, this role also reflects the necessity of translation in the process between the actors and the French-speaking Bel. While introducing the tasks, the translators make the devising process explicit by using such phrases as 'Jérôme then asked the actors to'. This repeated invocation of the absent Bel, Siegmund proposes, 'does not refer to the actual person Jérôme Bel. Rather, it refers to the (depersonalized, structural) *function of power* that organizes the field of performance' (2015: 23, original emphasis). Bel's contribution, according to this reading, is to establish and authorise the discursive frame within which the performance unfolds. Accordingly, 'the program notes list Jérôme Bel as responsible for the concept, whereas all the performers are given credit not only for performing but also for creating the show' (Siegmund, 2015: 23). This neat compartmentalisation of the respective contributions is reflected in the performance structure, in which the translator impassively articulates Bel's commands from the dimly lit sidelines, separated from the space in which the actors provide the central aesthetic content of the show. Bel's authority, Siegmund observes, does not therefore extend to choreographing the performers and, within each task, the actors 'are given agency to speak and act in their own right' (2015: 19).

After announcing each task, the translator calls the actors forward one at a time to undertake it. Once they have all done so, the translator then moves on to the next task. The one interruption to this simple structure is in the solo dances. These are self-choreographed pieces, for which the actors – who have little or no dance training – have chosen their own music and shaped their own routines without any technical or artistic input from Bel. Originally, the translator announces, Bel selected the seven best dances for performance, and these are presented as task four. As part of the fifth task, however, while giving his opinion of the show, the actor Gianni Blumer complains to the audience that he has been denied the opportunity to present his solo dance. Consequently, before the final task of taking a bow, the translator informs the spectators that Bel changed his mind and, at this point, allows the remaining dance solos to be seen.

Blumer's challenge to the director's authority has precedents in Bel's earlier productions. In *Pichet Klunchun and Myself* (2004), for example, Bel (as the eponymous 'Myself') exchanges experiences and choreography with Pichet Klunchun, a Thai dancer working in the traditional Khôn form. Countering criticism that the performance maintains postcolonial forms of appropriation, Siegmund points to Klunchun's open ridiculing of Bel's fame to argue that the French choreographer's 'discursive position enters into play and is now open for questioning, debate and criticism' (2017: 215). Similarly, Bel's directorial change of heart in *Disabled Theater* 'destabilizes not only his position of power, but also the stable position from which the audience judges what they see or hear' (Siegmund, 2015: 23). By allowing the spectators to observe the originally excluded dances, Bel opens up his artistic judgement, as well as his authority, for consideration.

The undermining of Bel's authority appears superficial under scrutiny, however. If the actors, for example, are 'given' agency, then the very contingency of this status suggests that they remain dependent in a way that inherently defers to the authority of the choreographer. Individual moments may invite a critique of Bel's judgement and authority, but his power always reasserts itself with the announcement of each task. Furthermore, other accounts of the process suggest that Bel exercised more directorial authority than is implied by the show's structure, exceeding the conceptual boundaries of his role in order to impose choreographic decisions.

Actor Remo Beuggert recalls that '[t]here was one actor who expressly did things on stage like waving to the audience and Jérôme told him three, four, or even five times and at some point he said, "If you do it again, you're out"' (Theater HORA, 2015: 89). Similarly, during performances of *Disabled Theater* actor Peter Keller remains on stage in the first task for much longer than the allotted minute. Yvonne Schmidt has described how 'at the beginning of the rehearsals, Keller actually remained on the stage far too long, only to walk off after almost exactly one minute at the next rehearsal. But Bel chose to keep the first version' (2015: 233). If such details of the performance were selected by Bel then the extent of the actors' genuine agency clearly diminishes. Furthermore, Bel's own account of why he relented and restored the excised dances has little to do with Gianni Blumer's opinion. Instead, he recounts that, after seeing the show in its original version with just seven dances, the French choreographer Xavier le Roy told him ' "[t]he piece is not accomplished if you don't see them all dance. It doesn't matter whether they are good or bad, the piece is about their singularity"' (Bel, 2015: 168). Despite the performance's implicit suggestion, then, that Bel's input is structurally limited to establishing the tasks, it seems as though a large degree of non-disabled control and influence is exerted over the aesthetic choices of *Disabled Theater*.

For Benjamin Wihstutz, alternatively, it does matter whether the individual dances are good or bad, as the question of what constitutes aesthetic quality forms the core conceptual drive of *Disabled Theater*, with Bel staging his change of heart in order to put his own judgement under scrutiny and provoke this very question. The show, Wihstutz argues, 'bids farewell to the fundamental principles of achievement and proficiency just as much as it challenges the conventional criteria of judgement. What is good and what is poor theater?' (2015: 45). This forms the basis of the show's political potency, since the actors' lack of virtuosity dismantles the concept of performance-as-achievement and so challenges 'a fundamental principle of neoliberal societies' (Wihstutz, 2015: 45). Within Bel's discourse, conventional aesthetics of dance are critiqued for imposing strict standards of virtuosity on the performers in ways that subjugate and subjectify them (Siegmund, 2017). The shows *Veronique Doisneau* and *Cedric Andrieux*, for example, explore how the titular performers have been shaped, as dancers and individuals, by their challenging experiences with the Paris Opera Ballet and Merce Cunningham respectively. Jasbir K. Puar notes a comparable ideological principle that operates in 'neoliberalism's heightened demands for bodily capacity' (2017: 1), such that exceptional physical challenges of the kind presented to balletic and contemporary dancers have now become a principle of everyday socio-economic productivity. Bel's interrogation of dance, therefore, contains an implicit political critique of neoliberalism.

For Wihstutz, this political project legitimises Bel's exercising of undue authority over the actors:

> It is fully justified to accuse Mr. Bel of exploiting the HORA actors. They *are* instrumentalized for an aesthetic concept that lies at the very heart of Bel's *œuvre*. The actors need to be presented on stage as disabled, for it is their very disability that serves as a tool to deconstruct the norms and rules of theater itself. However ethically problematic this may seem, the exploitation of the disabled cast thus enhances the political potential of the piece. (2015: 45, original emphasis)

Siegmund and Wihstutz agree that Bel's work is ultimately emancipatory and egalitarian, holding out, if not realising, the potential for new forms of subjectivity beyond those imposed by dance or neoliberal institutions. They disagree, however, on the role that disability plays in this project. For Wihstutz, Bel's critique requires the actors' disabilities to be presented and exploited as non-virtuosic in order to underline their contrast with normative theatrical bodies. Siegmund, alternatively, defends Bel in broadly the same terms that he approaches the accusations of postcolonial exploitation in *Pichet Klunchun and Myself*: the destabilising of Bel's power and degree of agency granted to the performers suggests that they are not exploited but emancipated within a performance that 'systematically destroys any kind of secure ground from which to differentiate between an appropriate or inappropriate representation of disabled people, […] between what is to be considered as abled or disabled' (2015: 30). Despite these differences, Siegmund's and Wihstutz's respective critiques rest on the impression of Bel creating space for a natural, non-virtuosic learning disability to appear. Bel's hidden influence over the aesthetic content, however, suggests that *Disabled Theater* constructs, rather than emancipates, a performance of learning disability. The resulting exploitation of the learning disabled actors deploys these constructions, and so operates through maintaining and exploiting conventional perceptions of learning disability. Thus, as Sarah Gorman notes, 'the performers' contribution is framed within an ableist paradigm' (2017: 97).

During the performance, the actor Matthias Brücker draws attention to the presentation of the performers as animalistic while giving his opinion of the show: 'It is super. My parents think differently. They didn't like it. After the performance, my sister cried in the car. She said that we are like animals in the zoo. Fingers in the nose, scratching, fingers in the mouth' (Umathum and Wihstutz 2015a: 225). The actors perform such 'animalistic' behaviours throughout by exhibiting behaviour that is apparently instinctive and culturally inappropriate, contradicting Siegmund's assertion that they are 'not doing anything freakish that would actively draw attention to their "otherness"' (2017: 246). While this may serve Bel's discursive drive to renegotiate the forms of physical behaviour that are permissible on stage, it also reinforces existing misperceptions of people with learning disabilities as socially undeveloped and uninhibited.

Fostering an impression of learning disability as animalistic has rather dangerous connotations in existing discourses about intellectual impairment. Eva Kittay recounts an exchange with the philosopher Jeff McMahan in 2008 in which she seeks to contest McMahan's thesis that 'the moral status of [people with profound cognitive disabilities] should be demoted below that of all other human beings [...] and that the appropriate comparison group is nonhuman animals, whose moral status should be appropriately elevated' (2010: 394). By aligning their moral status with animals, McMahan is questioning whether people with profound learning disabilities deserve the same rights as non-disabled people, including the right to justice and the right not to be killed.

Disabled Theater also constructs and exploits the performers as amateurs as well as animalistic, and this amateurism is pivotal in Bel's critique of the neoliberal insistence on performance-as-achievement. Gorman recognises Bel's intention to destabilise aesthetic conventions through a poetics of failure and reflects that the actors' perceived amateurism may be related to the art form, as they are trained actors and not dancers (2017). Nonetheless, Gorman is more critical than Wihstutz of Bel's exploitation of disabled actors in the pursuit of his aesthetic and political project and she argues that 'the suggestion that amateur bodies cannot transform themselves, or become "other" suggests that they are primarily identified by bodily "immanence" and a perceived failure to transcend the constraints or limitations of the body' (2017: 97).

If the piece explores the poetics of failure, then, it does so by employing a medical perception of disability in which failure is symptomatic of the actors' learning disabilities rather than an act of aesthetic choice or liberation. These particular actors, it appears, cannot reject virtuosity because they are already rejected by it.

I have demonstrated elsewhere that the function of learning disability within the symbolic order of liberal societies is to act as 'the static model of inferiority against which a non-disabled humanity measures itself' (Calvert, 2014: 187). Bel's decision to exploit the learning disabled actors by framing disability as amateurism constitutes a deployment, rather than a destabilisation, of the cultural and discursive norms established by (neo) liberal societies: learning disabled failure is the marker against which normative performance-as-achievement is assessed and valued. Furthermore, by only claiming credit for the concept, Bel personally sidesteps the poetics of failure, exempting himself from his own critique of performance-as-achievement. Within Bel's discourse on dance, then, this exemption and the failure to recognise the complexity of learning disabled discourse neutralises the critical potency of his project.

Under Bel's authority, the exploitation of the actors and the superficial engagement with learning disabled agency and representation are symptomatic of a lack of care. For Kittay, a key ethical feature of care is the necessity that 'the dependency relationship does not authorize the exercise of power except for the benefit of the charge [...] Should the dependency worker neglect her duties, the fate of the charge hangs in the balance, and some intervention is critical' (1999: 33). I will suggest below that similar obligations of care and dependency are necessarily operative, if usually hidden, in theatre. Bel, in framing the actors as animalistic and amateurish, neglects their interests as professional performers and as learning disabled people.

Kittay also proposes two urgent principles that philosophical discourse about learning disability should observe, and these seem appropriate to extend to Bel's function as the author of the conceptual and choreographic framework: 'first, *epistemic responsibility*: know the subject that you are using to make a philosophical point; and, second, *epistemic modesty*: know what you don't know' (2010: 401, original emphasis). In neglecting the complexities of discourses around learning disability, Bel's naivety both exposes the actors to undue risk and weakens his own discursive project.

What might happen, however, if we broaden our reading of the performance to consider *Disabled Theater* as a collaborative project, in which the performers' contribution exceeds Bel's ableist framework? Given the long-standing association between care and learning disability, could the combination of Theater HORA and Bel produce a meeting of two modes of interaction, one discursive and one caring? Under such a reading, the dynamics of care may become more complex and reciprocal, opening new insights into the making process that extend beyond the conceptual and subjective to the material and intersubjective. Before turning to this reading, it will be valuable to consider how such an approach is already articulated in another recent performance by learning disabled actors, Mind the Gap's *Contained*.

Contained

Contained is a touring production by Mind the Gap, a British theatre company based in West Yorkshire. Like Theater HORA, the company (which formed in 1988) works primarily with professional learning disabled actors and has an established history of touring original work nationally and internationally. For this production, it also worked with a guest director, Alan Lyddiard, noted for his ensemble practice as the former artistic director of Northern Stage in Newcastle-upon-Tyne. *Contained* shares some similarities with *Disabled Theater*: both shows begin with a bare stage apart from a row of chairs for the actors; and both stage elements of their own making processes within the performance with the actors appearing as themselves, rather than in the guise of characters.

At the same time, the productions are markedly different in tone, structure and content, with *Contained* invoking an open atmosphere of reciprocal care and collaboration in contrast to the more compartmentalised relationships presented by *Disabled Theater*. Built primarily on autobiographical stories told by the ensemble, *Contained* offers accounts of personal experiences and relationships that encompass struggle, achievement, pain, joy, victory, defeat and resilience, even within single narratives. The performers' disabilities carry particular significance in some stories, but not in others, although they usually inflect the perspective of the storyteller. Overall, however, rather than taking disability as its theme, the show opens up complex layers of human experience as it has been, and is, lived by these particular performers. Structurally, the stories are interwoven with each other and interspersed with original songs, written by cast member Jez Colborne and performed live by the ensemble. There are also dance sequences and video segments, which variously involve pre-recorded footage, live feed and green-screen technology. Accordingly, the bare stage soon gives way to a complex array of technical equipment that is assembled and disassembled by the performers throughout the show. My analysis is based on seeing the performance three times during its two-year tour: twice at Mind the Gap Studios in Bradford (October 2015 and April 2016) and once at La Condition Republique, Roubaix as part of the Crossing the Line Festival (January 2017).

The interweaving of the autobiographical stories with each other, and with different media, invites constant cross-cutting between the stories and performers as they glide in and out of view or individual narratives give way to concerted musical numbers that draw out shared threads and offer a thematic commentary on the material. The ongoing technical set-up and stage management compound the complexity and restlessness of the focus so that the performance never settles into seemingly finished routines in the way that *Disabled Theater* does. *Contained* is a work in flux that is perpetually making itself: indeed, as the performers' lives develop offstage, their personal narratives are continually updated.

Contained also involves the onstage presence of a non-disabled figure alongside the learning disabled performers who, like the translator figure in *Disabled Theater*, stands in for the director and the directorial process. This role is undertaken by Charli Ward, the academy director at Mind the Gap, who works permanently with the actors and whose engagement with them extends far beyond this particular project. Her role in the performance reflects some aspects of directorial authority in which she represents Lyddiard and his assistant, Mind the Gap's resident director Joyce Lee, by giving the actors onstage instructions and leading onstage warm-ups. Where the translator of *Disabled Theater* is restricted to managing the performance and its technical operations, however, Ward positions herself as a member of the ensemble, joining with the actors in the complicated technical operation of the show and, at times, performing alongside them in the dance routines.

At other points, she occupies a more supporting role. While many of the performers take charge of telling their own stories monologically, cast member Paul Bates is accompanied by Ward, who poses questions to him. Bates' impairment prevents him from fixing the story sequentially, so Ward's questions – which may vary from performance to performance – function to guide his narrative and negotiate a route through to the completed story. Similarly, Ward is visibly alert when Howard Davies, who may sometimes struggle with memory difficulties, tells his story. Unlike the neutral and detached tone of the *Disabled Theater* translators, Ward maintains a kindly and encouraging manner throughout. She is as immersed as the actors in the fluidity of the performance, managing the various staging processes and adapting to circumstances within her own role.

The exploration of the power dynamics between non-disabled facilitator and learning disabled performers is similarly fluid, as Ward moves between an authoritative position, a broadly equal contribution to stage and technical management and a supporting role that facilitates the performers' own authority. It is this latter role that most explicitly opens up the dynamics of care in the performance, as Ward's provision of support builds the performers' dependencies into the show.

Such support reflects Kittay's description of care as both a labour and an attitude:

> As labor, it is the work of maintaining ourselves and others when we are in a condition of need [...] As an attitude, caring denotes a positive, affective bond and investment in another's well-being. The labor can be done without the appropriate attitude. Yet without the attitude of care, the open responsiveness to another that is so essential to understanding what another requires is not possible. (2002: 259–60)

In the collaborative context of the performance, the labour of care combines personal care for the other with professional care: Ward's efforts are directed towards sustaining the performers *as* performers. This also demands an attitude of care, as Ward must be open and responsive to the needs of the performers in the live event, especially during her improvised support for Bates and Davies. In turn, this evidences Ward's epistemic responsibility at an intimate level, understanding the individual nuances and dependencies of these particular performers.

This combination of epistemic responsibility and attitude of care resonates with Nel Noddings' concept of engrossment, an essential element for qualitative acts of caring, through which the carer 'is *present* in her acts of caring. Even in physical absence, acts at a distance bear the signs of presence: engrossment in the other; regard, desire for the other's well-being. Caring is largely reactive and responsive' (2013: 39, original emphasis). Presence, of course, is a prized attribute of the live performer, and Noddings' concept opens up a potential mode of presence predicated on care that I will call theatrical engrossment. In this mode, the performer's engrossment during the live event does not signal immersion in the fictional world being created, but is externally directed, as a responsive and reactive attitude of care, towards sustaining the well-being or security of elements surrounding the performance itself, such as the other performers, the audience or the physical environment. Such care is intrinsic, on some level, to all theatre making, but is usually masked during performance.

Within the structure of *Contained*, such theatrical engrossment is openly presented: Ward's responsiveness to the performers, as a labour of care, is simultaneously an act of care for the performance itself, as its progress is also dependent on the quality of care paid to the performers within the fluid circumstances of the live event. As such, *Contained* is not concerned with a conceptual exploration of success and failure, but rather foregrounds the dynamics of care out of recognition that the well-being of the actors and the maintenance of the performance are equally dependent on the labour and attitude of care: indeed, the two are imbricated within each other.

The more rigid structure of *Disabled Theater*, divided along functional lines, struggles to meld care and performance in this way, as the compartmentalisation of director, translator and actors constrains theatrical engrossment. An accidental example, in which the established frame collapses, is illustrative. At the performance on 7 October 2017 at La Commune, the Theater HORA actor Julia Häusermann banged her head on the stage while dancing energetically to Michael Jackson's song *They Don't Care About Us*, forcing her to cut the routine short. The translator Simone Truong swiftly moved from the sound desk to check on and comfort Häusermann and then arrange for an ice pack to be delivered to the performer. For this moment, Truong's necessary and intimate engrossment in Häusermann conflicts with her role in the compartmentalised structure and so halts the performance. Her labour of care cannot accommodate either the aesthetic frame or the watching audience and so is not theatrical engrossment in which care for the live event coincides with care for the performer. Accordingly, the relationship between Truong and Häusermann, reconfigured as caregiver and dependent, overwhelms their given roles as translator and performer. If such dynamics of care operated during the making process of *Disabled Theater*, they have been erased by the metatheatrical frame of the performance.

A sequence towards the close of *Contained*, however, holds potential for acknowledging alternative care dynamics within *Disabled Theater* through its recognition of the learning disabled actors as caregivers rather than dependents. After the Mind the Gap actors Howard Davies and Zara

Mallinson have told the story of their personal relationship, Ward herself has the opportunity to tell an autobiographical story: 'Family is very important [to] me and I feel like now in my life that is what is missing. I desire a family. I want children, I want to be married, and I want a house. This is something I thought I was on track with until recently. My last relationship broke down because he didn't want this' (Mind the Gap, 2016: 34). The trauma of this relationship break-up was very recent at the time of early performances, and Ward could not contain the rawness of her own emotion, often breaking down as she tried to complete the story. Invariably, the performers around her responded with care.

The genuine emotion of both Ward and the performers was palpable to the audience, and Ward recalls how its intensity would vary according to her own level of difficulty:

> During the tour you can see the [performers' level of] support at its highest if I am really struggling with the story with hugs and constant 'you can do it' support. On those nights where it felt easier, there would just be a gentle touch of the shoulder for reassurance that they were there. I believe that in that moment, all the guys are with me and forget the audience, they are not performing. (Personal correspondence, 2016)

Ward here describes a highly responsive mode of theatrical engrossment, one that adjusts its intensity according to Ward's level of need and also reverses the established relations of dependency as the learning disabled performers now offer care to their usual caregiver. Unlike Truong's engrossment in Häusermann, however, this unplanned breakdown does not bring the performance to a halt, but is more readily accommodated within the dynamics of care already operating in the meta-theatrical frame.

The complex fluidity of roles, actions and narratives that underpin *Contained* thus extends to the dynamics of care itself, exposing the reciprocity within caring relations that Kittay acknowledges (2002). Her analysis does not, however, focus primarily on mutual care, which she calls 'exchange-based reciprocity' (Kittay, 1999: 68), exploring instead the more pronounced dependency involved in caring for a person with profound disabilities as a means of contesting liberalism's 'conception of the person as independent, rational, and capable of self-sufficiency. And […] of society as an association of such independent equals' (Kittay, 2002: 258).

Potentially more fruitful here is Jasbir K. Puar's 'broader politics of debility' that questions 'the presumed, taken-for-granted capacities-enabled status of abled-bodies' under neoliberalism (2009: 166). Kittay's critique of liberal societies sustains a distinction between disabled and non-disabled people according to the intensity, or longevity, of the former's dependency on the latter. For Puar, alternatively, disability no longer identifies an enclosed constituency grounded in its particular politics of identity and representation, but is connected to a wider critique of neoliberal regimes that privilege and demand capacity of their subjects, while simultaneously debilitating them. Such a context produces 'more fluid relations between capacity and debility' (Puar, 2009: 168) that problematise easy divisions into disabled and non-disabled. She examines the fluid dynamics of capacity and debility in terms of 'conviviality', approaching identity categories 'as events – as encounters – rather than as entities or attributes of the subject': 'In its conventional usage, conviviality means […] to be merry, festive, together at a table, with companions and guests, and hence, to live with […] [C]onviviality does not lead to a politics of the universal or inclusive common, nor an ethics of individuatedness, rather the futurity enabled through the open materiality of bodies as a Place to Meet' (Puar, 2009: 168). The open engagement within this concept of conviviality clearly resonates with Noddings' concept of engrossment and Kittay's attitude of care but, by replacing disability with the mutual navigation of each other's debilities and capacities, also allows for more nuanced and reciprocal meeting points between care and dependency.

Conviviality therefore suggests the attitude of care as fluid and mutual, constantly adjusting to the fluctuating vulnerabilities of interdependent people by 'rendering bare the instability of the divisions between capacity-endowed and debility-laden bodies' (Puar, 2009: 169). Ward's breakdown exposes this fluidity by revealing the emotional debility, and resulting dependency, of the presumed caregiver. In doing so, *Contained* resists distinctions between non-disabled and learning disabled debilities through which, as disability theorist Dan Goodley observes, diagnoses of cognitive impairment 'pathologise individually located behaviours and thoughts that stand in opposition to the rational, self-controlling and self-governing citizen so cherished by neoliberal societies' (2014: 88).

The fluid interplay of stories, status and care dynamics in *Contained* therefore produces a sense of restless engagement that marks this performance as convivial in Puar's terms. It is an event in which the performers meet and navigate each other's dependencies, collapsing the distinction between individuals as either wholly capable or wholly debilitated. While care is always a prominent component of learning disabled theatre making, arising from the historical understanding of learning disability outlined above, the explicit care in response to Ward's breakdown reveals an otherwise hidden, reciprocal care that constantly circulates among the ensemble in order to sustain both performers and performance. The conviviality and care that are necessary in collaborative theatre making become openly and aesthetically available to the audience, producing a distinct type of event that I would like to classify as 'convivial theatre'. Theatrical engrossment is an identifying characteristic of convivial theatre, in that the performers openly nurture the conditions surrounding the performance, through an externally directed labour, and attitude, of care. As such, each performance must recognise afresh the immediate debilities and needs of the performers, and meaning emerges from the audience encounter with, or experience of, the performers' highly responsive attitude of care within the live event.

Theatrical engrossment and Disabled Theater

Such insights into learning disabled theatre making have potential to extend the reading of *Disabled Theater* beyond the framework of Bel's discourse on dance, theatre and performance. Reflecting on the care dynamics in the show acknowledges the conviviality of the Theater HORA actors, collapsing *Disabled Theater*'s ableist framework and pursuing a subtler critique of neoliberalism in which the actors offer care to an absent, yet nonetheless dependent, Jérôme Bel.

Disabled Theater, while not explicitly pronouncing such care dynamics, contains traces of conviviality that open up a dialectical engagement with Bel's discourse. The performers briefly submit to necessary acts of theatrical engrossment that, in their contrast with Bel's meta-theatrical frame, are fleeting but noticeable. Focusing on these moments, instigated by the actors of Theater HORA, recognises *Disabled Theater* as a collaborative and interdependent project in which the Swiss company both pursues and subtly contests Bel's overarching agenda. Such acts of theatrical engrossment complicate the choreographer's abstract discourse, countering conventional liberal concerns with emancipation, equality and exploitation through an emphasis on openness, interdependency and responsiveness.

Critical appreciation of Theater HORA tends to emphasise the performers' energy and investment. Umathum and Wihstutz note a favourable response to 'the stage presence of the actors' (2015b: 7), while Siegmund proposes that '[w]hat makes the solos so compelling to watch is the actors' ability to lose themselves in the dance, to abandon themselves to the point of recklessness while at the same time trying to retain control over the form' (2015: 26). Häusermann's accident may be less accidental from this perspective: it is an inevitable risk, and consequence, of the personal recklessness that lends 'presence' to her performance.

Häusermann won the Alfred Kerr Prize in 2013 at the Berlin Theatertreffen, with judge Thomas Theime giving the award on the grounds of her authenticity in performance, which Sandra Umathum defines as 'forgetting the self' (2015: 111). Such observations on presence and abandonment of the self are reminiscent of characteristics of engrossment in Noddings' formulation. For the most part, the actors' engrossment here signals immersion in the act of performance itself, and so does not appear primarily motivated by care. There are, however, specific moments in which the actors display theatrical engrossment, the explicit and responsive attitude of care towards the conditions surrounding the performance that honours the interdependence of all involved.

One example is particularly illustrative. During the fifth task, in which the actors offer their opinion of the show, Häusermann states that she would like to dance to Justin Bieber instead of Michael Jackson. Bieber's song 'Baby' is then played by the translator, with Häusermann dancing and singing along. Following her accident during the Parisian performance, Häusermann concluded by saying '*Merci, Simone*' to Truong, who smiled and nodded her appreciation. This moment of gentle intimacy cut through the established framework of the show, shattering the demarcation of individual roles set up by the task structure to acknowledge the relationship between the performers. If Häusermann here acknowledges the care that Truong showed following the accident, in its tenderness and spontaneity the moment also feels like a reciprocal act of care, as though Häusermann senses that Truong has been unsettled by having to tend to her injury. Häusermann's gesture reassures Truong that she has recovered and, through this reassurance, eases Truong's concern for the actor and restores the translator fully to her role. It is through Häusermann's attitude of care, as an act of theatrical engrossment, that the equilibrium of both Truong and the show are restored.

At the same time, the sudden visibility of an attitude of care introduces a new register to the performance, which complicates Bel's framework. Truong herself is personalised by Häusermann's intimate gesture, which appreciates her as more than the physical representative of the absent Bel's structural and depersonalised power. The head injury, its treatment and its conclusion in Häusermann's gesture, reveals the interdependent humanity of both the actor and translator rather than their functional roles in Bel's conceptual discourse and political critique. The primary characteristic of this humanity is the necessity of care, as both Truong and Häusermann display the need for care and responsivity to the need of the other. In other instances of theatrical engrossment, such recognition of, and responsivity to, such human need is extended to Bel himself in ways that dialectically extend his conceptual exploration.

Also within the fifth task, the performers Gianni Blumer and Matthias Brücker both present negative criticisms of the show, but choose to soften their critiques. In calling the show 'super' before reporting his family's criticism, Brücker indicates that he does not wish to upset Bel. Similarly, while objecting to being omitted from the seven selected dances, Blumer tells the audience: 'I didn't dare complain to Jérôme Bel. Because actually he is very nice' (Umathum and Wihstutz, 2015a: 139). Their caveats form an act of care, designed to ensure that Bel is not personally wounded by the criticism. In order to enact this care, of course, Blumer and Brücker refer to the real Bel that they encountered in the devising and rehearsal process rather than Bel as the depersonalised authority shaping the performance and discourse. Just as Häusermann had to personalise Truong in order to restore the translator's equilibrium within the performance frame, so Blumer and Brücker must personalise Bel in order to fulfil the tasks he has set them.

These moments feel caring in that they respond to some perceived need within Bel himself. Given Bel's absence, it is difficult for the audience to know what needs Blumer and Brücker are catering for, and the intimacy between them and Bel is less intense than between Häusermann and Truong. Nonetheless, their care of Bel still evokes an intimate, interpersonal relationship, built on need and response, which is essential to the realisation of the performance. The fleeting glimpses of such relationships, which, again, contradict the individualistic and compartmentalised framework, offer important qualifications for Bel's discourse.

By opening up alternative registers, based on care and interdependency, Häusermann, Blumer and Brücker destabilise the proposition that Bel has simply established a structure that emancipates the individual agency, aesthetic control and self-expression of the actors. It is not simply that this structure obscures the extent to which Bel has exercised control over the actors' choices, but that these choices are not independent and may well themselves be inflected by the labour and attitude of care towards Bel, Truong or, indeed, each other. That is, the aesthetics of *Disabled Theater* may be driven by engrossment, shaped as much by the collaborators responding carefully to the perceived needs of the other as by the pursuit of a conceptual discourse, the choreographic authority of Jérôme Bel or the free expression of the actors. The apparent amateurism or freakishness of the actors may therefore be less indicative of the natural state of learning disability and more reflective of the actors' perception of, and performative response to, Bel's own aesthetic needs and desires.

These acts of theatrical engrossment therefore point to an underlying attitude of care that, perhaps, has most reverberations for Bel's critique of virtuosity, which, as with Puar's critique of neoliberalism, contests the impossibility of such demands, based as they are on idealised, non-disabled criteria. By presenting disabled aesthetics as an alternative, however, Bel does not trouble the more fundamental liberal insistence on individual freedom and independence. The theatrical engrossment of the Theater HORA actors, by contrast, resonates with Puar's conviviality in abandoning individual agency, independence and, indeed, the very notion of criteria itself as appropriate measurements of performance. Rather, performance here is not measurable as the successful realisation of Bel's concept, but emerges instead from the convivial encounter between collaborators, an open aesthetic that is guided by care as the actors, directors and translators negotiate each other's needs and debilities. The richness of *Disabled Theater* lies in the elements that both elude and nurture the framework of Bel's discourse, as much as what appears within it. Approaching the critique of liberalism from this perspective, in which interdependency is prized above individual contributions, Bel becomes incorporated into, rather than exempted from, his reflection on performance-as-achievement.

In attending to the traces of convivial theatre and theatrical engrossment in *Disabled Theater*, the distinctions between non-disabled and learning disabled artists become less significant, and the politics less concerned with questions of representation and reception. Instead, the politics of production reflect inevitable dynamics of care that are elemental in theatre making, particularly where this involves learning disabled actors, but are usually disavowed under a neoliberal system that emphasises individual capacity and productivity over mutual dependency. Recognising the reciprocal dynamics of care in the performance, and reading its meta-theatrical frame through this lens, complicates the conceptual drive of Bel's project by adding human complications and dependencies to his abstract discourse. At the same time, such concerns deserve consideration, not least because, as Truong's intervention following Häusermann's accident admits, these dynamics of care are already operative beneath the frame and to disavow them distorts Bel's conceptual and political critique. Moreover, they legitimately rebalance the discourse, and the outlined power relations, by acknowledging that Theater HORA, in providing the necessary care that is required to realise the concept, makes a foundational contribution to the project. This contribution of care, more pronounced in the history of this company and of learning disabled theatre in general than in Bel's own *oeuvre*, allows for the convivial collaboration to be understood as fundamentally interdependent.

Dan Goodley, like Puar, is interested in collapsing easy distinctions between disability and ability, reflected in his term 'dis/ability' (2014). He draws on Puar's theories to propose an active, rather than a critical, politics of debility:

> Debility invites new ways of thinking about and politically agitating around our (labouring) bodies of debility. Many of us fail to meet the demands of neoliberal ideals. And debility is to be found at that moment when dis/ability collides [...] Recognising our debility, creates a meeting ground, a dis/ability commons if you like, in which we each have [...] the transformative and creative capacities of our labouring bodies to fashion alternative modes of production, consumption and exchange. (Goodley, 2014: 95)

Both *Disabled Theater* and *Contained* meta-theatrically explore their own modes of production. *Contained* is most explicit about how this dis/ability commons, in recognising points of debility across the entire ensemble, can only be productive through mutual engrossment, a reciprocal attitude of care towards the debility of the other that, when directed towards the conditions of performance, results in convivial theatre. *Disabled Theater*, by contrast, appears more explicitly concerned with the conventional politics of representation, power relations, agency and identity. Recognising and applying the revelations of *Contained*, however, allows for a dialectical reading of *Disabled Theater* as fleetingly convivial, opening up the ordinarily contained dynamics of care to expose a more fluid and collaborative political critique than Bel intended, in which the destabilisation of clear lines of authority, capacity, debility and dependency challenge neoliberal ideals more profoundly by collapsing its ableist paradigm.

The attention to care that informs theatre that engages learning disabled performers perhaps makes it more attentive to these questions of debility, reciprocity and engrossment. In the case of *Contained*, this is central to the performance to the extent that it operates as convivial theatre, while in *Disabled Theater*, the learning disabled actors introduce brief instances of conviviality to the performance against the grain of Bel's more dominant discursive framework and the critical responses to it. Yet it is in these glimpses of conviviality that the production's political critique is at its most substantial, dissolving the distinction between disability and non-disability, acknowledging interdependence and opening up a shared negotiation of each other's debilities and capacities. Convivial theatre, which is, perhaps, more prominent in, although not limited to, the context of theatre and learning disability, offers resistance to the (neo)liberal prizing of individuality and independence at this more fundamental level.

Road care

Jen Archer-Martin and Julieanna Preston

> On a most general level, we suggest that caring be viewed as a species activity that includes everything that we do to maintain, continue, and repair our 'world' so that we can live in it as well as possible. (Fisher and Tronto, 1990: 40)

The origins of this chapter can be traced to 1990 and two disparate events: the redefinition of a feminist ethic of care by feminist political scientists Berenice Fisher and Joan Tronto and a woman's encounter with a roadworks scene. Where Carol Gilligan's (1982) ethic of care challenged the universal morality of patriarchal justice, embracing a feminine, relational voice of care, Fisher and Tronto's (1990) version extended caring from a human–human to human–environment activity, including world-making and maintenance labours. Understandings of care as a social activity, having influenced practices such as nursing, are now filtering across disciplinary boundaries into such fields as performance and design. The present edited collection picks up that discussion at the care/performance intersection, weaving a conversation around care and socially engaged performance. We seek to inject another voice – of non-human or more-than-human material ecologies – further expanding Fisher and Tronto's world care through contemporary post-human and new materialist thinking to explore the potential for affective care in material labours of repair. Emboldened by a post-human new materialist understanding of agency, we suggest that this is not just a species activity, but a labour co-performed by a caring ecology of ontologically diverse agents (Figure 6.1).

In this chapter, we critically reflect on our 2015 live art performance *bit-u-men-at-work*, developed as part of a performance-as-research project to become intimately acquainted with bitumen – a petroleum-based material of maintenance and repair – and its working ecology. The discussion unfolds through a series of encounters with various moments of the performance-as-research journey: the 1990 roadworks encounter, two events within our

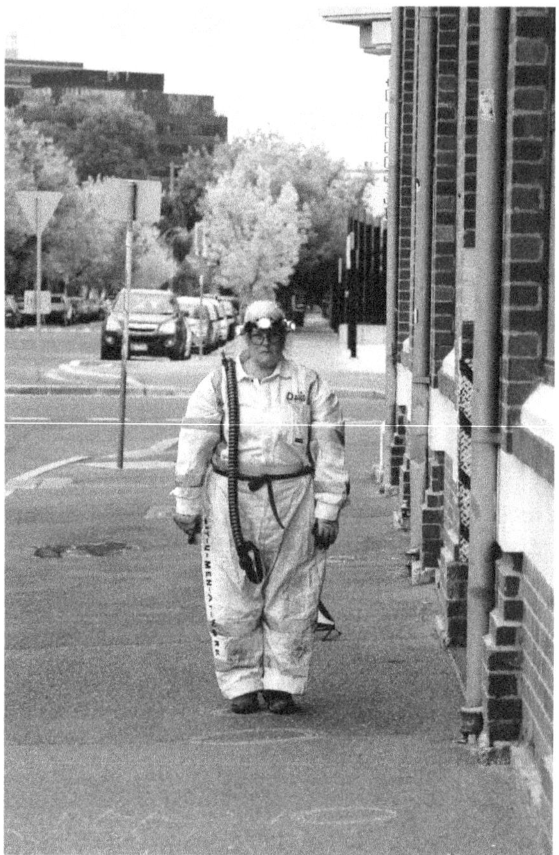

Figure 6.1 A woman-machine named Desiré, alert, poised, ready to start

concentrated research enquiry performed over the year preceding the public performance and the performance itself, which occurred over three evenings in October 2015 on a public footpath outside the Margaret Lawrence Gallery in Melbourne's Southbank arts precinct. Each evening, Julieanna Preston became a woman-machine named Desiré, performing a durational labour of repairing the cracked, pitted asphalt pavement with bitumen. The repetitive labour took place among a performance ecology that included the site, bitumen, orange safety triangles, two caretakers in high-vis vests, a critical witness (Jen Archer-Martin), passers-by and fluctuating assemblies of spectators. The work was part of the Performance Studies International (PSi) symposium *Performing Mobilities* – a city-wide event conceptualised by performance artist/curator Mick Douglas to rethink performance relative to shifting geopolitical and sociopolitical realities of mobility (Douglas, 2016).

We analyse these encounters and the performance-as-research process through a reflective conversation that confronts theories of care and affective labour with a new materialist, post-humanist, ecofeminist agenda. Augmenting existing notions of care and affective labour, we shift the focus from human-centred (social) to material-driven (ecological) caring labour. At the heart of this is an attempt to reveal the affective and gestural qualities of material caring labour in order to offer an expanded notion of the aesthetics of care proposed by James Thompson, which 'seeks to focus upon how the sensory and affective are realised in human relations fostered in art projects' (2015: 436). We suggest instead an aesthetics of care that critically departs from anthropocentric understandings to respond to affective material labours. Along the way, we wonder: What is it to care for something non-human, something as politically contentious, economically significant and materially abhorrent as bitumen? How might road repair be recognised as a world-maintaining caring activity – as road care? And how can the practice of developing and performing a work of live art propel this critical enquiry?

Context: people, practice, theory

Bit-u-men-at-work continued Julieanna Preston's series of spatial and performative interventions exploring intimate relationships with the materials of our built environment. This commitment to revealing the vibrancy of matter is grounded in the vital materialism of political ecologist Jane Bennett, who calls for more ethical engagements with 'vibrant matter and lively things' (2010: viii). Departing from the human–human responsibility of social ethics, Bennett suggests that 'perhaps the ethical responsibility of an individual human now resides in one's response to the assemblages in which one finds oneself participating' (2010: 37). Aligned with strategies of new materialist, post-human and ecological discourses, Bennett's framework shares a desire to dismantle ontological boundaries between nature/culture, animate/inanimate, revealing instead an interconnected web of relations. These non-anthropocentric assemblages decentralise the primacy of human agency and acknowledge the agency of non-humans, recognising humans as always already 'in', rather than acting 'upon', the world (Bennett, 2010). In her introduction to Julieanna Preston's *Performing Matters*, architectural scholar Hélène Frichot describes Julieanna's work as 'situated material learning', building on the diverse, localised and contingent nature of Donna Haraway's feminist 'situated knowledges' (2014: 11). Characterised by this process of following the material and learning material lessons along the way, *bit-u-men-at-work* employed the labouring, performing body of the artist to enter into ever closer and more responsive relations with materials.

In the case of *bit-u-men-at-work*, Julieanna collaborated with Jen Archer-Martin, whose practice also engaged with creating material-spatial opportunities for learning and providing hospitality, or care. Initially, Jen intended to perform the role of 'caretaking, hospitality and sustaining relief in a situation that finds me vulnerable and on my hands and knees patching potholes in laneways and footpaths, a kind of machine-becoming-animal critique of roadworks', as well as documenting the research process and performance. Jen's role, however, morphed into 'being a critical conscience' (Preston, personal correspondence, 2015). The collaboration became a dynamic dialogue of performing, documenting, talking and writing, from which emerged the performance score as well as the character and gestural language of Desiré. As the importance of the critical witness became apparent, we resolved that Jen would continue to provide that complicit outside eye to the performance itself, performing various modes of taking note and producing documented observations that inform the present recollection.

We take a moment here to expand on 'performance-as-research' and introduce some of the key voices that we summon to help frame the enquiry. 'Performance-as-research' is a field of scholarly artistic practice and the focus of PSi journal *PARtake.* Journal editors William Lewis and Niki Tulk describe it as a 'methodology for the organization and dissemination of knowledge – originating in the processes of making and analysing embodied and practiced performance work' (2016: 1). The goal of *bit-u-men-at-work* was not to produce 'a performance' that communicated the product of research to an audience, but to use the process of performance making as a research method and to create an opportunity for public encounter within that live and ongoing practice. In the spirit of Mierle Laderman Ukeles, whose efforts in carving out a space for the performance practice of 'maintenance art' we greatly admire, we 'consider the process as part of the art' (Ukeles, 2015: 18). Ours was not a linear process of making, performing and then analysing, but a reflexive, dialogic praxis that continually performs situated material-led learning.

The enquiry is framed by two main theoretical concerns – care and post-human new materialism. The first is by informed by Michael Hardt's *Affective Labour* and feminist theories of an ethics of care. Hardt posits the power of the qualities and nature of labouring practices to shape the 'processes of becoming human and the nature of the human itself' (1999: 90). Against a background of paradigmatic shifts in capitalist economies, Hardt suggests that workers, originally engaged directly in material practices, learned to act like machines and then think like computers. In the information economy, it is the immaterial labours of computerised (and we would add, almost twenty years later, networked or even intelligent) machines and people that 'produce collective subjectivities, produce sociality, and ultimately produce society itself' (Hardt, 1999: 89). Hardt draws a distinction between the symbolic-analytical tasks of the computer and the 'affective labour of human contact and interaction', which he associates with the care and cultural sectors (1999: 95). Though Hardt acknowledges the roots of caring labour as lying in feminist discourse on 'women's work', we desire to draw it more vigorously into the realm of feminist sociology, care, ecofeminism and biopower, turning in particular to a feminist 'ethics of care'.

Virginia Held's *Taking Care* (2005) helpfully surveys various definitions of a feminist ethics of care that have emerged since Carol Gilligan introduced care in the 1980s as an alternative to an ethics of justice or moral judgement. Gilligan's feminist ethics of care 'begins with connection, theorized as primary and seen as fundamental in human life' (1995: 122). Held asserts that 'care is both a practice and a value […] [t]he ethics of care builds relations of care and concern and mutual responsiveness to need on both the personal and wider social levels' (2005: 68–9). Held's extensive analysis of the state of caring relative to nursing, childrearing and childminding, justice, morals, ethics, obligation and empathy largely falls outside the scope of this chapter. Of particular interest to us is the contrast she draws between care as an intrinsically human, face-to-face activity (Noddings, cited in Held, 2005), and the broader definition supplied by Joan Tronto and Berenice Fisher, being 'everything that we do to maintain, continue and repair our "world" so that we can live in it as well as possible' (1990: 40). Held expresses concern that this definition of care as world repair, that would encompass such labours as house construction, is too broad and that 'the distinctive features of caring labour would be lost. It does not include the sensitivity to the needs of the cared for […] nor what Noddings calls the needed "engrossment" with the other' (Held, 2005: 61). It is precisely this concern that we wish to address.

In *bit-u-men-at-work*, the sought-after engrossment is with the non-human or material other. Another chapter would be required to celebrate the army of women who have shaped our understanding of what we refer to in short as 'post-human new materialism':

> Fundamental to this area of enquiry, including its redefinition of material not as something mute, but lively, vibrant and also politically entangled, is a debt that is owed to feminist thinkers. Luce Irigaray, Donna Haraway, Rosi Braidotti, Elizabeth Grosz, Moira Gatens, and more recently, the architect and architectural theorist Katie Lloyd Thomas, the feminist theorist Karen Barad, and the political theorist Jane Bennett have all drawn crucial attention to revitalised engagements with matter. (Frichot, 2014: 10)

Here, along with Bennett's aforementioned vital materialism, we reference Donna Haraway's (2008, 2016) post-human relations and 'response-ability' to the non-human other and, to a lesser extent, Karen Barad's (2007) influence on our understanding of Bennett's agentic material assemblages and support of Haraway's call for 'response-ability' within intimately entangled intra-actions (Barad, 2012). These concepts will be unpacked in relation to the performance in the proceeding reflection.

Encounters: scenes, machines, material, labours

Dusk, late spring, 1990, on an American desert road.
A snorting beast emerges from the dim remnants of the day's unrelenting light.
Headlamps, warning bleats, rank breath meeting evening air as gaseous exhalations.

Orange cones, MEN AT WORK signs, swarms of high visibility vests.
Sensations of speed replaced by enforced braking,
a disruption to the freedom of unchecked forward progress –
at least the insects in the path of my beams are afforded a momentary reprieve.
Tunes from the radio drowned out by grumbling engines.
A complex symphony of grinding, whirling, mechanical parts.
The queue in the rear view mirror grows.
Wasting time, sitting idle, nothing to do but take in the scene.
Engulfed by an oily black heat, a smelly, noxious haze,
the road-eating-bitumen-spewing mechanical creature creeps forward at 3 mph,
attended by a score of labourers engaged in mechanical physical exertions,
sweat making tracks on dust-caked skin.
Bored vision blurring, it appears as a mechanical whole,
bound together by a sense of purpose,
a vibrant web of lights, reflectors and fluorescent materials,
and a reverence for the steaming virgin black surface appearing in its wake.

'STOP' becomes 'GO', I proceed back into the night, the moment evaporates.
Impatiently accelerating, I think no further of the scene or my place in it.
Of the synthetic petroleum-based rubber tread of my tires.
Of the bitumen-bound surface they grip.
Of the exploitation of human and material resources in the name of mobility.
Of the strange satisfaction of all those moving parts working together.
Of the unexpected sensory appeal of the fresh bitumen.
It is behind me – before me is only open road. (Preston, field notes, 1990)

In this recollection of Julieanna's 1990 encounter with roadworks, the spatial, temporal, sensorial and material qualities of the scene are amplified as the suspension of forward motion makes way for an aesthetic experience. In this space of interruption, the mundane labours register as carefully choreographed performance. Years later, this memory surfaced as fertile inspiration to our affective relationship with the material bitumen. Through the lens of Julieanna's new materialist performance practice, the scene invited reinterpretation as a live performance – a socially engaged, material-centric, politically, environmentally and philosophically fraught piece of live art embedded in the everyday circumstances of modern life. With such sensibility and concern for material ethics, agency and vitality, an investigation of the material labours of road repair met the research aim to recognise the vibrancy of materials; the thing-hood and thing-power of a material usually assumed to be inert.

This agency is not located within a discrete entity but emerges within an ecological assemblage in which we humans participate as material configurations. In employing this material-ecological framework in both the performance and our reflection, we are not dispensing with the critical value of socially engaged performance but, rather, expanding the realm of social interaction to include a mutual entanglement with sentient and material others. These interactions do not occur between individualistic subjects, but emerge from within already-existing relations. Barad describes this as the intra-action of entangled agencies within a field as the locus of world making: 'phenomena – whether lizards, electrons, or humans – exist only as a result of, and as part of, the world's ongoing intra-activity, its dynamic and contingent differentiation into specific relationalities. "We humans" don't make it so, not by dint of our own will, and not on our own. But through our own advances, we participate in bringing forth the world in its specificity, including ourselves' (2007: 353). In the case of the roadworks encounter, the field is all of the things in the scene, including the spectators. The impatient driver is not outside of the act of world repair, but always-already entangled as a road user, resource consumer and world sharer – an implicated party with a vested, if not yet conscious or empathetic, interest.

Caring and maintenance labours operate within larger institutional systems – themselves a form of machine. How, then, to enter into the system of road repair in order to understand its capacity for care more critically? Artist Mierle Laderman Ukeles provides a precedent with her performance practice that critiques the social institutions of maintenance labours. As artist-in-residence with the New York City Department of Sanitation (1979–80), Ukeles developed 'maintenance art': a mode of artistic practice concerned with the politics, ethics and aesthetics of maintenance labours. Ukeles describes her aesthetic appreciation of maintenance work as 'trying to listen to the hum of living. A feeling of being alive, breath to breath […] it is like this repetitive thing that as much as you chafe at the boredom of the repetition is as important as the other parts' (quoted in Bartholomew, 2009). Maintenance is both a mundane labour that 'takes all the fucking time' (Ukeles, 1969: 2) and an opportunity for affective encounter with the everyday performances of living-in-the-world. Entering the space of maintenance work, Ukeles employs performance art to draw undervalued labour into a space of critical aesthetic consideration.

In *Touch Sanitation Performance*, Ukeles shook hands with 8,500 New York City sanitation workers over eleven months. Through this act, the artist-at-work met the maintenance-worker-at-work face-to-face. The importance of touch cannot be understated here: perhaps the most powerful gesture of care in Ukeles' work is the recognition of mutual humanity, through skin-to-skin contact, with the performer of a labour perceived as 'unclean' – a person in close contact with lively, hygienically dangerous, undesirable matter. The in-person social engagement with workers is at the heart of both the ethics and aesthetics of Ukeles' performance practice and characterises all phases of the project: 'Even if she had never shaken a single hand, the preliminary planning, listening tours, observation, research, and analysis required to imagine and implement the work would stand as key examples of late twentieth-century conceptual art' (Phillips, quoted in Steinhauer, 2017: 6–7). *Bit-u-men-at-work* followed a similar agenda while shifting from the primarily human or social aspects of maintenance work toward the material ecology. Through this more-than-human lens, human interaction became material intra-action. In order to come face-to-face with bitumen – to 'shake hands' – the labour was explored at the scale of one small, intimate act of road repair.

> Wellington, New Zealand: … well, there are different mixes … that's what I learned, going up at 5 o'clock in the morning to Ngauranga Gorge, to the plant, because the guy would go into the little hut, and say, I need a mix, and this is what I need it for, and the woman would say, well … today's temperature is this, and when are you going to pour it, and how long do you want it to last for, how big is the hole, you know … etc. … and those all would be factored in … and then I'd go up into his little control room which overlooks everything and you could see down to where the chute would dump it into the truck, and he would type in all these variables, and you would hear churn, churn, churn, churn, churn and you'd see it move up the conveyor belt and do all these things … it would be fluffed, it would be heated, it would be mixed, it would be condensed, you'd see the sand coming in, you'd see the gravel going in, the different kinds of gravel, and it all – talk about temporal – it all had to do with the temperature and the moisture in the air at that time, each batch has this life … and so you see this kind of thing being just processed like an intestine, which was what informed the costume … and then you'd see this 'phoohwhh' and then there'd be this cloud of steam coming up … this weight drop … like a big, giant, black, poop … just popped into the truck, and the truck would go away, and it would be steaming … 'cause it was, you know, it was the middle of the night, then … that was … that it must have been July … and it was just this very very theatrical thing, you know the rest of the world is sleeping, and here we are, digesting, regurgitating the bowels of the earth, the kind of veins of the earth squeezed dry of this stuff that is pure gold, but we spread it all over the surface of the earth. (Unpublished transcript of conversation between authors)

The research began with Julieanna seeking out ways to encounter bitumen: 'an attempt to come into relation with it, to get closer, to spend time together … to cultivate empathy or response-ability, to become attentive/attuned to its agency – political and aesthetic' (unpublished transcript of conversation between authors). Investigations explored how bitumen is mined and manufactured; the impact these processes have on land, people and climate; how roads are repaired; the industries that it supports; the economies of roadworks; how the material behaves and feels; health-related issues; and the contentious debates concerning the promulgation of oil-hungry appetites in the contemporary developed world. Much of this research comprised 'field work': visits to asphalt plants, discussions with manufacturers and many nights following road crews to observe the repetitious labours of moving the sticky black material with big machines. Bitumen was impossible to separate from its contexts of production and consumption, including their mechanical and human labourers. With all its noxious toxicity, the material proved difficult to get close to, hidden behind the trappings of health and safety that attempt to care for the humans who engage with it. Physical and institutional barriers served to exclude a mature, white-haired female academic artist from joining a road crew and gaining first-hand experience of working with the material in situ. These activities made the complex realities of bitumen evident, revealed the centrality of the machine in all its forms – mechanical, institutional, ecological – and shaped the performance.

With no room to romanticise the materiality of bitumen, the research adopted Haraway's technique of 'staying with the trouble': 'learning to be truly present, not as a vanishing pivot between awful or edenic pasts and apocalyptic or salvific futures, but as mortal critters entwined in myriad unfinished configurations of places, times, matters, meanings' (2016: 1). Getting close to the material was, most simply, about spending time with it – working with it, getting down on hands and knees to take note (and rubbings) of its texture, observing how the raw material responded to the touch of human hands and the cracks of pavements. Becoming horizontal, abandoning the vertical stance of the dominant human, brings one even closer: face-to-face, belly-to-belly. This zone of intimate proximity was where Julieanna began to cultivate 'response-ability' – 'face-to-face in the contact zone of an entangled relationship' (Haraway, 2008: 227). Barad contends that 'in a breathtakingly intimate sense, touching, sensing, is what matter does, or rather, what matter is: matter is condensations of response-ability. Touching is a matter of response' (2012: 215). Barad further extends this touching to theorising, claiming that all lively forms of matter 'do theory', with the idea being 'to do collaborative research, to be in touch, in ways that enable response-ability' (2012: 207–8). In this sense, the research assemblage or ecology could be said to include the material and material processes, the machines, the labourers, the theoretical texts and the researchers, all collaborating toward an emerging 'response-ability'.

On reflection, the gestures of coming close to bitumen through the research process begin to respond to Held's critique of Tronto and Fisher's world-maintaining vision of care. Invoking Noddings' condition of face-to-face interaction or 'engrossment with the other' as a prerequisite for caring labour, Held (2005) cautioned against the broadening of care to include world repair, expressing concern that this intimate quality was missing from relationships with non-human others. In our view, this is a particularly anthropocentric concern that denies the agency and vitality of non-humans and, in doing so, negates the possibility of a mutually caring relationship with the world. Through a new materialist understanding of agency and relation – one that recognises the liveliness of materials, their capacity to produce affects and our capacity to become 'response-able' – it becomes possible to imagine and enact coming face-to-face with bitumen. Through an expanded understanding of touch, we might understand that to spend time being present within the entangled relations of the road care ecology, as well as literally coming into close contact with the material itself, is to perform this necessary engrossment with the material other.

> I follow her down the corridor. She is dressed in a white boiler suit criss-crossed with silver reflective tape. Coiled around her torso and hanging over her shoulder is a plastic tube. It looks greasy on the inside, more

yellow-brown than clear – oily residue of bitumen. It waggles behind her as she walks – a tail, an intestinal organ, a protuberance.

Out in the courtyard, it is dark. I hear her slump to the ground. Switching on the torch on my phone, a jumbled pile of wrinkled and writhing reflective lines burst into view, tracing bodily contours yet resisting any reading of a human form. I can see the orange triangles that mark the extent of the work-site. Her headlamps, once activated, cast a strange three-eyed illumination on the ground in front of her. Abruptly she starts making noises – I didn't know there was going to be sound. The sounds accompany actions, but they feel forced. At one point she sounds like a duck. How should it end?

With more light the figure is more obviously human, although the gestures, along with the prosthetic appendages and strange vocabulary of noises, is starting to hint at something other – glimmers of the woman-machine, not-yet-formed. What is becoming more apparent, though, is that there is a clear sequence to the labour: identify areas in the worksite to be re-paired, excrete bitumen from the tube, then pack it down. Each step entails a coming-closer – to the ground, to an intimate relationship, to the possibility of enacting desire. (Archer-Martin, unpublished notes, 2015–18)

The character of Desiré and the performance aesthetics – gestures, vocalisations, costume and score – emerged out of an iterative process that included test performances and reflective conversations between the authors, informed by the initial fieldwork and ongoing engagement in the discursive ecology of the research. In these conversations, we traversed notions of becoming machine, otherness, empathy and desire, against the established background of feminist, post-human, new materialist thinking. Some central understandings unfolded:

1. Desiré was neither human nor machine; she was 'both-and'. She was woman – was Julieanna – but was also other-than, more-than woman; gendered neither-nor, both-and. She was the road worker, rendered masculine in dominant culture, but she was also machine and ecology. She was trying to hold them together as different kinds of bodies, and look for empathetic relationships between them. Our understanding was by way of Haraway's notion of the cyborg: 'hybrid entities that are neither wholly technological nor completely organic, which means that the cyborg has the potential [...] to disrupt persistent dualisms that set the natural body in opposition to the technologically recrafted body' (Balsamo, 1999: 11).

2. Bitumen was not characterised in the work as 'unnatural'. Binaries of live/inert and natural/artificial were problematised through notions of material agency – the material was entangled in an ecology that was both natural and artificial (or 'neither-nor'). It was also not characterised as inherently 'bad'. Meeting the other 'as they are', we attempted to suspend moral and aesthetic judgement. This resonates with a move toward the more relational, situated, contingent ethics of care.

3. Desiré's labour was both to repair the pavement and to explore a desiring relationship with bitumen. There was something about fondling the material that got us thinking about the desiring-machine: if you could get to that place with the material that doesn't have that first primary sensibility about it, that you will have maybe transcended its abhorrent qualities or recognised the abhorrence of what is happening with it. The desiring-machine is a Deleuzean concept, lifted from Anti-oedipus:

> Desiring-machines are binary machines [...] one machine is always coupled with another. The productive synthesis, the production of production, is inherently connective in nature: 'and [...]' 'and then [...]'. This is because there is always a flow-producing machine, and another machine connected to it that interrupts or draws off part of its flow [...] [and so on] [...] Desire constantly couples continuous flows and partial objects that are by nature fragmentary and fragmented. Desire causes the current to flow, itself flows in turn, and breaks the flows. (Deleuze and Guattari, [1972] 1983: 5)

    While we recognised the riskiness of desire as a word (and a name), with its tints of possession of the other, we were drawn to the possibility of desire to activate a flow of affect.
4. The idea of falling in love with bitumen, of intimately desiring it, may appear a ridiculous notion. Being open to moments of humour was a tactic: 'admit[ting] a playful element into one's thinking and [being] willing to play the fool' (Bennett, 2010: 11). Being thought foolish is nothing when the possibility of knowing the material otherwise is at stake. With that in mind, we embraced the possibility of the sounds and gestures of the machine to be read as absurd, clownish or preposterous; witnessing strange (yet curiously familiar) beeps and growls, or the woman-machine humping or pummelling the pavement to flatten the pile of bitumen, invoked empathy even if eliciting dis-ease.

The aesthetics of the caring gesture has, on reflection, stood out to us as central to the work. Desiré's movement language progressed from Julieanna attempting to 'act' like a machine, to a stripped-back programming of behaviour that responded directly to the task at hand. While this initially resulted in fairly functional movements of standing, scanning and reversing, the quality of the gesture shifted when Desiré came into contact with the material, circling defects with chalk or working the bitumen belly-down on the pavement – qualitative feedback from the materials, registered in the performing bodies, provoked response. This was not an imposed choreographic decision so much as something that emerged in relationship with the materials – chalk, pavement, bitumen, suit and human flesh. It suggests that an aesthetics of more-than-human care and affective material gesture might be considered possible through a post-human new materialist lens.

The more that we attuned our sensibilities to care and desire, the more the gesture expressed an affective quality. In hindsight, this could be read as the emergence of a contingent aesthetic of caring material gesture – not in that the material itself was performing the gesture, but in that it was agentic in co-producing the response.

> a scene:
> reflectors, headlamps, visibility markings …
> utterances of steam and engine and reverse signals …
> of affection and longing and desire …
> a woman-machine:
> the functional qualities of a machine …
> human contours accentuated by a white boiler-suit …
>
> a labour:
> the figure identifies the parts that need repair,
> marks those areas,
> fills the imperfections with bitumen,
> presses the material in …
>
> But still I want to write of smells and mouths, of being close, of skins touching –
> because this is how the road and machine/woman-woman/machine come to know one another.
> the figure murmurs lovingly to the road,
> heaves and undulates over the markings that need attention,
> speaks to it in indecipherable loving tones,
> caresses it, warms it and humps it with her belly …
>
> But to say 'belly' and to gender it is to lean too heavily on the human and on dominant structures that try to order the world.
> there is a kind of perversity in this sensuality which induces discomfort …
> the interchangeable qualities of human and machine, organic and inorganic …
> the artist embodies the machine but also bodies-forth human desires …
>
> this is a private and intimate moment unfolding in public …
> this intimacy complicates the relations between road, machine, and human …
>
> this is vital:
> the audience must endure this work
> so that they might access these indeterminate spaces of human, machine and road
> as they are held together by flesh, breath and bitumen. (Adapted from Glisovic, 2016: 77)

Over three Melbourne evenings, Julieanna became Desiré, a hybrid woman-machine, set to work surveying a stretch of pavement for defects to repair with bitumen. Desiré was something more than Julieanna, who enacted a becoming-other, however, the labour was real. There was no script, only a set of parameters and a score that programmed the labours of Desiré, garbed in a white boiler suit, work boots, coiled bitumen-filled hose and a trio of headlamps. Two caretakers (Scott Morrison and Kerensa Diball) were hired to watch over Desiré/Julieanna and to take care of the start and finish of each durational labour – setting out two high-vis orange triangles (one with a go-pro recording-appendage) to demarcate the work site, and manoeuvring Desiré into position. Not 'in character' as in theatrical performance, they had received only the necessary briefing needed to don their high-vis vests and do the job like any conventional road worker, free to engage with the public as they supervised proceedings.

The work was encountered by a diverse audience including programme-toting symposium delegates and passing members of the public, not explicitly called out as 'a performance' but simply happening in the fray of life as does most roadwork. With a loose start time and indeterminate duration dictated only by the labourer's stamina, few experienced the work as a 'complete' performance with beginning and end, with three exceptions: the two caretakers and a woman in a red hat – Jen, the complicit witness, observing and documenting, simultaneously inhabiting the critical enquiry of the work as it unfolded and experiencing it from the outside. As she observed, Desiré worked, the caretakers hung about, people (and dogs) passed by. At times, some gathered on the road and footpath, lingered and dispersed. Interactions ranged from complete disinterest to active expressions of concern for the woman on the ground. For many, the nature of the scene as performance or maintenance work appeared to remain ambiguous.

As in our rereading of the original roadworks encounter, we offer a reading of this scene as an ecology of performance (or of labour, work, repair) in which everything is implicated – site, materials, performer/machine, crew, spectators, symposium organisers, civic bodies, political and theoretical discourses on ecology, care, labour, repair, mobility and so on. From her inside-outside position as critical witness, Jen observed a dynamic scene of diverse response and attentiveness to the labour, which, through duration and repetition, became background. This blending into the site or situation of roadwork was amplified at night, when the contours of bodies disappeared and the scene materialised as a networked assemblage of lights and high-vis materials. Headlamps, reflective strips, vests, safety triangles, street lights and car lights were all drawn together as a set of moving and static points operating in relation to one another, the individual bodies to which they were attached melding into a single connected field of dark but lively matter. A shift in aesthetic and empathetic response occurred over the duration of the performance labour: as the demands on the bodies of both the performer and spectator began to take their toll, a relationship of shared endurance emerged in which everything but the sensation of the pavement and the repeated gestures of the labour fell away.

The machine started without me. Does it feel the difference? Does it know I'm here?

People walking, cycling, skating past. Some glance, some smirk or laugh, raise an eyebrow.

Someone leaves their bag with me. Because I'm sitting/immobile?

A person wanders up and stops. I think she intended to be here.

Two people standing behind, slightly beyond. Talking, not watching.

Someone stops to look from other side of street, then keeps walking.

A lady looks at me instead of Desiré. Smiles.

I think I am too close to the work site. Moving.

What is the mobility of the machine? Of the material?

From across the road it looks more strange.

A woman in a white suit lies prone. Two people in high-vis look on. She looks like she's having a conversation with the footpath.

A circle forms around Desiré … the most intimate moment yet. Light comes on inside the gallery! Circle maintains then breaks. Some leave. Some want a different perspective.

The machine only gets the perspective it's given. I move again.

It's a person! I thought it was a doll (– kid)

A man in a people mover pulls up as Desiré is humping the ground. I think he might be concerned she is having a medical episode.

A person walked past and didn't even look. Minders weren't there but Desiré was, lying on the ground. Close to the wall though, maybe looks like she's supposed to be there, fixing something?

Woman and dog pass by. Dog looks. Woman keeps walking. Dog keeps looking back over shoulder.

It's getting cold. I wonder if Desiré is cold. It was more sheltered over by the wall though.

No one around to see Desiré reversing. Only minders, chatting casually, not looking. Only me.

Machine seems angry. Have I done something? Missed something?

Is this okay? Am I doing it right?

The machine seems tired. Sore. (So am I – the pavement is hard and bits of gravel stick in my palms.)

It hasn't been worked this hard before. Are we driving it too hard?

… my soul sees a soul in the machine. But does the machine see me? perhaps it sees the machine in me.

… does the material, the stuff, see the stuff in me?

I need to wee. I wonder if Desiré does. She still has work to do. I can go when I want …

I'm back from the bathroom.

There was a piece of rubber hose in there, like a shed skin or banana peel or half a dead worm.

I think it might have fallen off Desiré.

I was distracted talking to a caretaker about the performance feeling more machine-like, especially after I went away and came back. The machine was still working, without needing me there to witness it. The contractual obligation of me as witness or audience or observer was broken. The performance is reduced to a banal, albeit odd, act of labour. It seems strange to keep watching now, as if I should just leave her to her business, but yet there's

something more that compels me – a feeling – a strangely intimate connection visible in the way she works the material.

    That's it, right there. It's just work, but done differently, made new.

    (Archer-Martin, unpublished notes, 2015–18)

Conclusion: toward a material-led aesthetics of care in ecologically engaged performance

Our reflections on *bit-u-men-at-work* have posed a number of challenges in terms of the present conversation on performance and care, and, in particular, the aesthetics of care. Primarily, this edited collection aligns care with 'socially engaged performance' through an interdisciplinary interrogation of the relationship between creative or aesthetic practices, and the ethics and practices of care. Much of the existing discourse focuses on the qualities of caring human–human relationships. We have made the case for more voices, asking what might happen if we were to consider care through a post-human new materialist lens. In this scenario, agency is extended beyond the human to material ecologies in which humans are implicated but not dominant. Extending the call to matter, things and material assemblages, invoking the likes of Bennett, Barad and Haraway, we have begun to refigure the topic of concern from 'care and *socially* engaged performance' to 'care and *ecologically* engaged performance'.

    Bit-u-men-at-work employed a performance-as-research methodology, exploring the making of and public encounters with live art performance as modes of enquiring into or enacting care. Whereas various modes of participatory performance take the social co-production of experience as a central tenet, the ecological co-production of experience poses a different challenge. Framing the enquiry within a post-human new materialism worldview, we considered materials and machines as participants in the research assemblage and the performance ecology it informed, prompting different ways of thinking about and experiencing performance that recognise the agency of non-humans in the co-production of affect: a first step toward developing a post-human new materialist performance-as-research methodology.

    Central to both the enquiry and our reflection on it has been an emerging vocabulary of gestures and affect. In a material-led rather than human-led performance ecology, we have had to think otherwise about the agents at play in producing the affects that might be said to comprise an aesthetics of care. If the capacity for caring relations extends beyond the human, then a study of an aesthetics of care must necessarily include non-human actors and the affects that they co-produce as part of agentic assemblages. We are a long way from being able to define what an aesthetics of post-human new materialist care might look or feel like. Rather, we have begun to attune our embodied sensibility to the qualities of gestures and affects produced by these trans-ontological assemblages, cultivating a new 'response-ability' and

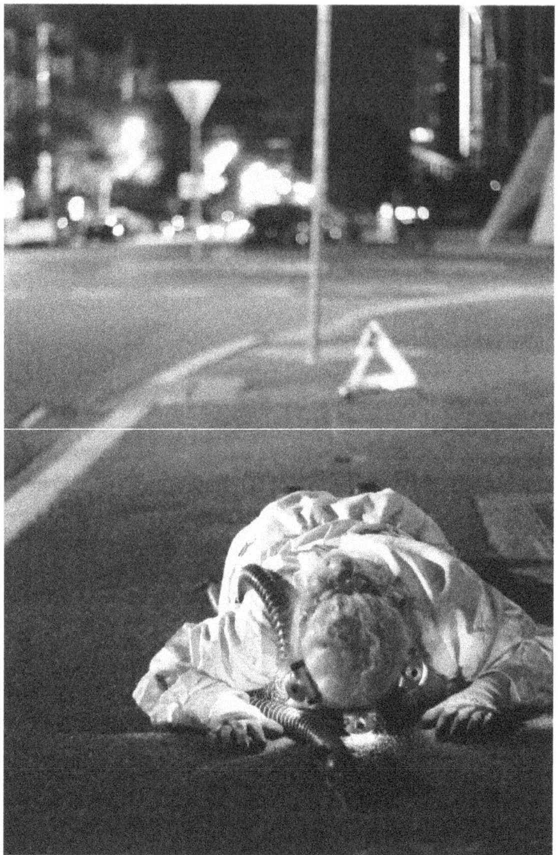

Figure 6.2 Desiré, a tangled pile on the pavement, face-to-face with bitumen

positioning affective material labours as performances of care that maintain and repair our world.

We end with two questions around the role of desire in the aesthetics of care: Who defines the terms of reference in a desiring relation and what does that mean for the relationship between aesthetics and desire? In opening the performance of care to the non-human or material other, we have found it necessary to become open to aesthetics of the other. We challenged ourselves to work with an undesirable yet wilfully exploited material, taking seriously Haraway's call to 'stay with the trouble' (2016). On a superficial but affectively powerful level, bitumen did not appeal to our senses. The dirty and monotonous labours of people and machines engaged in acts of road repair did not sing out to us as being beautiful. Nevertheless, we proceeded, unafraid to play the fool, with the notion of desiring and becoming intimate – and not just in the sense of proximity – with this material through up-close and personal caring labour. We attempted to suspend our human judgement in order to meet the ontological other as they are. An aesthetic did emerge, but it was not one defined by some socially constructed ideal of beauty. Rather, it was born out of time spent together, of hard labour and shared suffering and of joyful moments when everything seemed to just work together. It was at once ridiculous, disgusting, imperfect, strange, sensual – and caring (Figure 6.2).

CARE DEFICITS

Clean Break: a practical politics of care

Caoimhe McAvinchey

Clean Break, founded in 1979 by two women serving sentences in an English prison, has developed over the last four decades into an influential theatre, education and advocacy organisation, positioning narratives of women affected by the criminal justice system centre stage. In this chapter, Joan Tronto's work on care, markets and justice ([1993] 2009, 2013) informs my reading of Clean Break's organisational practices as care. From its distinctive approach to developing new writing for theatre, to its enduring commitment to reach audiences through partnerships with criminal justice, cultural and voluntary sector organisations, Clean Break creates structures of care for women who have fallen beyond the reach of state systems of welfare: the subjects of stigma, regulation and punishment. In this chapter, I argue that Clean Break not only critiques the intersectional oppressions that shape the lives of many women who experience the criminal justice system but, through its responsive and interconnected practices, attends to a care deficit in society, integral to the company's commitment to equality and justice.

A radical articulation of care

In *Moral Boundaries: A Political Argument for an Ethic of Care* ([1993] 2009), Joan Tronto argues for a reconsideration of care as a central rather than peripheral concern to society, a valuable moral and political concept that, through practice, engenders social equality and justice. Tronto's earlier work with Berenice Fisher establishes caring as central to our lived experience, 'a species activity that includes everything we do to maintain, continue and repair our "world" so that we can live in it as well as possible' ([1993] 2009: 40). In this context, care is a practice (a process you do) rather than a disposition (a way you feel), upon which we are all interdependent. However, in a world where autonomy and independence is valued more than negotiation, collaboration and *inter*dependence, care is sidelined and devalued. It is relegated as 'women's work', firmly positioned in the realm of the domestic and hidden, rather than the public and visible, a site with little agency and even less power. In a neoliberal world that values productivity and the free movement of goods in global markets, ideas of care are discredited ideologically and economically: relational acts of caregiving – parenting, looking after friends and family members who are living with long-term illnesses, disability or the effects of age – are under-recognised contributions to society. In the case of the UK, where the state may issue a carer's allowance, carers often find themselves discredited and viewed as an economic drain on society, despite the fact that their hidden work saves the government over £123 billion a year on health and social care (Carers UK, 2015). Additionally, as Tronto notes, where care work is paid, it is often gendered, raced and classed and that 'those who are least well off in society are disproportionately those who do the work of caring, and that the best-off members of society often use their positions of superiority to pass caring work off to others' ([1993] 2009: 113). This marginalisation and devaluing of care work further facilitates the construction of 'otherness' – of both the carer and cared for – through power and privilege.

Tronto disaggregates the idea of care from women's work and women's morality and repositions this species activity that maintains, continues and repairs the world as a 'care ethic' – something to be foregrounded and valued as part of the collaborative, processual act of society. A centralising of the value of care, of care ethics, would, she argues, enable societies to reframe and envision the world differently, 'so that the activities that legitimate the accretion of power to the existing powerful are less valued, and the activities that might legitimate a sharing of power with outsiders are increased in value' (Tronto, [1993] 2009: 20). This radical rethinking about the relationship between care and justice, equality and power exposes the limited reach of government policy addressing social injustice. Clean Break's theatre practice *with* women affected by social inequality, and the work it does around consciousness raising through theatre *about* the enduring structural inequalities that shape their experience is, I argue, a political, social and cultural intervention that breeches this gap. Fisher and Tronto's identification of the elements of care offers a pertinent framework with which to examine Clean Break's nuanced, robust and responsive practice: 'caring about, noticing the need to care in the first place; taking care of, assuming responsibility for care; care-giving, the actual work of care that needs to be done; and care-receiving, the response of that which is cared for to the carer' (1990: 127). In her later work, *Caring Democracy: Markets, Equality and Justice* (2013), Tronto expands this framework to include, 'caring with', arguing that 'caring needs and the ways in which they are met need to be consistent with democratic commitments to justice, equality, and freedom for all' (2013: 23). To think about care beyond primary, dyadic care relations offers an opportunity to think about how care functions socially and politically in a culture. This is imperative when considering societal perception of and political response to women with experience of the criminal justice system. These are women who are often reduced and delimited through stigma, shame and regulation as 'bad girls': contributors to society's problems rather than individuals whose lives are disproportionately affected by social injustice. Cast as such, these women are deemed, individually and collectively, beyond care.

Beyond care? Women, criminal justice and criminalisation

The prison population continues to soar. At the time of writing, more than eleven million people are incarcerated across the globe. There is a considerable body of research detailing the political and economic imperatives for this phenomenon (Coyle *et al.*, 2016; Mauer, 2016). The rise in crime and sentencing reflects an expansion in the number of human behaviours identified as unlawful (particularly in relation to technology and immigration) and greater state intervention by policing and judicial bodies. Despite the democratic ideal that everyone is equal before the law, in the USA and UK particularly, there is a disproportionate percentage of the prison population who experience social inequality through their experience of poverty, racism and limited social mobility (Mauer, 1999). Wacquant highlights the interrelationship between poverty and punishment in neoliberal societies. He argues that in neoliberal states, 'welfare and criminal justice are two modalities of public policy toward the poor' and that 'the linked stinginess of the welfare wing and munificence of the penal wing under the guidance of moralism are profoundly injurious to democratic ideals' (Wacquant, 2011). While Wacquant evidences his argument with specific reference to the USA, the fundamental issues about the punitive regulation of those who live in poverty is also evident in countries whose actions reveal an increased deployment of incarceration as punishment, despite successive governments' rhetoric to tackle crime and reduce it: countries like the UK, where the work of managing and administering the state business of punishment is, increasingly, carried out by private companies in a global corrections industry. These companies' escalating profits show little sign of diminishing as governments continue to find funds in the name of security at a time of aggressive cutbacks in health, education and social care (Stern, 2006; Garland, 2018).

The feminisation of poverty (Bradshaw, 2002) and the elision between welfare policy and penal policy means that women are particularly vulnerable to political forces of regulation and punishment. Globally, women make up less than 10 per cent of the prison population, and the vast majority of crimes they commit are non-violent, resulting in short-term sentences (Kennedy, 1993; Gunnison and Bernat, 2016). It is most significant that the characteristics of women in prison reflect, largely, the profile of women who live in poverty – women who are unemployed, who have experienced homelessness, who live with poor physical and mental health (Fitch *et al.*, 2011). Shame and stigma attach themselves to women who are seen to be unemployed, unemployable, 'living off the state', women who are criminalised – either due to a formal sentence or because of perception. Valentine's work on *Inequality and Class Prejudice in an Age of Austerity* (2014) details a marked decrease in societal compassion and empathy for those who are perceived as the 'undeserving poor', as 'morally deficient', an attitude further entrenched in relation to women with experience of the criminal justice system. For them, a criminal record and the limited access to employment that this ensures means that many women continue to be further punished – economically and socially – beyond the term of their sentence.

Clean Break

In attending to the needs of women who have experience of the criminal justice system through its distinctive organisational practices, Clean Break addresses wider issues of gendered social inequality and gendered social injustice. It models an ambitious and enduring resistance to the critical lack of care – even 'care-lessness' – in state policy and cultural representations of criminalised women. Clean Break values 'compassion, collaboration, respect and relationship-making' (Perman, 2018) and this informs all aspects of its work, from direct intervention with women with lived experience of the criminal justice system through its education programme and consciousness raising through the commissioning, producing and touring of productions that place stories of these lives centre stage. These values are the antithesis of coercion and control, they are a distinctive practical politics of care, addressing social injustice and a care deficit and have been evident from the genesis and subsequent development of the company over the past forty years.

Clean Break theatre company was established by Jacqueline Holborough and Jenny Hicks while at HMP Askham Grange, an open prison in the North East of England. In its early years, Clean Break was a collective of women with experience of prison, who devised, wrote and performed plays about their experience, the impact of this on their lives and the lives of their families. These productions toured to theatres, prisons, educational and community centres across the UK and, on occasion, to the USA and the Netherlands. By the mid-1980s, the company had established a unique voice in contemporary British theatre, continuing to raise challenging questions about identity politics, gendered experience of criminal justice and modes of theatre production. During the 1980s, the availability of government funding for the arts was increasingly conditional on organisations demonstrating hierarchical management structures that reflected more traditional business models, and the collective identity of Clean Break was necessarily expanded to include artists and arts professionals who shared a commitment to the mission of the company, rather than the shared lived experience of incarceration. After years of financial instability, with the company working with box-office splits, small grants and considerable volunteer labour, Clean Break was finally supported by the Greater London Council and Arts Council England. This wider recognition of the unique work of the company was consolidated in 1995, when the company secured funding for the building of a women-only theatre, education and social space in Kentish Town, North London, where the company is still based. Between 1997 and 2018, Clean Break was led by Lucy Perman. At the time of writing, the company is making significant changes in its organisational structures and programmes, decentralising its power structures and increasing collaboration with members in the planning and realisation of the company's work.

Clean Break's women-only building has been an integral part of the company's less-visible but core work, offering extensive and free education, training and support for thousands of women referred by prison, probation and voluntary sector services. Over 70 per cent of graduates from Clean Break's education programme have gone on to further education, employment or training (Abraham and Busby, 2015). The impact of Clean Break's work has been far-reaching – not only for the individual women who have worked with the company but in shifting public understandings about gendered inequality across a network of organisations in arts, education, criminal justice, the voluntary sector and government who have partnered with it.

In addition to this necessarily less-visible work, Clean Break has, over the last four decades, made a significant contribution to contemporary British theatre through the commissioning of new writing focusing on women and criminal justice, staged and produced by women-only casts and creative teams. The range of playwrights commissioned during this time is extraordinary, some established and others at earlier stages of their careers: Bryony Lavery, Sarah Daniels, Paulette Randall, Rebecca Prichard, Winsome Pinnock, Lucy Kirkwood, Theresa Ikoko, Alice Birch and Chino Odimba. The company's relentless commitment to expose the hidden narratives beyond the stereotypes of women and crime details an expansive and interconnected range of social injustices in over sixty plays including: mental illness (*Sounds Like an Insult*, 2014, Vivienne Franzmann), enduring poverty and social immobility (*Spent*, 2016, Katherine Chandler), racism (*24%*, 1991, Paulette Randall), drug abuse (*Pests*, 2014, Vivienne Franzmann), family rupture (*Billy the Girl*, 2013, Katy Hims; *House*, 2016, Somalia Seaton) and sex trafficking (*it felt empty when the heart went at first but it's alright now*, 2009, Lucy Kirkwood). This brief selection of plays illustrates some of the ways that Clean Break has invited the public to attend to the experience of women whose lives are often masked by stereotype and lazy cultural representation. The company's commitment to reach a broad range of audiences is evident as, in addition to touring work to mainstream major theatres including the Royal Court and the Royal Exchange, it also tours to smaller venues, festivals, prisons and specialist conferences on criminal justice and women's services. This is critical cultural work. But why, after forty years, is this work still – urgently – needed? Clean Break's commitment to a practical politics of care presents a particular challenge to the company, continually negotiating a landscape where the pace of sociopolitical intervention is glacial. In the following section, I detail how public and political engagement with women and criminal justice continually fails to acknowledge the practical care needed to support the lives of women who have been disproportionately affected by social inequality. This sociopolitical inertia surrounding women and the criminal justice system has led to the neglect, dismissal and disruption of any significant interventions of support. For four decades, Clean Break has refused to be complicit in this apathy, not only critiquing it but responding to it – developing care-orientated practices that adapt to the needs of criminalised women, finding ways – and audiences – to address them despite economic, social and political torpor.

More 'troubled' than 'troublesome'

> The light dancing on the Thames floods into the river-terrace function room at the House of Lords, the second chamber of the United Kingdom's Houses of Parliament. Three women in prison-regulation grey tracksuits, stand at one end of the room, commanding the attention of the audience of more than one hundred politicians, prison governors, National Offender Management Service staff, police and crime commissioners as well as staff from Women's Centres. One of the women speaks:
>
> They're saying I've made myself intentionally homeless by coming into prison. Where am I going to live when I get out? How am I going to survive?
>
> I talk to women here, in the kitchens, on the wing, and from what I can understand, and I'm not a politician, but their problems have started with lack of housing. So you've got vulnerable women, leaving prison unsafe, homeless, struggling to stay clean from drugs and alcohol, at risk of domestic abuse.
>
> And, No support.
>
> It's not rocket science, they'll end up back in.
>
> When the woman declares herself 'not a politician', there is a ripple of laughter, an acknowledgement from the audience that this has been said in a room full of politicians, of people with influence on government or who are the frontline of implementing Ministry of Justice policy on law, policing and prisons. (Bruce, 2017)

The women in the above extract, actors from Clean Break, were performing *Hear*, a short play written by Deborah Bruce, informed by the voices and opinions of women serving sentences, who had recently participated in a writing residency with the company. *Hear* was commissioned by Women in Prison for this event at the House of Lords, celebrating the ten-year anniversary of the publication of the Corston Report (2007), a landmark review of the treatment of women in the criminal justice system. The report acknowledged that, while women make up 4–6 per cent of the overall prison population, the majority of women serve short sentences for non-violent crimes, that prison is not always the most appropriate form of punishment and that a prison sentence can do more societal harm than good. In short, the Corston Report exposed how the treatment of many vulnerable women in prison failed to live up to Her Majesty's Prison Service's 'duty [...] to look after [those committed by the courts] with humanity' (Coyle, 2003: 10). Corston decimated the perpetuated, lazy stereotypes of women in prison as 'bad girls', exposing the deep-rooted, intersectional social injustices that shape the lives of many women who commit non-violent crime: women who are 'more "troubled" than "troublesome"' (2007: 16). Racism, poverty, histories of neglect, abuse, poor mental health, homelessness and limited access to education and employment are some of the structural, recurring issues faced by many women in the criminal justice system. In addition to wider concerns about the use and effectiveness of incarceration as punishment, Corston detailed the devastating social and economic consequences of women's incarceration on individuals and families that endures for generations including children being removed from their mothers, the loss of homes, limits on employment possibilities and enduring poor health.

Despite previous government reports (Ramsbotham, 1997) and the enduring advocacy of organisations, including Women in Prison and the Penal Reform Trust, it took the deaths of six women in HMP Styal in 2006 for the Labour government to take action. In taking on this review, Corston was explicit in her exasperation at the status quo:

> I have been dismayed at the high prevalence of institutional misunderstanding within the criminal justice system of the things that matter to women and at the shocking level of unmet need. Yet the compelling body of research which has accumulated over many years consistently points to remedies. Much of this research was commissioned by government. There can be few topics that have been so exhaustively researched to such little practical effect as the plight of women in the criminal justice system. (2007: 16)

A decade later, however, little has changed for women who are at risk of entering or returning to the criminal justice system. At this House of Lords' event, Women in Prison launched *The Corston Report 10 Years On: How Far Have We Come on the Road to Reform for Women Affected by the Criminal Justice System?* (2017). This report reviewed (in)action undertaken in response to each of the recommendations. Once again, despite cross-party acknowledgement of the value of the report's findings, successive governments' action continues to be patchy and sporadic: austerity measures and regulation threaten the very viability of interventions, including Corston's highly successful community-based Women's Centres, supporting a wide range of needs for women at risk of entering or returning to prison (Howard League, 2016).

Corston's call for societal compassion, her frustration at the lack of political commitment and the continued need for urgent penal reform is echoed, ten years later, by the voice of another character in *Hear*, who states, with incredulity, 'My God, the cost! The cost of putting the kids in care. The cost of our incarceration. What sense does it make to cut the services that support us? You'll end up paying ten times further down the line for the chaos it causes. No one's looking at the bigger picture are they?' (Bruce, 2017: 5). The potency of *Hear* is heightened by the audience's understandings that the play is informed by the voices of women currently living in prison and performed by actors, graduates of Clean Break's education programme, who have experience of prison. The question, 'No one's looking at the bigger picture are they?' was particularly powerful in the context of performances for audiences of politicians and policy makers at the House of Lords and staff at the Ministry of Justice, where *Hear* was performed as part of International Women's Day celebrations the following day. Both the Corston Report and *Hear* expose a 'care deficit' – a structural gap between the recognition that care is required (caring about) and knowing that the caring needs have been met (care receiving). This gap reflects Tronto's observation that caring about and taking care of are often 'the duties of the powerful while care-giving and care-receiving are left to the less powerful' ([1993] 2009: 114). This gap ensures an interruption in care: a failure of care to be received by those who most need it, despite the best efforts of individuals on the front line of care services pushed to the brink of collapse. This is the terrain of Clean Break's 2015 production, *Joanne* by Deborah Bruce, Theresa Ikoko, Laura Lomas, Chino Odimba and Ursula Rani Sarma. The dramaturgical structure of the play, shaped by five writers collaborating on separate monologues that connect to reveal the overarching narrative of Joanne's life and final hours, was the first time that Clean Break had worked in this way. The writers developed a timeline that created a narrative with potential characters – people from front-line services such as the National Health Service (NHS) – but there was no prescription as to who the character would be. Informed by research into the impacts of austerity on the lives of those who are particularly vulnerable (Ali, 2015) and interviews with people who support women when released on a day-to-day basis, *Joanne* is an example of the way in which Clean Break's practical politics of care has supported the development of new dramaturgical structures. *Joanne* is a state-of-the-nation play, capturing the long moment of critical impact when the state refuses to take responsibility to care about or care with those who are most vulnerable within it.

Joanne: *a fatal interruption of care*

Joanne stages the final twenty-four hours in the life of a young woman after she is released from prison. We never meet the eponymous Joanne but aspects of her life are revealed through the testimony of five women, played by the same actor (Tanya Moodie in the original production). Each of these five characters has a role to play in organisations and institutions that Joanne comes into contact with, before and after prison: school, the police, the NHS, a charity that supports prisoners as they prepare for release and a hostel that provides accommodation for homeless prisoners. Throughout each of the five monologues, the audience is given insight into Joanne's life and the hours before her death: they reveal moments of a life untethered through grief, self-harm, drugs and, most damagingly, isolation – a life with no family or friends to turn to. The monologues also give insight into the personal and professional lives of Stella, Grace, Kathleen, Alice and Becky – women who work on the front line of care services; women who, in their personal lives, have significant caring responsibilities. Focusing on three of these monologues gives insight into the labour of care and the formal care systems that are under acute and unsustainable pressure, where individuals employed within them feel compelled but constrained to offer responsive care beyond what the system anticipates and plans for.

We meet Stella on her last day of work, giving a farewell speech to colleagues in a charity that supports prisoners preparing for release. She has been made redundant because the charity's funding has run out. As a woman with a criminal record, Stella's employment opportunities are curtailed, 'If it wasn't for this job. If it wasn't for them believing in me. Anyway you know what I mean. Not many options to put my "experience" to good use if you know what I mean' (Bruce *et al.*, 2015: 3). Stella is the person who meets with Joanne in the weeks before she leaves prison and is there for her the moment she walks out the gate, who intercepts her before the lingering drug dealers do, who navigates services with her, 'Probation. Doctor. Homeless Unit' (Bruce *et al.*, 2015: 8). We also learn that Stella cares for her mum who has complex needs, 'I'll feed her, wash her, and sit in the house with her watching TV all day cuz she's too scared to go out, too scared to wash her hair, too scared of everything' (Bruce *et al.*, 2015: 9). With an absence of any family support, Stella becomes Joanne's sole but temporary guide to the world beyond the prison gate: she helps Joanne access her medication and battles, in vain, to ensure that Joanne is not put in a wet hostel with drug addicts and alcoholics. Despite the demands of home and work and facing imminent unemployment, Stella's ethic of care continues to fuel her engagement with Joanne, 'This is the bit of the job I love. Loved. The human-contact bit, the breaking-the-ice bit. The breaking-into-a-smile bit. And there's that feeling. The reason why we do it. That thing that makes you wake up every morning to do it' (Bruce *et al.*, 2015: 6–7). Stella's concern for Joanne goes beyond the parameters of her job, it is interpersonal and, in Tronto's terms, interdependent – it is, as Stella says, 'that feeling … The reason why we do it'. However, at the end of this particular day, Stella has no job, no official responsibility to Joanne but she worries, 'Who's going to check on her tomorrow? […] Who cares now?' (Bruce *et al.*, 2015: 7).

When Joanne gets into a fight at the hostel because someone steals the Mickey Mouse watch her dead father had once given her, the police are called. Grace is a police officer with the London Met, and she arrives with her partner Harry, a 'nice decent bloke … believes in doing things by the book' (Bruce *et al.*, 2015: 5). As her monologue unfolds, Grace reveals her pathway to the police, one that is very different to what could have been: teenage years wrecked by grief, numbed by alcohol and sex and forever scarred by not intervening when she was part of a gang that bullied a girl who then attempted suicide. As a teenage mum, Grace witnessed 'nine-year-olds smoking weed in the stairwells and twelve-year-olds pushing prams of their own' (Bruce *et al.*, 2015: 15). The thought of her daughter being caught up in this world made Grace take action, leave and train for the police. When Grace encounters Joanne, she should, according to the rules, report the incident. But Joanne is so distressed by the prospect of returning to prison that Grace steps beyond the parameters of the official rules of her role and acknowledges the person before her:

> And suddenly I see her, the moments that have defined her, that have led her to this kitchen tonight, standing in front of me, shaking, saying going back to prison will break her […] I tell Harry we'll keep this one between the two of us … and he doesn't like it […] We have to follow procedure … No we don't, we fucking don't, all we have to do is what we think is right. And this is the right thing. I'm sure of it. (Bruce *et al.*, 2015: 17)

Grace's distinction between procedure (playing by the rules) and doing the right thing (responding to the human before her) illuminates the care labour that characterises so much work on front-line services. It illustrates the sharp distinction between care that an organisation plans for with procedures that are managed, and care work that is responsive, attended to by an individual who becomes open to another through this encounter, resisting the professional administration of care that processes and categorises aspects of a person's behaviour rather than considering the person in the entirety of their being. *Joanne* exposes the unresolvable tension between the two.

The social and personal impact of this lived-with tension is even more heightened in Kathleen's monologue. Kathleen is an accident and emergency (A&E) receptionist in an NHS hospital. When Joanne appears before Kathleen she is distressed, suffering side effects from the wrong medication and suicidal, asking to be sectioned. As Kathleen tries to attend to Joanne she is accosted by a man, 'Aggressive, proper nasty', who 'comes right up to the grid, presses his mouth right into it […] "What do you care? […] With ya cuts and ya community plans and ya broken promises." I can feel the wetness on my chin as his spit sprays on the face of the NHS' (Bruce *et al.*, 2015: 26). By the time Kathleen attends to the man with a professionalism that she has learnt to armour herself with, Joanne has disappeared. Kathleen's concern for Joanne, for all the people in crises she has met over thirty years of

A&E night shifts means that she is tormented by her work, by the chronic and unmet need she witnesses daily:

> They're all there, curled up on the bed next to me, squeezed into the drawers of my bedside cabinet, in my glasses case, wrapped around the legs of the bed.
>
> With their broken toes and high temperatures and domestic incidents and split lips and cracked heads and stomachs needing pumping and hearing voices and handcuffed to police. The schizos and psychos, knives hidden in socks, the boys wanting their mums. Rumbling appendixes and no GP appointments and infected dog bites and third-degree burns, the pub fights and chest pains, the luckless and the poverty struck and the poor lonely live-alones with no one to tell them to take two aspirin and get an early night. (Bruce *et al.*, 2015: 26–7)

This litany of human hurt is the daily business of care workers, people like Stella, Grace and Kathleen who are the public face of state and voluntary service care. They are the women who stand on the front line, making direct contact with people whose lives are in crisis, a buffer between the messy needs of lives and the management systems that administer professional care at a distance to the bodies themselves. They are, as Róisín McBrinn, the joint artistic director at Clean Break identifies, the 'very brittle army, kept fighting through good will and human endurance' (McBrinn, 2015: n.p.). These are the women who witness the crises of care in which Joanne – and other nameless, faceless women who leave prison on a daily basis – is fatally enmeshed: they witness the complexity and fragility of a life that is barely visible to the public, that is made even more vulnerable in a context of cuts to services in the name of prudence in an age of austerity. In *Joanne*, Clean Break asks the audience to attend to what we – individuals and the state – don't, or won't, see.

Towards a practical politics of care

For Clean Break, theatre is both the medium to address social injustices experienced by criminalised women and the means to make a direct intervention in the individual lives of women they work with. Alongside its commitment to producing new plays that directly engage with issues of women and criminal justice, Clean Break offers training and education opportunities for women who have experience of or are at risk of entering the system. Clean Break's unique education programme, which ran for twenty years until 2017, offered women a range of courses specifically related to theatre making – performance, backstage craft, writing for performance – alongside courses that support personal development – anger management, literacy and mental health and well-being. Women travelled to the programme from across London's thirty-three boroughs and, at times, beyond. Some of the women had completed prison sentences, others were released on temporary license (ROTL). Some were referred by women's and health services who recognised them as being 'at risk' of offending, others encountered members of Clean Break's student support team when they were visiting prisons, probation, bail hostels or community-based alcohol or drug projects. While the offer of Clean Break's education programme was appealing in principle, many women faced practical barriers that could easily prevent them from leaving home, let alone travelling across the city and engaging with any formal education or training programme. A major part of the work of the education programme took place beyond the studios, ensuring that women were supported in being able to take up the invitation to participate: women were offered financial support for travel, a hot lunch and, when needed, hand-holding assistance to get to the building (Perman, 2016). In the early 1990s, when Clean Break's new women-only centre was being planned, there was a conscious decision not to have a crèche in the building to ensure that the women had time and space to attend to their own needs; however, Clean Break provides support in both setting up and paying for childcare. Once the women make it to through Clean Break's door, there is substantial support that ranges from food-bank vouchers to counselling, from careers guidance to housing support. These structures of care have been rigorously thought through, attending to a range of interlinked challenges to be negotiated. For Lucy Perman, Chief Executive of Clean Break from 1997 to 2018, care is integral to the company's values:

> It is in all our practices: how we talk to the women; how we interact with them; treating them for who they are and what they want to share with you; respecting them, their history, their story […] It's creating the relationship and environment for a woman to be able to share everything and anything that is in her life that is a barrier to her participating in our offer and supporting her to move on with her life in the way she wants to. (2016)

One of the many remarkable things about Clean Break is how it fosters relationships between members and between members and staff. There is a strong sense of Clean Break as being a point of focus – as a place, an idea and a community – to which people have a strong attachment. This has been apparent in conversations with students, graduates, writers, actors, staff from partner organisations in prisons and theatres and members of staff who no longer work there. The company's commitment to theatre as a means to navigate, critique and understand the world is reiterated through the practical acquisition of skills; the emphasis on personal development; the valuing of collaboration that invites people to contribute in the way that they are able to at a particular moment; the collective witnessing of people making constructive changes in their lives; and the playfulness and rigor of the theatre that is shared with a wider Clean Break audience.

Care and inter/dependence

One of the challenges the organisation is keenly aware of is negotiating when the support offered to the women through the structures and relationships in the company tips the balance towards dependency. It is imperative that the organisation facilitates the women in their self-care and steps towards independence. In the context of Clean Break, care is something that is both structurally planned for *and* responsive, creating a model of relational practice, committed to negotiating the challenges of human interdependence in the attempt to imagine and realise a more just society. This model of organisational practice and culture takes time to evolve and maintain. Lucy Perman identified the ongoing challenge the organisation faced maintaining a culture of care when society is

> under siege from government cuts to education, health and social care. In a time of austerity, the women's sector, a sector that is founded on caring for 'vulnerable women', is under massive pressures and is having to behave in a way that is the antithesis of that because of Transforming Rehabilitation and funding cuts. The environment of the building and the values which underpin our practice feel under threat, they could seem old fashioned. […] There's something about time which is under pressure in this period – it takes time to allow relationships and trust to grow, for brilliant, creative and fruitful things to happen. (2016)

At the time of writing, two years since this interview took place, Clean Break is in a period of transition. The company began a restructuring process after a lengthy consultation process with its staff, board members, current students, graduates and stakeholders. A number of factors informed this: the external environment, particularly the combined impacts of Brexit preparations, the impact of austerity with cuts across criminal justice, women's services, education and the arts, along with, more positively, the company's ongoing reflection of how best to support women with experience of the criminal justice system through theatre. While previously, Clean Break had four identifiable strands of work – artistic, education, engagement and leadership – in the newly proposed model, the company has assimilated all its activity into one artistic programme. Within this, opportunities for personal development, education and training that were once delivered through a structured programme of separate courses have been integrated, bringing Clean Break Members (previously students and graduates) to the 'heart of our theatre-making and organization' (Clean Break, 2018: 3). Additionally, the hierarchical model of power with a single figure of ultimate authority, the role of the chief executive, has been recalibrated with three people/roles taking equal responsibility for the company. In an interview in 2018, in the week before leaving the company after leading it for twenty-one years, Lucy Perman, reflected on these changes:

> With this new structure and the theatre produced, we are trying to do more consciousness raising with the women rather than on behalf of or for the

women. That's going to be a work in progress for some time. But there are moments where you can see it already happening – like Deborah Bruce [Clean Break's current writer in residence] saying, we have a writing circle, we don't have a writing course. In the writing circles that she runs, she writes with the women and that's quite different […] and that is exactly the change that we are wanting to make – artists alongside Members collaborating and making work together. The more we get the women involved in making decisions and coming up with ideas, the more it'll feel different. We won't know what these ideas will look like, but they won't look like the ones we're dreaming up now and that's great. It's about more of an equal distribution of power – not an old style paternalistic way of doing things of behalf of the 'less fortunate', the 'traumatised' or the 'vulnerable'. (2018)

This restructuring is a further reiteration of Clean Break's practical politics of care. For the organisation to continue to do work that contributes to making 'a society where women can realise their full potential, free from criminal-isation' (Clean Break, 2018: 6), it demands negotiation, collaboration and interdependence working *alongside* the women it seeks to represent through theatre. This resonates with Tronto's care ethic in practice, with an organ-isational structure and approach that purposefully disrupts the accretion of power to those who have it (in this case, social capital and a life without the stigma of criminalisation) and legitimates the sharing of power with 'out-siders' (Tronto, [1993] 2009: 20).

Conclusion

While researching with the company for over three years, I have witnessed Clean Break's ethic of care in its daily practices: from the creative writing residencies in prisons, to the graduation ceremonies of students in the edu-cation programme; from the post-show conversations that invite a general public's engagement in issues about the criminalisation of women, to the ways in which staff and members talk with each other in hallways, theatre foyers and workshops.

Clean Break's approach to women and criminal justice is, in effect, an approach to supporting women made vulnerable through societal structural disadvantage. Is it fueled by compassion and an ethic of care – it mirrors Tronto's acknowledgement of care as an approach to personal, social and political life that acknowledges that *all* human beings need, receive and give care to others – that we are interdependent ([1993] 2009). But to be inter-dependent, to witness and respond to others who are vulnerable, who live in volatile worlds, is a major political and social commitment. It demands a relational approach, a dialogue with those who are othered. An ethic of care is an approach that struggles to win any political votes with an electorate conditioned to be fearful of crime and those who are criminalised, where austerity, cuts to public services and increased costs of living encourage individualism and protectionism. Each element of Clean Break's work is part of coherent and holistic commitment to negotiating the challenges of human interdependence in the attempt to imagine and realise a more just society. It has also, as identified in relation to the new organisational structure and practices, ensured the structure, approach and reach of the company continues to evolve.

It has been less than a decade since the idea of the Big Society was proposed in Britain as the cornerstone of the 2010 Conservative Party manifesto, an ideology that would, supposedly, redistribute power from central government to local communities to enhance civic responsibility, volunteerism and local action. Critics argued that the Big Society was an excuse for government not to take responsibility or invest in much needed structures or services to support those in need but rather it would hand this responsibility to voluntary and charitable organisations who were already committed to doing this work, organisations like Clean Break. The company has attended to the needs of thousands of individual women who have participated in the education programme and training opportunities, supporting their transition into education, employment and desistance with a model of care that reflects the organisation's investment in support structures for them. However, it is important to recognise that Clean Break is, first and foremost, a theatre company. It has made a critical intervention in the lives of women who have been failed by the state but it cannot and must not take the place of it. Lucy Perman (2018) reflected on this tension:

> Recently care hasn't been a particularly positive term. It's linked with social work and people in care. The connotations and profile around that sector is that it is stretched and starved and that has resulted in failings in care provision. We identify ourselves with the theatre sector, we wouldn't see ourselves as part of the care sector but we do have a duty of care, we do provide care, we are caring and it's very much ingrained in the organisation's values. But it becomes problematic when you define the organisation in that way because you then become part of the system; it defines how people who are part of the care sector might relate to you, it doesn't feel a particularly equal relationship. The company has intervened when the state fails but with the recent changes in the company we have made a clear and determined shift towards consciousness raising and more theatre output – and away from so much 'direct provision'.

In May 2015, Clean Break hosted a Long Table event inviting students, graduates, staff, associate artists and teachers as well as board members to reflect on the organisation and their relationship with it. One of the graduates spoke about Clean Break as 'they'. Later in the conversation, another woman came to the table and rejected this term, proposing that 'us' is more appropriate. I conclude this chapter with a quotation from this woman as she articulates how Clean Break realises Tronto's vision of 'care with', of interdependence, 'consistent with democratic commitments to justice, equality and freedom for all' (2013: 23):

I was drawn to come to the table every time I heard the word they because Clean Break is us [...] Home is where the heart is and the heart of Clean Break hasn't changed although so many other things have. Clean Break gave me access to theatre. It gave access to women like me and that's what Clean Break continues to do [...] As an organisation Clean Break didn't just embrace me but many, many other women – whether it's a woman who has come here to go on a course, to audition to take part in one of the professional productions, whether you are on the Board or a member of staff here – we all come here because we have a real belief in the work. I think it's really evident when we look around the room today that that job has been done, and done wonderfully, by us. *Us*, not they. (Clean Break Associate A, 2015)

Performing a museum of living memories: beholding young people's experiences and expressions of care through oral history performance

Kathleen Gallagher and Rachel Turner-King

Prelude: towards 'hope', 'care' and 'civic engagement'

To be 'care-full', in these times, is to move against the grain; it is to announce oneself or one's project as ready and able to put others' needs in the foreground, to *lose time* caring. In this chapter, we will argue the obvious, which is also, strangely, the radical: caring will, ultimately, *save* us. And those of us who have been engulfed in a 'care-full' arts ecology know too well that the following is true: our art, our social relations, our intellectual contributions are all served by the fierce privileging of care. To act as though this is true is to be a part of a revolution.

In the introduction, Stuart Fisher explains that this edited collection places 'care in dialogue with performance'. This invitation has caused us, as co-authors, to reflect seriously on one of the fundamental reasons why we have both spent our professional lives making theatre with young people: it has the pedagogical potential to be a laboratory of care, a care that is not undemanding or simplistic, but complex and earned. As we have taken our step back from the swirling creative and research acts of our work together, in order to reflect on this central provocation, it strikes us that we are trying here to separate out into two languages an experience we shared that spoke in one language alone. It was 'care-full theatre making', 'caring performance', 'performances of our shared cares'; rather than dialogic, then, rather than the merging or relationship between two meaning systems, the creators and social actors of our project, occupying different roles, were nonetheless speaking a shared language and operating from an astonishingly lucid and singular meaning system.

In this chapter, we attempt to deconstruct what we experienced as a relational mode of being with others (Held, 2006) that we lived through as holistic, systemic and ecological. Perhaps the mere proposal of such an argument seems ludicrously optimistic when the lives, and life prospects, of young people have been so destabilised by global economic and political uncertainty. Indeed, we have worried over reproducing a kind of writing about theatre that is altogether too celebratory and uncritical. But, we did experience something unusually caring and generous through this collaboration that was most certainly heightened by the surrounding cold-heartedness and self-interest of the larger social and political context, specifically the 2016 Brexit referendum in the UK and the rising popularity of divisive populism in the USA. Our chapter focuses on an oral history performance project in which the pedagogies of 'youth theatre' and 'youth work' coalesced, enabling new ways of understanding the aesthetics, pedagogy, politics and sociality of caring, in these most 'care-less', global times.

Youth, Theatre, Radical Hope and the Ethical Imaginary: An International, Intercultural Investigation of Drama Pedagogy, Performance and Civic Engagement (2014–19)

Our multi-sited, ethnographic research study funded by the Social Sciences and Humanities Research Council of Canada is the project through which we have collaborated over the last five years. Gallagher conceived of this study in order to think about disengagement in schools, and from civic life more broadly, as a precursor to, and driver of, youth social unrest around the world. Using a socially engaged and collaborative model of research, the project asks what makes the theatre workshop/classroom a forum of civic engagement in the present as well as an experience that may cultivate civic engagement later in life. Collaborating across universities, schools, theatres and youth community spaces in Toronto (Canada), Lucknow (India), Tainan (Taiwan), Coventry (England) and Athens (Greece), we examine how youth theatre making can cultivate practices, relationships, contrariness, dispositions and values that orient young people towards, and support them in, engaged and full citizenship. One early finding of this intentional pairing of performance and civic engagement has made clear that our understandings of civic engagement remain anaemic unless they recognise the necessary *relationality* of it, and we return to this idea in this chapter.

As demonstrated in Table 8.1, the larger *Radical Hope* project took place over five consecutive years. We have drawn upon a different model of drama or theatre pedagogy each year to investigate how these specific theatre-making practices with young people might give rise to their thinking about, expression of, or caretaking of their own and others' lives. The project was launched through a week-long collaborators' meeting in Toronto, where we aimed to make our distinct sites appreciable to one another.[1]

Each year of the research, a different researcher-collaborator informed the mode of practice undertaken in all five sites. Each researcher-collaborator had creative agency to interpret these modes of practice and adapted the structure and content to suit their research contexts. Connecting

TABLE 8.1 Overview of the *Radical Hope* project 2014–19

Year	Mode of collaborative theatre making	Lead collaborator(s) guiding the mode of practice
Y1 (2014/15)	Verbatim	Artist Andrew Kushnir (creative director of Project: Humanity), Dr Gallagher and the Toronto Research Team, Canada
Y2 (2015/16)	Oral history performance	Dr Wan-Jung Wang in Taipei, Taiwan
Y3 (2016/17)	Devising and ensemble-based practice	Dr Myrto Pigou-Repousi and artist-practitioner Nikos Govas in Athens, Greece and Dr Rachel Turner-King at University of Warwick with artist-practitioner Jouvan Fucinni from the Belgrade Theatre, Coventry UK
Across all years	Feminist dialogic-performance practice of 'critical dialogues'	Dr Urvashi Sahni in Lucknow, India

these global/local investigations, Gallagher's Toronto research team visited and spent time with each of the different collaborators and their research participants in their specific locales. Andrew Kushnir, the embedded playwright for the *Radical Hope* project, and creative director of Toronto-based, socially engaged theatre company, Project: Humanity,[2] has produced a verbatim play, *Towards Youth*, created out of the data across all of the five sites of the study.[3]

In this chapter, we share findings from our Coventry site in the UK, specifically in year two of the wider international study when Turner-King partnered with the Belgrade Theatre's Canley Youth Theatre (CYT) and Coventry Youth Services to produce an 'oral history performance'. Turner-King led the planning and facilitation of the project in collaboration with Jouvan Fucinni, CYT director, and with the support of Angela Evans, youth worker for Coventry's Children, Learning and Young People's Directorate. Out of the Belgrade's seven youth theatre companies, CYT was the only group to have access to a trained youth worker. Evans' long-standing relationship with the local authority and her embeddedness within the socio-economically deprived area of Canley, meant that she was uniquely positioned to encourage new members to join the youth theatre, including a number of young people in the care system (Turner-King, 2018). Here, we focus on one such youth participant, Bruce, whose particular experience of being 'in care' made its way into the rehearsal room and the final public performance.[4] Turner-King considers the ways they struggled and experimented with the aesthetics of oral history performance in order to revisit and share significant memories of their pasts by focusing on the playful, relational and affective dimensions of improvisation. Immediately after this creative process, Coventry City Council announced severe cuts to its youth services, directly affecting the youth theatre group and its wider community (Lepper, 2017). This led to an inspiring political awakening in Bruce who initiated a multifaceted campaign against the proposed cuts. Bruce's story acts as a hopeful counter-narrative to accounts that 'seek to label, pathologise or categorise' young people in care (Spence, 2007: 308).

Finally, we zoom out from Bruce's particular story to offer a contextualisation of the wider sociopolitical context in which this project took place. Gallagher also adds details of her Toronto team's visit (principal investigator Kathleen Gallagher, playwright Andrew Kushnir, research assistants Dirk Rodricks and Nancy Cardwell) to Turner-King's research site in Canley, 21–30 June 2016. They observed the creative and caretaking rehearsal and performance work of the local team, during the week the UK voted to leave the European Union.[5] Through our cross-comparisons of field notes, video footage from the weekly workshops and participant interviews, we aim to draw out the interrelationships between 'hope', 'care' and 'civic engagement' through our rendering of the relationality that was intrinsic to the oral history performance work and the nurturing of an arts ecology of care.

A theoretical frame for care

Gallagher's previous study revealed that social support or care *given by adolescents to others* was positively correlated with their sense of engagement and achievement in school (Gallagher, 2014). Being deeply curious about these earlier findings, in evidence in both the quantitative and qualitative results of that study, Gallagher and her Toronto team aimed to turn towards a more robust examination of care in the current study and to do so with others across a range of different cultural, political and theatre-making contexts. Care is a much-debated concept in the subfield of philosophy and ethics in education with little agreement on a universal theory of care, despite much writing on the topic from such care theorists as Nel Noddings (see 1992; 1999; 2010b; 2010c, 2013). Noddings imagines a kind of caring relationship in education contexts where the carer is called not out of duty, but desire, to care for others, 'acts done out of love and natural inclination', she writes (1999: 219). Hedge and MacKenzie (2012) have rightly critiqued Noddings' account of care for its failure to operate from a more comprehensive political theory or set of moral principles, and Houston (1990), before them, similarly challenging that care is not a stand-alone ethic. Importantly for this chapter, Noddings' body of work seems to suggest that our capacity for care is finite and teachers ought to focus on what is before them, what they might realistically be able to care for, rather than risk 'empathic exhaustion' by focusing too much on 'unknown victims of poverty or injustice in some far away land' (2010b: 12). This particular idea is especially provocative as Gallagher and her team attempted to make some sense of the kind and quality of care they witnessed as ethnographic researchers in Turner-King's context of CYT. They felt that the care they witnessed seemed neither limited nor terribly inward-looking, despite having every reason to be inner-directed in the days immediately following the extraordinarily difficult Brexit referendum vote result and the remarkable sense of uncertainty that followed it.

Sociologists Kathleen Lynch, Maureen Lyons and Sara Cantillon, drawing upon extensive feminist literature on care, put forward a view of the 'care-full' citizen that recognises the care and love labour, and solidarity work that is not generally part of normative formal education trajectories. They consider the importance of 'other-centred work, the work arising from our interdependencies and dependencies as affective, relational beings' (Lynch *et al.* 2007: 2). They lament especially the lack of attention paid to 'other care' due to traditional education's preoccupation with educating the rational, autonomous, subject, writing that: 'The citizen carer and the care recipient citizen (and most people are both one and the other simultaneously) are only recognised in the educational arena when professionals are being trained as social workers, nurses, therapists, teachers, psychologists, social care workers and/or counsellors/therapists' (Lynch *et al.* 2007: 4). Traditional education's more pernicious neoliberal agenda, they argue further, concerns producing the resilient, self-sufficient or entrepreneurial citizen, capable of human capital acquisition. This 'care-less' model is focused instead on the privatised citizen, educated primarily for themselves; and education itself, a market service to be delivered. Intimate care work is, from this standpoint, a private matter. In short, whether it is classic liberalism or contemporary neoliberalism, the primacy of educating the autonomous, rational subject (clearly also one important aspect of education) has occluded the enormously important dimensions of human interdependency.

Even within the spheres of well-intentioned youth work, Julie Tilsen argues persuasively that an 'individualist framework' within education has drawn focus away from our 'social/relational complexities'. She goes on to say: 'Our attention is given to what is one's "authentic self", what is "in their heads" or "in their hearts". With our interest solidly placed in this idea of interiority (that is, the stuff "inside" of people), all our efforts to shape, change, inspire, or otherwise influence others are directed at people's "insides"' (Tilsen, 2018: 14). Tilsen calls for youth workers to engage in a form of a critical pedagogy that goes beyond 'essentialist notions of identity' (2018: 16). While Tilsen's 'narrative approach' to youth work emphasises well-rehearsed notions of social constructivism, her discussion of 'storying' is most intriguing. She argues that youth work is all about the 'co-creation of meaningful stories and experiences through collaborative conversations with young people' (Tilsen, 2018: 52). She likens the dynamics of this relationship to a 'jazz improvisation' where 'performers listen and respond in the moment' (Tilsen, 2018: 63). This resonates with Richard Sennett's discussion of the ability to 'listen well' as a feature of cooperation that can manifest in non-verbal exchanges such as musical rehearsals (2012: 14). Tilsen suggests that when the youth worker and youth participant are engaged in the structured yet responsive process of 'storying', identity is 'multiple, fluid and emergent' (2018: 16). Likewise, the devising process, characterised by its potential dynamism, permeability and possibility, *can* provide young people with supportive space to play, experiment and rehearse their emerging youth identities (Gallagher and Mealey, 2018).

While developing CYT's 'voices' and each individual's sense of self was a key aspect of Fucinni and Evans' intersecting caring practice, there was a shared ethos around fostering the group's sense of interconnectedness, not just to each other but to their wider world.[6] This played out in subtle, gentle and non-coercive ways. If a young person volunteered a story about something that had happened during their week, Fucinni and Evans would often relate by offering something from their own lives, asking the others what they felt and/or by drawing connections to current social and political issues. Critically, they made time and space within the structure of their workshop plan for conversations to intersect, diverge and transgress. This open and responsive type of 'hospitality' within the informal youth space is often sorely lacking within the confines of the formal education system (Turner-King, 2018). The potential 'liminal space' presented by youth clubs, Sevasti-Melissa Nolas argues, 'offer young people the opportunity of identity development and the crafting of biographical narratives, both in terms of being and becoming, as old identities are shed and new ones adopted' (2013: 34). Our project with CYT aimed to offer them opportunities to explore and *reperform* their emerging 'biographical narratives'.

Barry Freeman has recently argued, using an example of Indigenous theatre makers in Canada, that theatre does not simply represent the world, but models 'alternative ways of being in the now' (2016: 25). How could oral history performance, through its focus on personal narrative and past memories, open up a space for CYT members to explore 'alternative ways of being in the *now*'? In no way could we have envisaged the extent to which one youth participant, Bruce, would shift his identity from being the often-quiet, unassuming member of the group to the group's strongest community activist.

Care as civic engagement: 'I consider it as a home'

To tell the story of Bruce, we have to start at the end of our project. In July 2016, just one week after our public performances, Coventry City Council announced severe cuts to its youth services, directly affecting the CYT and its wider community.[7] While the Belgrade Theatre was committed to sustaining this youth theatre group, the wider services and some of its key sites were facing closure. Bruce, a fourteen-year-old at the time, took it upon himself to create an online petition, part of which stated: 'I am utterly devastated and I will do everything and anything I can to prevent it. I attend Canley Youth Theatre, a group which has inspired hope, laughter and tears. In the centre there lies so many memories and I consider it as a home. It is our centre and the Coventry City Council cannot close it down' (12 July 2016).[8] The poignancy of Bruce's words is heightened by the fact that he is a 'looked-after child' (LAC). He had been in the 'care system' for just over four years and was encouraged to join CYT in 2015 by his foster mother, who recognised that he needed to develop his self-esteem and confidence. As the resident youth worker for Canley, Evans engaged directly with Bruce and his foster family. She described her work as 'behind the scenes care' but this was all too modest on her part. Obvious to all were the skilful ways she would continually yet subtly encourage Bruce to feel welcome in the group. Likewise, Fucinni made little openings within the context of the drama work for Bruce to participate. Unbeknown to Bruce, Fucinni and Evans would provide feedback to each other about their mutual efforts to engage him. They were all too aware that his attendance at the weekly sessions was precarious and that they had to earn his trust.

Helen Nicholson suggests that trust, underpinned by an ethic of care, is performed through the outward gestures and 'particular actions' of the body, 'trust is a performative act, which is publicly visible in social action' (2002: 88). These micro-gestures of care performed by CYT's leaders modelled a sociality and conviviality that was reflected in the youth group's behaviour towards each other. Repeatedly, the young people spoke about the friendliness of CYT, compared to their different experiences of school. Through a continual and negotiated process of engagement and relationality, Tilsen argues that in youth work, 'each relationship becomes a place of caring' (2018: 37). However, as Noddings reminds us, 'in order for the relation to be properly labeled caring, the cared for must somehow recognize the efforts of the carer as caring' (2010c: 391). We can begin to get a sense of Bruce's felt experience of care by considering the extent of his subsequent civic actions. After receiving over eight hundred signatures on his petition, Bruce wrote a letter to his local Member of Parliament (MP); participated in a 'silent protest' in the city alongside other youth groups; publicised his campaign in an interview for a local newspaper; spoke at a number of council events across the city and visited Parliament to protest against the cuts. Bruce's public display of care for the centre is indicative of the strength of the positive relationships fostered throughout his time in CYT.

While this project was not driven by an instrumentalist agenda to 'produce caring citizens', we are nonetheless interested in the ways our creative process and performance *may* have affected Bruce's sense of agency and voice. In the Introduction to this volume, Stuart Fisher suggests that 'the debates in this edited collection lay the ground for new modes of being together and a growing understanding of how certain performance practices can promote and aspire to a more caring and just society' (p. 14).

These proposals orient our analysis of a creative process, which moved interchangeably between the ontological and epistemological. The ways we behaved toward each other, related to each other and played together were linked inextricably to the generation of knowledge or, in this case, the material we *chose* to perform publicly. This was typified when Bruce's story about being in care became an integral part of the final performance. While it is impossible to trace back through the messiness of the devising process to find any linear narrative that might have led Bruce to care so actively and passionately about the closure of the youth services, we focus on two particular scenes of care that were created out of a tapestry of different moments from the hours spent together.

Encountering objects of care: Bruce's 'archive of memories'

Inspired by the methodology of 'oral history performance' outlined by one of our international collaborators, Wan-Jung Wang, we invited the youth group to bring in a 'significant personal object' (2010: 563). A well-known game in 'improv theatre', often associated with the work of Augusto Boal (2002), involves participants taking an object and reimagining it by gesturing its new function. For example, a cricket bat can become a paddle. Through play, we can create new ways of seeing an object. In oral history performance, however, the 'objects' are also the *subjects* of the drama; they carry meaning for the individual owners and, therefore, playing with the objects comes with a degree of risk. In our early explorations of the objects' meaningfulness, we arranged them around the space, explaining that the rehearsal room had become a museum of artefacts. The group members were invited to examine the objects, without conferring with one another. We emphasised to the young people that these objects mattered to someone but it was up to them to imagine why. Following this, they took up an object (not their own) and performed a possible moment that might have led to this object becoming significant. We then started to connect the different objects and images together by placing them into groups of three. We invited the group to interpret these new multilayered images and make random connections between their stories. This exploratory work was critical in opening up discussions about how and why 'things' have value and power. A recurring theme in each of the imagined stories was that these objects were gifts of some kind and this had made them valuable. Caring for a thing, an object, is often deeply rooted in our connectedness to others. In Jane Bennett's discussion of 'vibrant matter', we learn that non-human forms, the stuff and things of everyday life, are indeed full of life. This 'thing-power', she explains, is 'the curious ability of inanimate objects to animate, to act, to produce effects, dramatic and subtle' (Bennett, 2010: 6). Indeed, when Turner-King first noticed a 'Nintendo DS' among the collection of anonymous objects, it evoked feelings of irritation and disappointment. The group had been told to bring in something of *significance*, not a games console! So, when the objects were returned to their owners and their stories revealed, the following exchange was surprising:

> **Bruce:** This is my Nintendo DS. I got it in 2011 about three months after I went into care. It's cool because lots of people pooled together to get it. I took loads of pictures on it, and I like to look back at them as memories because … they are pictures of someone out there I don't see anymore, some people, memories, places, and stuff; it's kind of basically like an archive of memories … as well as for playing games [he smiles].
> **Rachel:** I didn't know that you could store pictures on there. I had no idea.
> **Bruce:** Yeah you can …
> **Theo:** I wouldn't have known … I would have just thought you used it for games but … the fact that it's got a sort of different identity in the way that you use it … it's sort of different.
> **Rachel:** Yeah we could just go 'Oh it's just a game' but actually it's a bit of treasure … what did you say Bruce? It's an archive of memories?
> **Bruce:** Yeah …
> **Rachel:** Beautiful. (Transcription from workshop, 7 June 2016)

In her discussion of the performative framework involved in capturing 'oral histories', Della Pollock argues that the 'ordinary conversation' becomes 'momentous' (2005: 3). In light of this, what makes a fleeting moment in a drama workshop feel momentous? In this instance, Bruce's capacity to articulate the story about the Nintendo as his 'archive of memories' was moving and arresting. The room seemed to swell with knowingness. Until this point, Bruce had never shared his experience of being in care. By choosing to share this story, the Nintendo was no longer *just* a games console; it was imbued with Bruce's story. As fellow group member Theo explains, the Nintendo, and perhaps Bruce too, now had 'a different identity'. When describing the political potential of oral history performance, Dee Heddon explains that:

> Performing stories about ourselves might enable us to imagine different selves, to determine different scripts than the other ones that seem to trap us […] Performing the personal in public might allow a connection between the performer and the spectator, encouraging the formation of a community or prompting discussion, dialogue and debate. (2007: 157)

We felt convinced that, if Bruce agreed to it, this story *should* be made public. However, recreating this moment for performance was challenging, both ethically and aesthetically. How could we 'take care' to recreate the sense of intimacy of our rehearsal space on a public stage? Could we expect the audience to care in the same way? And what about Bruce? We wanted to convey this significant memory of his past while also doing what Helen Nicholson describes in her applied theatre work as 'engaging in the present and imagining the future' (2016: 256). By performing these words again about his absent parents, did we risk 'retraumatisation' (Gallagher *et al.*, 2012: 37)? Or, if another member performed the words on his behalf, would the potency and poignancy of this moment be lost?

Handle with care: reperforming Bruce's story

When grappling with how to represent Bruce's object story in performance, we returned to the multiple notes and recordings of the weekly sessions. In her discussion of 'performed ethnography', D. Soyini Madison suggests that 'recording rehearsals is most helpful to remember and play back what in the moment might have felt inconsequential, but seeing it again in recordings, you might find something useable and profound to be carried forward to audiences (2018: 144). Two recurring themes from our workshops were the group's capacity to listen to each other and their sense of playfulness. The script had to convey and honour the joyful ways we had interacted and attended to each other as an ensemble. We returned to the initial dismissiveness Turner-King had felt about Bruce's Nintendo DS as an inspiration for a key transitional moment in the performance. As shown in this script excerpt, the group played with the idea that their objects were meaningless, things to be either ignored or mocked:

> **Luke:** This is *just* a cane
> **Maya:** This is *just* a sarong
> **Brian:** This is *just* a ukulele
> **Amy:** This is *just* a pendant
> **Ophelia:** This is *just* a badge
> **Lorrie:** This is *just* a quilt
> **Bruce:** This is *just* a Nintendo DS
> **Connie:** This is *just* a blanket
> **Theo:** This is *just* a picture in a frame
> **Mike:** This is *just* a home-made toy. (Unpublished script, 2016)

The group took great pleasure in performing these subversive 'uncaring' moments, which were enhanced through the use of a thumping, sinister musical backbeat and gloomy lighting effects. However, they could not have *played* with the objects in this way without having spent considerable time within our workshops caring for and investing in each other's objects. They understood that this was a moment of antithesis deliberately set up to create an atmosphere of tension immediately ruptured by the intimate and sensitive retelling of their memories.

When dealing with Bruce's object memory, we did not want to root Bruce in the past as this would not have been representative of Bruce's optimism about his future. Throughout our devising process, we had been drawn to the idea of *living* memories. We had discussed the ways we tell stories to keep memories alive and that, paradoxically, we are always in the process of creating memories and that this somehow keeps us facing towards our 'future selves'. When gathering stories about significant role models, Bruce had spoken about how participating in classes, run by the youth services, had supported him through a difficult period: 'I started to do, like, dance and drama to build my confidence to help myself. I had counsellors that I confided in … we played games and talked … I didn't feel embarrassed anymore to say I'm a foster child' (Field notes, 3 June 2016). Bruce had gained this sense of empowerment through the care that had been shown by others and through his own strength of character. We felt this story should also be included in the public performance. And finally, during another improvisation when we were searching for ideas, Bruce had suggested that a piece of fabric could be lifted over the heads of the participants, mimicking a 'crowd-surfing' move he had witnessed in one of his dance classes: 'Did you know that in dance there's this move that you do where you can, like, lift people over your shoulders?' (Field notes, 14 June 2016). This was a vivid memory for Turner-King and her collaborators who were struck by Bruce's readiness to contribute and respond to his fellow peers. Though this utterance was totally disconnected from his discussion about being a foster child, Bruce's urge to share this idea captured an important and positive part of his emerging identity as a more confident ensemble player, and this felt important to represent.

In the final performance Bruce agreed to retell his Nintendo DS story. He climbed on to an empty chair positioned next to an audience member and spoke: 'Did you know that in dance there's this move that you do where you can like, lift people over your shoulders?' With that, his fellow group members arrived on stage while he called out, 'I'm not embarrassed anymore to say I'm a foster child' (Unpublished script, 2016). His teammates lifted him up and carried him aloft across the stage – the complex look of fear, concentration and victory etched on the young actors' faces – a daring choreography and care taking on display. As Nicholson suggests, it is unlikely that trust will be fostered through 'decontextualized trust exercises' (2002: 85); it manifests through the participants' investment in the drama itself. As depicted in the images taken during the dress rehearsal and the live performance (see Figures 8.1 and 8.2), they trusted each other not to let Bruce fall and Bruce trusted them because, collectively, they wanted to tell this story and tell it well. Echoes of this very caretaking of and through the drama emerged in other research sites, as Gallagher and team members have written (Gallagher *et al.* 2018). Performing this lift, in front of Bruce's foster family, was particularly poignant for Evans who later reflected that, 'it was a metaphor for Bruce's journey with us and all he's been through' (Personal communication, April 1, 2017).

By repositioning Bruce's object memory with verbatim lines from two other workshops, we hoped to honour Bruce's past memories while also representing Bruce's emerging identity. The audience had no knowledge of the significance of the 'back stories' that had played out in our rehearsal space; it was, however, important that the young people felt just how much we had valued their contributions. The final performance, therefore, was a realisation of the multiple expressions of care we had experienced over the weeks spent together. As critical pedagogue bell hooks suggests, an engaged pedagogy 'insists that everyone's presence is acknowledged […] there must be an ongoing recognition that everyone influences the classroom dynamic, that everyone contributes' (1994: 8). We attempted to perform care to Bruce

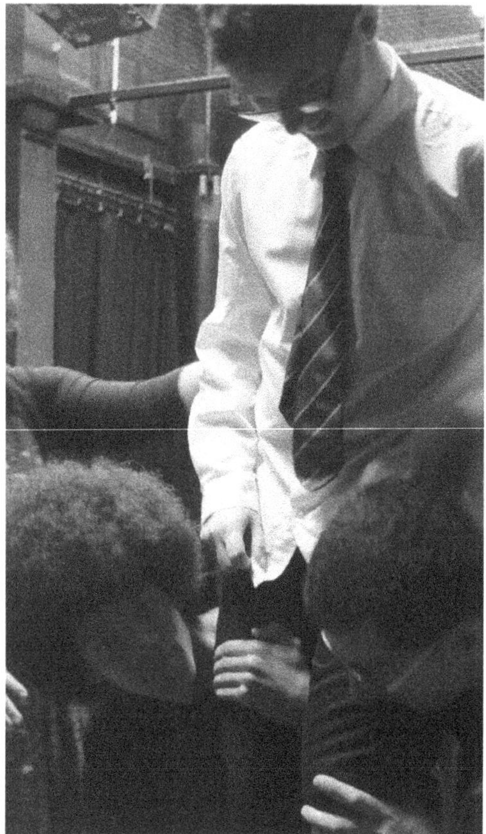

Figure 8.1 CYT members rehearse the lift with Bruce

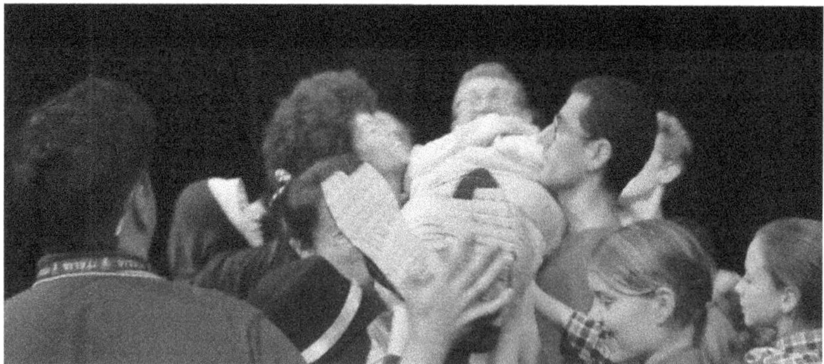

Figure 8.2 CYT members carry Bruce aloft during the live performance

and the rest of the group by demonstrating that we recognised them, we were living each moment *with* them, we had listened to them, their ideas mattered to us and they had affected us. Pollock proposes that the dialogic relationship between the interviewer and interviewee in oral history performance is 'cocreative, co-embodied, specially framed, contextually and intersubjectively contingent' (2005: 2). Our process of telling stories was *polyvocal* and the roles of 'interviewer/interviewee' were constantly shifting: members were invited to listen to each other's stories on multiple occasions. In this hybrid form of ethnography and devised theatre, the script we produced was a composite of our shared and multiple exchanges, and we were able to use the theatrical space as a heightened, symbolic version of our workshop space. As Wang argues, in oral history performance, 'personal narratives are retold and restructured due to the collaborative aspects of the performance. The "new perspectives" help the storyteller to see the stories differently' (2010: 572).

Just after the performance event, Gallagher and her Toronto team conducted a series of focus group interviews:

> **Kathleen:** Can you think of anything, however big or small, where you understood more about people, because of that work together?
>
> **Theo:** Yeah it's just, this uh, project was making a statement like, don't underestimate things, sort of cause like, all of these objects and, they weren't, they didn't look that special, but things have a story behind them, everything has a story behind it. And I just think, that was, I was like, when I first saw all these objects, I was like, well, what's so important about them? And then, when people told me these stories I was like, so shocked, and, how, how complex and how much these people cared for these things. (Transcription of interview, 30 June 2016)

Theo's first encounter with Bruce's Nintendo memory had remained and resonated with him. Perhaps this was because Theo himself was an adopted child and had also shared stories of his experiences. Whatever it was that had triggered this moment of connection and recognition, it is worth dwelling on the potential space that theatre creates for us to appreciate the world in ways that are more 'complex'.

Between the local and global: seeking love and care in uncaring times

Gallagher has recently argued for the value of love in research, 'a politically committed, seriously playful love, embedded in a reflexively relational methodological practice' (2018: 106). Building from Dale Tracey's (2017) theory of compassion from twentieth- and twenty-first-century 'witness poetry', which produces a 'feeling with' rather than a 'feeling as' an other, the effort is about getting to a place of nearness rather than likeness. As research collaborators in this multi-sited project, we have travelled worlds together in our efforts to make sense of empirical moments of caretaking and care receiving, of creative generosity, of youth story-telling through theatre that have much to teach us about living the present differently and building a future fully conscious of, and better for, our ultimate inter-dependence.

Indeed, this 'feeling with' was so critical in the week we spent together when the Toronto team visited the Coventry site. The first thing the Toronto team experienced in Coventry was a lovely evening in Turner-King's garden where we shared a meal, caught a post-rain rainbow and laughed heartily with the key adult players (Jouvan Fucinni and Angela Evans, research assistants and student participants, Rachel and her husband) in their 'universe of care' (Sahni, 2017). We borrow this term 'universe of care' from our Indian collaborator Urvashi Sahni. In our early collaborator meetings, she set the bar for the kind of 'care-full' schooling and theatre making to which we all aspired through the example of her girls' school, Prerna, in Lucknow, India. She speaks particularly of 'a web of mutually supportive relationships' that we also experienced strongly in our Coventry site (Sahni, 2017: 64). This 'adult caretaking' was all the more welcome as it was unfolding on the evening following the UK's European Union referendum results. The following day, the local group invited the Canadian visitors into their 'storytime' circle, a practice meant to be a brief sharing of feelings/experiences since the last meeting. We could see from the start that the rehearsal room was making space to acknowledge that we are all coming into the room with different preoccupations. This seemed a small but important attempt, a punctuation mark of sorts, to acknowledge that each of our lives is full and complex but we are now coming together and *listening* to each other before we create.

Kushnir's play, *Towards Youth*, moves across the five sites of the study and, when it came to representing the work in Coventry, and the Canley Youth piece, *The Museum of Living Memories*, the character 'Kathleen' turns to the audience and simply says, 'Something aesthetically stunning has to happen right now'. But nothing does. The character stares at the audience, waiting; the audience stares back. In other words, there would be no lame reproduction that could adequately convey to the theatre audience what had been witnessed in Canley's youth-produced performance. No matter what unfolded on the stage at that moment, we knew that it would not be able to deliver the aesthetic simplicity yet sophistication, the deep and abiding trust among that young company of performers and the larger 'universe of care' that so evidently surrounded them. This question of 'trust' had been reflected back to us by an audience member during the Q&A after one of the Canley Youth performances:

> **Audience member:** It strikes me that there is a lot of trust between you all and I just wondered, has that been hard work to get to? Have you had to really work on the trust bit? Does that take a while to achieve?
>
> **Connie (a young performer):** I don't know. A little bit. But every week, when we come together, we get closer each time. So you tell stories like John said and like, get to know each other a bit more each week. So, a little bit.

Theo (a young performer): And also we'll do like trust exercises. Like to do that lift with Bruce, that was quite a big thing. He had to trust us. But like, we've done it before, we've practised, and we've told him a lot about ourselves and he can trust us. (Transcription of discussion, 29 June 2016)

At another of the post-performance focus group interviews with the Gallagher team, one young performer turned the gaze back upon the visitors:

Theo: Uh … What did the play mean for you?

Kathleen: Oh my goodness … Um, I felt like I was in a room with people who I didn't know before and who didn't know me, and I felt quite warmly embraced. It made me feel hopeful, in a really deep way, because, we've come from Canada and we arrived at the time that your country is in a little bit of a mess, and there are lots of unknowns, and there's quite a lot of unhappiness and uh, fear, and so the fact that that was all going on and then we got to go into this magic place where people who had big important relationships with each other could open up the circle a little bit and say 'come look at what we're doing' – it kind of gave me a faith that I wasn't expecting to find.

Nancy (research assistant): I also saw that you guys couldn't really get hurt because you were taking such good care of each other throughout these rehearsals and process and performance and I felt so lucky to catch that. (Transcription of interview, 30 June 2016)

Our time together allowed us to see vividly the relationships between adults and young people, and among young people themselves, as instances of caregiving and care receiving (Hedge and MacKenzie, 2012) cultivated through creative and collective models of drama, in this most unsettling of weeks in the UK context. In particular, it helped us scrutinise what youth citizenship means beyond the logic of electoral/referendum politics when these young people were only beginning to understand their inheritance of a referendum within which they had had no vote or voice. In turn, this brought into focus the 'habits of the everyday through which subjects become citizens' (Isin and Neilsen, 2007: 17) and enabled us to examine the ways care and citizenship manifest as everyday practices. The play making and community-building process of the CYT was one of 'nearness', among young people and between them and their adult caregivers, theatre facilitators and local and visiting researchers. It was a space of intimacy and creative experimentation. In the uncertain days following the Brexit referendum, young and old alike felt in touch with their susceptibility to larger and unfeeling political forces, whatever 'side' they may have been on. After the divisive political rhetoric leading up to the vote, in which this very group of young people would inherit a future for which they held no decision-making power, many felt unsure about who their 'community' was. But, the Canley youth, by that time, had together built a caring ensemble they were determined not to lose.

Performance itself is an act of vulnerability. So, 'to care' in and through that vulnerability is one way to move through this precarious world, not perfectly, not without struggle, but with creative intention and political agency. In the post-project interviews, we invited the members to reflect on the ways 'care' was performed as a group:

> John: I think we've all had to care for each other … and you, Jouvan and the other helpers, have all had to care for us … and Angela of course … cos erm … otherwise we can't get through it without that … because, obviously, you need to take an interest in *us* … and it was really nice cos when I was having that down day, everyone seemed to notice. (Transcription of interview, 5 July 2016)

For John, care was *vital*; it enabled the group to 'get through' things. Critically, he experienced care through the interest shown by others. Care, like love, is unequally distributed among human beings. But the Coventry experience for all of us – in the heedless and dislocating days that followed the Brexit referendum result – was a fine example of 'care-full theatre making', 'caring performance' and 'performances of our shared cares' for locals and visitors alike. In *our* ecology, care and performance were simultaneously experienced and became, in the end, quite inseparable. Love and friendship drove the research methodology as well, making a virtue of our differences of social, generational and geographic location and becoming critical and fierce friends to one another.

While 'love' is not imparted by the state, 'care' *is* recognised as an official duty and government responsibility. Joan Tronto (2012) reminds us though that the nature of the care given is subject to the ideology of the current government as well as the constant flux of external socio-economic factors. As James Thompson laments, 'the habit of caring for others is devalued, placed at the whim of the market and radically under resourced' (2015: 435). Bruce had come to experience this first-hand through the Council's proposals to close down the very places he held dear. In his online petition, he wrote: 'Not only would you be taking down a building, you would be taking down a museum of living memories. People need to realise that not all kids are reckless juveniles and our centre proves that' (Field notes, 12 July 2016). Bruce's decision to rename the youth centre with the title of our performance, *The Museum of Living Memories*, is indicative of the impact it had upon him. Bruce's subsequent letter to his local MP is demonstrative of his awareness that the type of 'care' *now* being offered is not the same level of care he had benefitted from: 'One-to-one sessions will make vulnerable kids feel more vulnerable because they'll be excluded and singled out from kids they could potentially get along with. Isolation cannot help troubled kids; they need to release their problems by being able to have fun instead of sitting in an intimidating office being asked personal questions' (20 October 2016). The care that Bruce experienced in youth theatre is fundamentally about the experience of relationality. Being a 'looked-after child' in an official capacity, therefore, is an entirely different experience to being 'looked after' in the convivial site of the youth theatre workshop. Indeed, the care given, received and performed in this space is an important form of resistance to top-down, governmental notions of care. It may even crucially signal to us all 'alternative ways of being in the now'.

As for the wider *Radical Hope* research collaboration – the many local partnerships of academics, theatre makers and community organisations that comprise the global research network – we have taken the decision to move forward together into a new project, adding in a new partner in Colombia. The contagion of care has swept us all up and, as we look forward, we will turn more directly to the idea of youth artist-citizens performing for socio-ecological justice. A fitting turn for our expansive community that has faced adversity in a variety of local forms and now aims to create for the survival of the planet.[9] It is no small objective, but our intergenerational energies are well primed to approach the 'inextricable entanglements' of the environment, society, subjectivity and our own actions (Neimanis *et al.* 2015: 68). Our singular meaning system of care and performance compels us forward.

Notes

1 For an introduction to the international collaborators, see www.oise.utoronto. ca/dr/Research_Projects/Youth_Theatre_Radical_Hope_and_the_Ethical_ Imaginary/index.html (accessed 14/02/19).
2 See Project: Humanity website at www.projecthumanity.ca/towards-youth (accessed 09/03/19).
3 To date, that piece has enjoyed a development process in Banff, Alberta, at a playwrights' colony where Kushnir and Gallagher spent a week in May 2017. Subsequently, Crow's Theatre, a professional theatre in Toronto, supported a two-week development process in December 2017, culminating in two public readings of the script. Now, a full production of the play, its world première, co-produced with Kushnir's company Project: Humanity (see www.projecthumanity.ca/towards-youth, accessed 09/03/19), took place at Crow's Theatre in March 2019 (see www. crowstheatre.com/whats-on/view-all/towards-youth-a-play-on-radical-hope, accessed 09/03/19).
4 All youth names used are pseudonyms.
5 Turner-King's research team included two PhD students: Emily Temple, who worked as an assistant ethnographer and Hanzhi Ruan, whose role was to document the process using photography, audio and video recording.
6 The Belgrade's community and education team has a commitment to 'building confident, articulate young citizens with an active interest in the world around them'. For more information, see http://belgrade.co.uk/take-part/youth-theatre (accessed 21/03/19).
7 In a UK context, 'youth services' is an umbrella term for the plethora of systems, organisations and initiatives that serve young people, supporting their physical, emotional, social and cultural welfare. Youth services are provided by both voluntary and statutory sectors.
8 See www.change.org/p/coventry-city-council-stop-coventry-youth-centres-from-being-closed-down-and-turned-into-family-hubs (accessed 16/10/18).
9 For further detail about the new research project, please see www.oise.utoronto. ca/dr/global-youth-digital-citizen-artists.

9

'Still Lives': Syrian displacement and care in contemporary Beirut

Ella Parry-Davies

The title of this chapter, 'Still Lives', borrows the name of a series of photographs taken by a girl of about eight years old (who I will refer to as M) on the evening of 11 July 2015, in Lebanon's capital Beirut. M's first image shows a blurred photograph of a bunch of red roses. The stems are packed together in a plastic bucket, and each one is wrapped in cellophane protecting a full crimson bloom. The photograph is taken from above, so that each perfect nest of petals faces towards the camera, picturesque. In the background, on the tiled floor on which the bucket stands, are two pairs of feet. One larger, in black high heels, seems to belong to a woman walking past or dancing. The smaller feet, in flat pumps and stripy socks are M's, at the bottom of the frame. The second image is a close-up of the roses, blurry again. The next is in better focus, just two of the perfect blooms filling the frame. In the following image, M seems to be holding the bucket stably between her knees, handling the camera more securely, the bunch of red flowers gorgeous in the centre of the frame. The series of photographs continues: an extended, conscientious study evocative of the floral painting tradition referenced by its title.

M's photographs have been shown to me by the Lebanese community artist Dima el Mabsout.[1] They form part of a collection of images taken by Mabsout and a group of children (including M) in the Hamra area of west Beirut over six months in 2015. The photographs were produced as part of *Fleeing and Forgetting*, a project Mabsout devised in response to the post-2011 conflict in neighbouring Syria. *Fleeing and Forgetting* focused on the transformation of urban spaces in Beirut enacted by the presence of new populations who had come to Lebanon from Syria as refugees. In June 2015, Mabsout began to compile a collection of photographs – mostly taken on streets in Hamra, a mixed neighbourhood with a particularly high refugee presence – that resonated with her focus.[2] Supporting herself financially as a part-time waitress in a restaurant on Hamra Street, Mabsout formed a friendship with a group of Syrian children who sold flowers at night outside the restaurant. Using her camera phone while Mabsout was at work, the children contributed to a body of almost two hundred photographs, including those in 'Still Lives' described above, which document their experiences in the nocturnal life of the neighbourhood.

In this chapter, I explore the photographs collected through *Fleeing and Forgetting* in order to think through the performances of care that subtended this project, and the broader questions that these pose about art and scholarship produced in relation to experiences of displacement. While a visual art analysis of the images may (generatively) celebrate their qualities as aesthetic objects, I adopt the perceptual coordinates offered by performance, which emphasise the actions and processes that have enabled and conditioned their production. A focus on performance thus attends to the social and aesthetic care that the images perform and depend upon. This propels my problematisation of a historical tendency in some performance theory to associate migration with liminality, and with transgressing the interdependency of living-as-usual. In this chapter, I argue that to perform scholarship 'care-fully' (Thompson, 2015: 438), by recognising the specificities and complexities of experiences of migration, must also allow the latter to challenge the dominant hermeneutic and ethical paradigms through which research encounters practice (and vice versa). As Judith Hamera has argued, for scholars to act 'response-ably' and make ourselves 'accountable to others' bodies' we must support the 'vulnerability' of our ethical and methodological positions (2013: 306–7). The particular challenge presented by *Fleeing and Forgetting*, I will suggest, demands that we pay attention to stillness, reciprocity and care, which as the project demonstrates can be just as pertinent to experiences of displacement as upheaval and transformation.

I begin this chapter by introducing *Fleeing and Forgetting* and the conditions of its production. I then turn back to a lengthier exploration of 'Still Lives', the series of photographs described at the opening of the chapter. I mobilise the dialogues around performing care staged in this edited collection in order to suggest that, even as it evidences the conditions of precarity experienced by the child photographer M, 'Still Lives' requires and performs relational infrastructures of care that seek to work against this precarity. I use the term 'infrastructure' after AbdouMaliq Simone, whose attention to 'people as infrastructure' denotes intersubjective and complex 'combinations of objects, spaces, persons, and practices, [...] providing for and reproducing life in the city' (2004: 408). I trace a disciplinary history in which migration has been celebrated as a metaphor for transgression and examine the ways in which apprehending the images instead through an 'aesthetics of care' (Thompson, 2015) might defamiliarise these tropes. A 'care-full' approach, I suggest, would respond to the two-fold injunction of Thompson's argument: first, to notice the acts of care that performance practices depend on; and in doing so, to enact care in our hermeneutic responses as researchers. In the context of *Fleeing and Forgetting*, a 'care-full' approach recognises the children photographers as subjects, rather than objects, of representation; and as givers, as well as receivers, of aesthetic and intersubjective care. Finally, I turn to a second series of images from the collection entitled 'Home', concluding that it indexes a complex, non-dichotomous relationship between 'home' and 'displacement', and reiterates the importance of attending to sustained, embodied and reciprocal care in addressing art making by or about displaced persons.

Postcards from Hamra

Over six months in 2015, I was regularly emailed 'postcards' by the Beiruti community artist Dima el Mabsout, consisting of individual or grouped photographs, each accompanied by a date, title and short text written by her. I first began working with Mabsout when she successfully applied to be artist-in-residence at 'Beirut: Bodies in Public', a three-day programme of conference activities and performances in public spaces in Beirut that I co-convened in 2014 with Eliesh S. D., a performer and founder of the Lebanese NGO Organisation du Développement Durable (Organisation for Sustainable Development). These projects took place in conjunction with several years of my own research on performance practices in Lebanon. To reiterate Hamera's (2013) terms, my affective and critical 'vulnerability' to *Fleeing and Forgetting* partly owes to the duration of my engagement with the project and my proximity to Mabsout as my colleague and, increasingly, friend. Mabsout and I maintained close correspondence through emails, instant messages and video calls throughout *Fleeing and Forgetting*, and I returned to Beirut from London towards the end of the project. Mabsout's collection of postcards was exhibited in December 2015 at the community art venue Mansion in Zoukak el Blatt, Beirut, alongside a shared meal and public forum discussing questions relating to urban public space in the context of the recent large influx of people leaving Syria for Lebanon as refugees.

Lebanon still experiences the after-effects of its own 1975–90 civil war (in the form of high levels of inequality, extant sectarian hostility and irregular public services, among others) and at the time of writing hosts an estimated 1.5 million refugees from the current Syrian conflict, in addition to hundreds of thousands of others from around the region: one in three residents in Lebanon in 2015 was a refugee.[3] In her texts and in our correspondence at the time, Mabsout expressed concern about how the images might be viewed, cautious both of the hostility to Syrian refugees prevalent in both Lebanese and international media, and, on the other hand, the reductive stereotype of the victim (which I will go on to discuss later in this chapter). Remarkable popular initiatives providing support to refugee populations in Lebanon have been counterposed by mediatised images of refugees as burdensome and threatening additions to an already strained national infrastructure. Despite much active support for refugees, the Lebanese government has perpetuated a fear of the Syrian presence and its apparent risk for national security, blaming crime and public service breakdown (in particular over waste management, which I discuss below) on the Syrian influx (Al-Saadi, 2014; see also Mroue, 2014; Chit and Nayel, 2016).

Mabsout's postcards, numbering over forty and comprising almost two hundred photographs in total, were displayed at Mansion in 2015 as A4 prints on long tables. The chronology of the postcards was sporadic, and the text so miniscule that that the objects had to be brought close to the eyes to read, making it difficult for viewers to feel they could assume a panoramic perspective on the collection, or, by extension, ascertain generalised reflections on either Mabsout's experience or the children's. Mabsout's texts read as confessional and extemporaneous rather than explanatory, often a candid – and uncomfortable – reflection on the ethics of representation inherent to the project, and rarely a direct explication of what the images depicted. The 'postcard' form, juxtaposing text and images, gestured towards the constraints of the page space and the polyvalence opened up by this adjacency of visual and verbal modes, pointing to the unknown context, actions and affects that extended beyond the frame. Alongside the photographs, Mabsout's texts spoke from a deliberately personal and self-reflexive perspective. Rather than superseding the photographs in a dominant narrative mode, her writing pointed towards the incompleteness of both image and text, and the ultimately subjective nature of their respective interpretation.

In the collection, the children frequently photographed themselves, each other and their flowers, sometimes in long series of images (such as 'Still Lives') that show them playing with the camera during Mabsout's shifts at work in the restaurant. The images also attest to the positive affects of their time together, and to the care that Mabsout and her co-workers attempted to provide for the children, frequently (as is shown in the postcards) appropriating food and bottles of water from the restaurant for them, sketching portraits together, intervening during incidents of aggression they faced on the street or accompanying them when they crossed the city at night. Revolving around the children's night-time labour selling flowers, however, the postcards are frequently also reminders of the violence they face. The postcards make numerous references to physical harassment of the children by local shopkeepers and from within their own families, fights between some of the children over food and the exhaustion they experience selling flowers at night, often falling asleep on the pavement or stairs outside the restaurant.

The context of Mabsout's concurrent activity – the other kinds of paid labour and political action that formed the social world in which *Fleeing and Forgetting* was realised and exhibited – also manifested timely concerns regarding institutional accountability and infrastructural, relational care. Alongside *Fleeing and Forgetting* and her hospitality work in the restaurant, Mabsout was involved in designing and building a playground with children living in refugee camps in the Beqaa Valley, with the non-profit group CatalyticAction.[4] As she related in our correspondence, she was also participating in and documenting protests that took place in response to a breakdown in public waste management. In July 2015, residents living close to the

Na'ameh landfill site south of Beirut successfully brought the closure of the (supposedly temporary) site due to public health and environmental hazards. Without an alternative landfill option, however, rubbish collected on the streets of Lebanon's most populated zones, Beirut and Mount Lebanon. Demonstrations took place in late July and early August contesting corrupt government relationships with the private waste-management company Sukleen and the political stalemates that had precipitated the crisis (Anon, 2016). Demanding an end to government corruption and to the dilapidation of public services, these demonstrations emphasised the importance of accountable state institutions and the necessity of infrastructural maintenance to social and environmental well-being. They also enlisted a large degree of social coordination across identitarian and interest groups, emphasising the concerted, cooperative nature of the particular political action that was efficacious at this time.[5] Mabsout incorporated documentation of the demonstrations into the collection of postcards, and the demonstrations would also have been in the forefront of the minds of many of the visitors to the exhibition and forum. Contemporaneous events thus inflected the artwork with the significance of maintaining communal and accountable infrastructures of service and support.

Concurrently, Mabsout was also facilitating an ongoing project called *The Naked Wagon* (originally developed in 2013), which uses a bare wooden cart pulled by bicycles as a peripatetic platform to stage creative events in public spaces. She used the Wagon, for example, to hold a memorial for Fares – a child who also sold flowers in Hamra – who returned to Syria and, as she writes in a postcard entitled 'Nightingale', was killed by an American missile. Fares was known in Hamra for reciting a poem about a *bulbul*, or nightingale. The images in 'Nightingale' show the Wagon strewn with red roses, and children placing candles on the wooden boards. In the text accompanying the image, Mabsout writes that over a hundred people attended this street-side memorial to Fares at short notice, bringing flowers, candles and personal offerings. 'The roses were then collected and sent to Fares by sea' (Mabsout, 2015a). Postcards such as this – and the broader social and artistic context in which *Fleeing and Forgetting* took place – stage actions and affects of intersubjective care. They attest, then, both to precarity, disenfranchisement and violence at multiple levels, and also to efforts to counteract this through activist and artistic performances of sustained, communal caregiving.

A gallery of flowers

The interrelated dynamics of precarity and care evidenced by the postcards are acutely exposed in the series of images described at the start of this chapter, 'Still Lives'. In the accompanying text, Mabsout writes: '[K] and his sister took my phone and were busy photographing and filming for hours until the battery died. I am looking through the documents and there are tons of material I have yet to post. But here is a gallery of flowers his sister took' (2015b). Mabsout's title, 'Still Lives', and her description of the series of photographs as a 'gallery' are thrown into relief by the evidence that the photographs were not taken in stillness. While the term 'gallery' indicates that Mabsout conceives of M's photographs as artistic works, the images have evidently not been produced in the traditional, meditative space usually associated with visual art production or display. The first blurred and off-centre images are indicative of an authorial body in motion, and the two pairs of feet in the frame evocative of a passing opportunity, resting the bucket on the floor before moving on through a space of walking or dancing. The other meaning of 'Still Lives' suggests a broader paradox of transition. M and her brother K are still lives – still alive – but they have survived conflict, forced migration and now the labour of selling flowers at night on the streets of Hamra. This labour is profoundly dehumanising, because the children's very existence *as* lives is ignored by many of the people they try to engage. Selling the roses (for 2,000 Lebanese lira, or £1 each) is possibly their family's only source of income, and it means that they do not attend school in the daytime. Stillness, then, additionally evokes the impasse that forced migration has brought about in their lives. M's evident pleasure in the beauty of the roses, and the aesthetic care that is manifest in her growing dexterity as a photographer, are poignant reminders that the flowers are also the objects of her labour. The time she takes to photograph them adds to the hours in which she has to sell them before she is allowed to return home. Mabsout's title, then, alludes to M's vulnerability, but also to her demonstration of skill and joy in the production of beauty, and her capacity to enact care as well as to receive it.

Attending to M's own performance of aesthetic care is not intended to suggest a straightforward conflation of art making with social empowerment, nor to erase her severe disenfranchisement through over-emphasising the pleasure and skill the photographs manifest. Yet I would suggest it is also worth forgoing the impulse to reduce her experience to victimhood and abject helplessness. Refugee populations – and particularly children – are associated with a heightened visibility as the objects, and rarely the subjects, of image making, yet the photographs collected in *Fleeing and Forgetting* trouble this norm. They index a range of performances, including manifestations of grief and anger by the children, but also of joy and the strong, reciprocal bonds of friendship they formed with Mabsout and her peers. Certain postcards in the collection include reams of 'selfies', sometimes comprising as many as forty images taken consecutively, in which the photographers joke around and pull silly faces, trying to make each other and Mabsout laugh when they return the camera phone to her after work.

The children's humour and skill as performers goes some way towards challenging the lack of self-representation prevalent in depictions of refugee populations, and especially of those departing Syria and the region since 2011. As Katty Alhayek has noted of recent media images of Syrian women, 'In this dominant media representation, Syrian refugee women are robbed of their agency and are constricted to a representation of a single faceless victim/woman' (2015: 1). This 'invisiblise[s] their complex and various stories of struggling for freedom, suffering from violence and war, and resisting inequality and injustice' (Alhayek, 2015: 2). As Alison Jeffers has similarly claimed, audiences of refugee performances are often 'better prepared to accept an image of depressed passivity' because 'the alternative is to portray refugees as [...] angry, as active agents of change' (2012: 139). Though the postcards do at times show anger in the children, there is also agency in their performances of humour, affection and care. I suggest, then, that resistance and subversion are not the only means by which agency might be expressed. Recognising the varied conditions within which people can manifest ethical or political action points towards the social value of interdependence.[6] The children's photographs are funny, tender and increasingly confident, and through them, they present themselves as agents of self-representation and as givers (not just receivers) of care.

New conversations bringing together performance and care enact a helpful intervention in approaching 'Still Lives' in light of these concerns. In advocating for an 'aesthetics of care', James Thompson (2015) traces a critical framework in which the work that sustains art making is not concealed by the culminating product, nor seen as subsidiary to it, but rather is an integral and constituent component – and must equally be in its analysis. In this, I read a double imperative to at once recognise the caring practices that enable and constitute aesthetic production, and, in so doing, to enact care in our own work as scholars or critics, allowing the specific practices and subjects we engage with to challenge dominant hermeneutic priorities.

Performance is a helpful analytic focaliser since it encourages us to look beyond two-dimensional images such as those presented in 'Still Lives' and towards the actions and material conditions that enable (and are in turn shaped by) them. The images collected in *Fleeing and Forgetting*, in this sense, index much broader infrastructures through which care is performed. These were present in the context in which the photographs were taken, but also in their presentation and curation, and in their analysis in this chapter. Participating in a chain of performances that affect one another mutually, such moments of creation and display all have the capacity to manifest care. I agree with Thompson when he argues that writing about performance practices makes scholars powerful storytellers, with a consequent ethical responsibility to perform care ourselves in our research and writing (2004: 150–1). Taking the visual analysis of the postcards therefore as the starting (not ending) point of the discussion, I seek to adopt what Shannon Jackson refers to as the 'disciplinary perceptual habit' (2011: 4) of performance to attend to process and labour, the material and social infrastructures that make possible the creation of aesthetic works. As she argues, 'Performance's historical place as a cross-disciplinary, time-based, group art form also means that it requires a degree of systemic coordination, a brand of stage management that must think deliberately but also speculatively about what it means to sustain human collaboration spatially and temporally' (Jackson,

2011: 14). Though the relationships formed between Mabsout and the children were challenging to maintain and at times disrupted, it is crucial to attend to this sustained and systemic effort that underpins images of and by the children in this project and that can also be read as speculating a greater degree of self-representation available to the subjects of the photographs.

As M's photographs of the roses in 'Still Lives' make evident, aesthetic production and the labour and maintenance of the body are bound together inextricably; indeed, this is signalled by the title of the postcard and the very moment at which the photographs themselves were taken. During such moments both M and Mabsout were performing other kinds of paid work (hospitality and flower-selling), a confluence of labour and art making that is mirrored in their practices and joined through mutual relations of care. In Thompson's terms, this attests to the visibility of the artwork's 'preparation' in the moment of its 'exhibition', which can thus 'demonstrate and model a form of mutual regard' (2015: 438). The postcards' many references to labour (both to Mabsout's and to the children selling flowers), to shared meals syphoned from the restaurant and to embodied protection and the de-escalation of street violence, emphasise this enmeshing of aesthetic practice with the survival and care of the body and its material needs.

With Jackson, Thompson has argued that '"supporting infrastructures" are not the hidden mechanism of creative endeavours but a valued component of the aesthetics' (2015: 438).[7] This underscores the creative quality of infrastructural support and caring labour, emphasising that the substrates and conditions of possibility for the aesthetic are not given, but themselves imaginatively (and often collaboratively) made and effortfully maintained. The 'mutual regard' elicited here encourages us to encounter the children as subjects and as art makers who enact, as well as receive, creative care. Performance is helpful, then, in naming a 'doing' that enfolds and enmeshes the work of creative, sustaining and caring practices, challenging the relegation of these to separate spheres (such as the aesthetic, the activist, the social or the domestic), and emphasising that care is often reciprocally practised by multiple subjects in art-making processes.

Uncoupling migration and freedom

In the case of *Fleeing and Forgetting*, then, mobilising Thompson's 'aesthetics of care' helps to recognise the children photographers as subjects of self-representation, whose agency is interwoven within broader relational infrastructures of aesthetic and intersubjective care. In the particular context of art making by and about refugee populations, this stands to challenge not only dominant representations of refugees as victims (as suggested with Alhayek and Jeffers above), but also to problematise critical narratives in which migration and displacement have been employed as metaphors that celebrate rupture and transformation. As Sara Ahmed notes in her book *Strange Encounters* (2000), which interrogates the discursive co-constitution of the figure of the (migrant) 'stranger' in dialectical opposition to the (localised) 'epistemic community': 'Migration is employed as a metaphor within contemporary critical theory for movement and dislocation, and the crossing of borders and boundaries. Such a generalization of the meaning of migration allows it to be celebrated as a transgressive and liberating departure from living-as-usual' (2000: 80). As such, migration (and with it the exemplary 'figure' of the migrant) become tropes denoting a certain type of sociopolitical radicality that prioritises social disruption over social cooperation. Misleadingly, such tropes come to stand in for the lived diversity of migratory experiences: for Ahmed, 'this act of granting the migrant the status as a figure (of speech) erases and conceals the historical determination of experiences of migration' (2000: 81). Extrapolating from lived displacements to metaphors suggesting the movements of ideas and theories can be productive, though as Caren Kaplan has similarly argued, such 'affiliation is political, however, and cannot simply be assumed through […] the deployment of generalized metaphors' (1996: 105). Such metaphors risk effacing concrete, historical disparities in the conditions faced by migrants and refugees, as well as disparities between places in the world that they depart from and arrive.

In performance studies, Ahmed's diagnostic has special relevance given the historical tendency of the field to celebrate experiences of liminality and transgression. In an example of what Jon McKenzie has called the 'liminal norm', the efficacy of both the focus and the method of performance studies has been defined by 'a mode of activity whose spatial, temporal, and symbolic "in-between-ness" allows for social norms to be suspended, challenged, played with, and perhaps even transformed' (2001: 50). Many years after McKenzie's observation, liminality continues to be enlisted in the (paradoxically normative) valorisation of both performance practice and its study as subversive, interstitial activities. Liminality relies on pervasively spatial metaphors, as deployed by Arnold van Gennep (1977) and then Victor Turner to describe a 'gap between ordered worlds [in which] almost anything may happen' (Turner, 1985: 13). Foundational narratives of performance studies, such as those authored by the theorist-practitioner Richard Schechner, have also visualised the field's liminal constitution through exceptionalist metaphors of mobility; for example, by comparing performance studies to a sidewinder rattlesnake characterised by indirection, disorientation and dissimulation 'as it sidewinds its way across the deserts of academia' (Schechner, 1998: 358).[8] These metaphors imagine performance as evincing exceptional change through movement and social rupture. Correspondingly, stillness and social interdependence come to be pejoratively associated with stasis, normativity and unfreedom.

The disciplinary history of these paradigms, denoting conditions of institutional privilege in a North Atlantic context, are limited in what they are able to make legible about actual migratory experiences. As Ahmed has suggested: 'The naming of theory as nomadic can be understood in terms of the violence of translation, a form of translation that allows the theory to name itself as a subversion of conventions', yet 'what is at stake here is a certain kind of Western subject, the subject of and in theory, as a subject who is *free to move*' (2000: 83, emphasis added). In measuring freedom according to the mobility of an individual, heroic and privileged subject, we risk overlooking the unfreedoms that many experience through migration, as well as different forms of agency that may, for example, be constituted through stillness or continuity, rather than mobility and liminality. As Jackson has suggested, in much avant-garde art and performance, freedom has been 'increasingly equated with systemic *in*dependence' (2011: 28, original emphasis). Yet performance, she suggests, 'both activates and depends upon a relational system' and thus recognises that 'to avow the supporting acts that sustain and are sustained by social actors is to avow the relational systems on which any conception of freedom rests' (Jackson, 2011: 30, 36). My reading of *Fleeing and Forgetting* insists on the recognition of reciprocal performances of care as crucial and life-sustaining in certain conditions of displacement. In this sense, the perceptual 'habit' of performance is helpful in rethinking the correspondence of mobility and freedom, and pointing instead towards the systemic, 'care-full' interdependencies through which agency, well-being or joy can be founded in art practices.

'Home'

One of the final postcards in the *Fleeing and Forgetting* collection points towards the intervention that attention to performances of care might make in recognising the diverse ways in which subjective agency can be expressed by displaced persons. I conclude this chapter with an exploration of this postcard, suggesting that it encourages us to complicate oppositions between mobility and stillness, and so too the ethical valences that each of these concepts denote. Noticing the performances of care indexed by the postcard conversely foregrounds the varied experiences that art making by or about displaced persons might articulate.

The postcard – comprising three photographs and a short text – is entitled 'Home' and dated 4 September 2015. It contains a 'selfie' photograph taken by Mabsout: she appears in the foreground in her apartment in Hamra, with K and M in the background, who are looking at the camera phone and laughing, in the middle of a meal. There is another photograph of K showing a large painting he has created of what seems to be the inside of a house, with open, multicoloured windows and a framed portrait showing three or perhaps four faces hanging on the wall. The final photograph included in 'Home' shows two buckets of roses, one bigger and one smaller, put aside on a bench in Mabsout's apartment. The only accompanying text reads: 'That night I invited [K] and [M] home for the first time' (Mabsout, 2015c).

Like many of the postcards, 'Home' leaves space for – indeed, draws attention to – what it does not disclose. The postcard does not express how long K and M were at Mabsout's home, nor what they did except eat and paint together, nor whether this first time inaugurated her apartment as a more consistent space of their relationship that continued beyond the temporal scope of *Fleeing and Forgetting*. Beyond the references to a shared meal and K's painting, it is difficult to gauge the degree to which this experience extends or supports any broader well-being on the part of the children, and I do not seek – and indeed am unable – to draw generalised conclusions about the wider effects that Mabsout's project and the friendships it generated may have had on the children's lives. Despite the support system maintained by a wider group of Mabsout's peers and collaborators, who have responded to the needs of Syrian refugees and the repercussions of their entrance into Lebanon, this postcard is perhaps disconcerting in expressing an unboundaried provision of care for the children: for implying both their needs (for food, rest and creative play) and the personal demands placed on Mabsout in responding to them, both material and affective. Given the professionalisation of practitioners in the fields of 'applied' and 'community' arts and in a humanitarian context, the photographs are perhaps also troubling for the blurring of roles and spaces they index. This postcard insists on the private and intimate sphere of the home as a space of care and social action, and the affective intricacies and attachments this manifests. As Thompson has argued, however, 'intimate care [...] can be connected to an affective solidarity and felt sense of justice, and ultimately might be foundational to the ethics and aesthetics of a theatre and arts practice that seeks to engage with communities' (2015: 432). 'Home' refuses to 'bifurcate a world of public justice and private care' (Thompson, 2015: 432), an intervention that can be both disorientating and hopeful.

The postcard itself seems to allude both to the importance of home as an enduring site of rest, food and creativity, and to its precarity, particularly in the final photograph. The two buckets have been put aside temporarily (for the moment they are 'still') but they are a reminder of the children's labour, which must be carried out to permit their time eating and painting at Mabsout's apartment, and that will also eventually separate them from her. A nostalgic image of home might metaphorise and figure it oppositely to mobility or transgression, either with positive or pejorative connotations. This postcard, however, suggests that 'home' is expressed as a specific material, spatial and affective relation. Instead of positioning private care and public justice oppositely, or figuring home dichotomously to mobility, the postcard suggests that displacement can occasion complex but not necessarily devoid or divorced relationships to the idea of home and the care associated with it. A migratory 'figure' that is 'premised on universality in the very loss of home' (Ahmed, 2000: 79) would perpetuate the reductive theorisations of migration described above. Yet in this postcard, home is both profoundly precarious and passionately supported by migratory *and* 'local' individuals, suggesting that the home can be one possible site for realising interdependence and reciprocity supported by mutual and effortful care.

In my exploration of *Fleeing and Forgetting*, I have aimed to both recognise and mobilise performances of care. These joint aims respond to what I see as the double imperative operating within Thompson's articulation of an 'aesthetics of care'. The first of these works towards avowing the systems of support and interdependency that can underlie expressions of agency within social settings, suggesting that agency and freedom cannot be disentangled from the material and intersubjective conditions in which they are expressed. Agency, then, is bound up with performances of care, manifest, for example, in the aesthetic care shown by M in 'Still Lives' or the material and affective care demonstrated by Mabsout in 'Home' and other postcards. Second, mobilising care in critical scholarship asks us to work 'response-ably' (Hamera, 2013) to the specificities of contexts, artworks and experiences, and allow these to interrogate the dominant paradigms that shape our hermeneutic work.

These conjoined goals are particularly pertinent, I suggest, when writing about art made by or about displaced persons. While scholars in the field of performance studies have deployed metaphors of mobility to privilege liminality and transgression, an 'aesthetics of care' problematises such tropes. It points instead towards how displaced persons often give and receive systemic and sustainable care, and towards the ways in which political action can take place not only through social transgression or resistance, but also through social coordination and interdependence. Performing care, then, entails attending to the resolutely embodied and radically differentiated possibilities of movement and refuge available to subjects, and the ways in which these might be 'care-fully' addressed in art practices and scholarship.

Notes

1 The names of the children in this chapter have been removed to protect their anonymity. While no strategy of anonymisation is ideal, and this one risks de-personalising the individuals concerned, the most appropriate strategy for protecting their identity has been taken here in consultation with Mabsout.
2 There are eighteen officially recognised religious sects in Lebanon, and most areas of Beirut are predominantly associated with particular sectarian, ethnic or political groups. With a mix of residential and commercial use, two prominent universities and an established scene of cafés, bars and restaurants, Hamra is distinctively diverse in its class, ethnic and sectarian make up (see Khalaf and Kongstad, 1973; Seidman, 2012).
3 Terms such as 'migrant' and 'refugee' are not neutral and have important ideological valences as well as legal definitions. I describe the children concerned as refugees since, in having been forced to leave Syria due to violent conflict, they fall into the UN Refugee Agency UNHCR's definition, even if they have not been personally registered as such. For insightful analyses of the performative and theatrical constitutions of the category of 'refugee', see Nield (2006), Jeffers (2012), Wake (2013a) and Yoxall (2018). I use the term 'displacement' in this chapter to signal an affective experience as well as the geographic one suggested by migration (cf. Kaplan, 1996). At the time of writing, there are 259,849 Syrian refugees in Beirut registered with the UNHRC and 986,942 registered in Lebanon, approximately half of whom are children (UNHCR, 2018a; UNHCR, 2018b). However, registration with the UNHCR was suspended as per

instructions from the Government of Lebanon on 6 May 2015 (at which point the number registered reached over a million), so this data does not include unregistered individuals, estimated to raise the total number to 1.5 million (Human Rights Watch, 2017). On the Lebanese government's response, see el Mufti (2014).

4 The Beqaa region has received more UNHCR-registered refugees from the Syrian conflict than any other area of Lebanon (at the time of writing, 35.9 per cent as opposed to 26.3 per cent in Beirut), and there are currently over 350,00 Syrian refugees living there (UNHRC, 2018c).

5 The protest movement brought together demonstrators from multiple sectarian and class backgrounds and built on existing networks of activists in Lebanon: it thus wove into itself a diversity of interests and concerns including those around public space, environmental sustainability, police brutality and feminist movements (Abu-Rish, 2015; Mikdashi, 2015).

6 This argument builds on the work of Saba Mahmood, who in *Politics of Piety* asks: 'Does the category of resistance impose a teleology of progressive politics on the analytics of power – a teleology that makes it hard for us to see and understand forms of being and action that are not necessarily encapsulated by the narrative of subversion and reinscription of norms?' (2005: 9; cf. el Zein, 2017).

7 This claim echoes the insistence of some Marxist feminists on social reproduction as a terrain of unwaged labour that is invisible, and yet foundational, to the workings of capitalism (see Federici, 2012; and cf. Jackson, 2011: 75–103).

8 For Caren Kaplan, 'Euro-American recourse to the metaphors of desert and nomad can never be innocent or separable from the dominant orientalist tropes in circulation throughout modernity' (1996: 66). As Ella Shohat (1991) has similarly shown, visualisations of heroic mobility through deserted terra incognita (such as Schechner's) are often historically constituted through imperial fantasies of conquest.

PART IV

CARE AS PERFORMANCE

Verbatim practice as research with care-experienced young people: an 'aesthetics of care' through aural attention

Sylvan Baker and Maggie Inchley

> I've literally become a catalogue of statistics, and just irrelevant facts and info. And it's dehumanising to be honest. If adults don't really view you as a human then how can you view yourself? … Right now, according to the system, kids have become just another number, another statistic, and it's not whether a child is being cared for, it's whether they're being dealt with. (Leah, fourteen years old, TVF Audio Archive: 2015–18)[1]

The Verbatim Formula (TVF) is an ongoing verbatim theatre-based participatory research project founded in 2015 at Queen Mary University of London (QMUL). The project started out as a collaboration between the authors of this chapter, Maggie Inchley, a senior lecturer in drama at QMUL, and Sylvan Baker, then an associate director at arts and social justice organisation People's Palace Projects (PPP) and now a lecturer at the Royal Central School of Speech and Drama. Behind its inception was a desire to find ways of using artistic and pedagogical practice that would shed light on how young people perceived the experience of entering and being in social service-based care in the UK. Our preliminary research had revealed that the experience of young people during and after local authority care interventions was marked by exclusion from education, social deprivation and increased risks of engaging with oppressive and criminalised behaviours. For example, research carried out in the UK between 2008 and 2015 indicates that only 6 per cent of care leavers entered higher education compared to 30 per cent of that age demographic nationally. Furthermore, 49 per cent of young men who had had some contact with the criminal justice system and 25 per cent of those who were homeless were found to have been in care at some point in their lives (National Audit Office, 2015: 4–6). In addition, evidence suggests that the physical and mental health and well-being of many young people entering care is a matter for serious concern. A UK

Parliamentary briefing paper produced in 2015, for example, indicates that, in general, social service's first engagement with 'looked-after children'[2] was as a result of abuse or neglect in 61 per cent of cases (Zayed and Harker, 2015: 4). In 2016, an Education Committee report found that almost half of children in care have a diagnosable mental health disorder (Education Committee, 2016: 3).

The disproportionate levels of criminalisation, social and education exclusion, and mental health challenges revealed in this statistical catalogue were extremely shocking, and point to what seems to be a dereliction of care for these most vulnerable of young people. Our desire to 'do something' in response to such apparent systemic 'care-lessness' led to the development of TVF, a project that explores, with care-experienced young people, their suggestions to improve the care they receive and their hopes for the future. In this sense, the project's methodology sought to discover personal experiences that lie behind the statistical evidence and to place the young people and their knowledge at the centre. Accordingly, we chose to frame our participatory research project around the practices of verbatim theatre, a form of theatre practice that promises to convey in performance an 'authentic' or 'word-for-word' account of its subjects' voices and that, as we will argue in what follows, can be used as a practice that treats the experience of young people and their reflections on it with due respect and care. Crucially, our decision to use verbatim theatre was not to align our practice with that of the therapeutic storytelling that James Thompson, among others, has argued risks recycling a speaker's trauma (2009: 45). Instead, we wanted to use verbatim theatre techniques and strategies to acknowledge the expertise of the young people and to support an implicit process of self-narration of their paths into adult life. As the project progressed, we began to recognise the potential impact of our verbatim-based practices both in relation to the potency of performed verbatim material that addressed the young people's experiences of being cared for by the state, and because the performance of the verbatim testimonies led to caring encounters and dialogues between the young people and their professional carers.

The initial invitation to be part of the early stage of the TVF project was to young people aged fourteen to eighteen who were currently living in foster or residential social care in the UK to meet and work with students and young adult facilitators, and to experience life on a university campus by taking part in a week's residential at QMUL. As it has developed, TVF has become a much wider collaboration that includes adult colleagues from a range of disciplinary areas, notably from the field of ethical management and creative evaluation, as well as with participatory officers from local authority children's services.[3] Since the project began in 2015, we have gathered a broader range of testimonies, notably from foster carers and social workers who share the professional contexts and conditions of their work in the care service. These have become components of our 'living archive' – the bank of recorded material that we draw upon for sharing at TVF events, which have taken place in a range of spaces beyond the rehearsal room and university studio, including conference halls, theatres, museums, meeting rooms, offices and libraries. At TVF events, the testimonies are performed by our project participants, alumni and facilitators to invited and public audiences or to particular groups such as social workers or university staff. Following the performance, the facilitators curate direct dialogue between participants and audience members, which is itself recorded and becomes part of the living archive. In this way, we argue, both the performed verbatim material and the curated exchanges between participants and audience members operate together to become performances of care that explore and illuminate the caring encounter.

The desire to recognise and respect the experience of the young people we have worked with is also behind our decision to adopt the term 'care-experienced young people', rather than to use the ubiquitous term 'looked-after children'. For, as they soon revealed, many young people do not feel 'looked after' at all when they are in the care of their 'corporate parents' (the term adopted by UK state bodies and local authorities to describe the social workers and organisations responsible for the young people placed 'in care'). Each of the young people we have worked with has a unique background and individual set of circumstances. Each one of them is experienced in the services they have accessed for care and education. For this reason, within all the sessions we have led as part of TVF, we have aimed to subvert the uneven power dynamics of academic practice and traditional research processes that tends to place researchers in the position of experts and participants as unknowing subjects. Instead, we have aimed to underpin the design and trajectory of our research with an ethics and practice of care that positions the young people as co-researchers, *with* whom we share verbatim theatre-making techniques, and *from* whose expertise we are learning. Placing young people in the role of co-researcher also enables them to develop and value their own interrogatory skills, which can be used to challenge the systems in which young people all too often feel that it is the adults who hold all the agency and all power. Most frequently, it is the young people themselves who conduct peer interviews with foster carers and social workers, encounters that themselves can be important interventions in young people's own sense of receiving and giving care and that also provide further testimonial accounts of the ways in which these caring adults carry out and perceive their own practices.

During TVF sharings, the verbatim testimonies we have gathered are performed using headphone technique, a practice where performers listen to clips of recorded interviews loaded on to iPods, speaking them out to the audience as they hear the words through their earpieces. This technique ensures that personal testimonies, reflections and opinions can be conveyed as closely as possible to the exact words of the original speaker, whose anonymity is preserved as another person performs their testimony. We frequently redistribute and interchange the audio clips so that a facilitator might perform the words of a care-experienced young person, or a young person might share a testimony that was given by another project

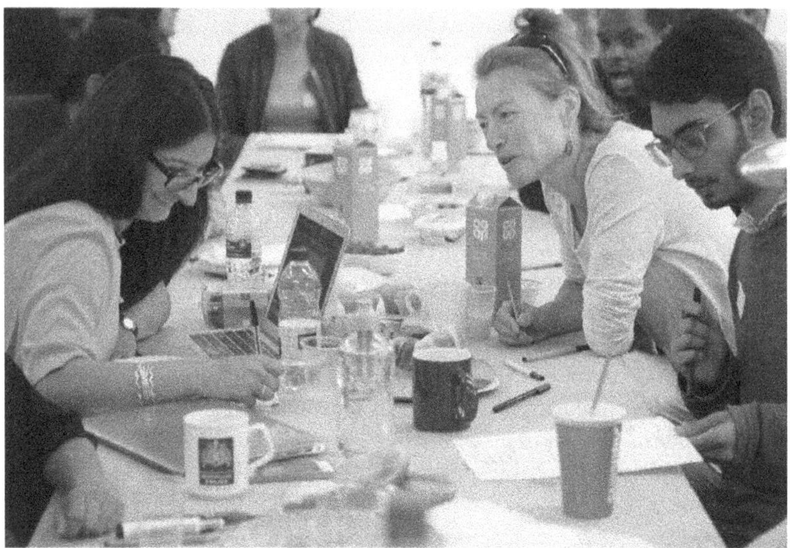

Figure 10.1 TVF welcome breakfast

participant or adult care professional. We find that the shifting of the testimony into the 'mouth' of another can heighten the engagement with which our audiences listen to the testimonies. This is particularly so if the identity of the person sharing the testimony is different in some way, such as with respect to age, race or gender, to that of the giver of the testimony. While the headphone form that we will discuss further below has been previously used to create plays by verbatim playwrights for theatre, we have adapted its approach in ways that we argue facilitates forms of caring, participatory practice and performance. The shift enables a 'care-full' and caring form of speaking and listening to be part of an ethical encounter between adult carers and young people. This palpably demonstrates that the latter have substantive contributions to make in the ongoing debate around practices of care, while allowing us to frame dialogue in spaces and contexts where they feel they are being heard.

Later in this chapter we examine how TVF might be understood as a performance of care that enables its participants/co-researchers not only to narrate their experience of caregiving and care receiving, but also to engage with a mode of attentive care through their participation in the process of theatre making itself. What TVF explores, we suggest, is an affective mode of engagement with the young participants and their testimonies, where care is present in the act of listening to and sharing their words and, crucially, for the young people, in the experience of being heard and listened to. We therefore consider how *listening* emerges in this project both as an aesthetic but also as a care-based participatory and political practice, inspired by the principles and practices of good care that we have observed and researched, that aims to empower care-experienced young people to intervene

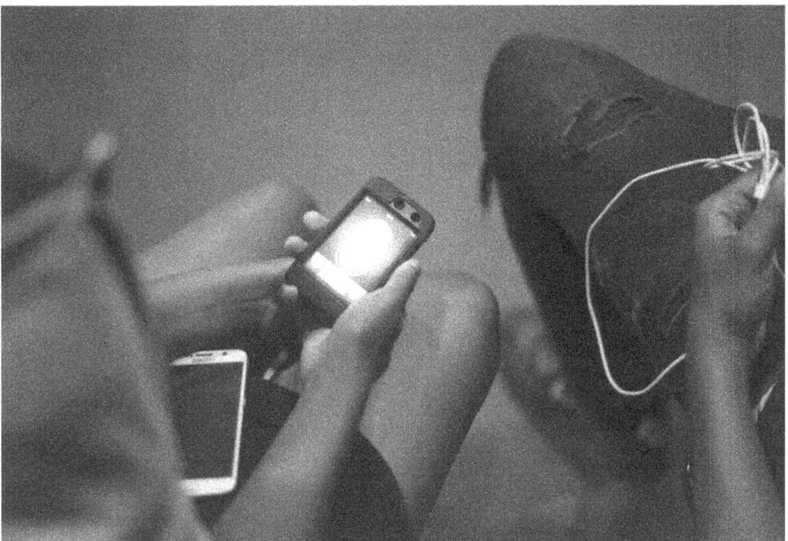

Figure 10.2 Making verbatim

in the structures that represent them and to support adults to *honour* their experiences and needs. It is important to note that we use the word 'honour' here, both in the sense of respect or esteem, but also as a fulfilment of an obligation – to act on what has been agreed.

We have constructed the TVF methodological process by starting with an awareness that within state-based care services in the UK, listening is a legal requirement and understood as an important relationship-building tool that should be positioned at the centre of social work practice. Drawing from this, we argue that when forming part of an ethical participatory process, listening can become a mode of care for the other and a sensory practice of knowing, which can be heightened aesthetically though verbatim theatre-making processes that support a more informed and generative dialogue between young people and adult professionals. In some senses, our project directly responds to some of the provocations of feminist care ethicists, whose theorisation has influenced our reflections on listening as a mode of caring. In *Moral Boundaries* ([1993] 2009), for example, Joan Tronto identifies the practice of 'attentiveness' as one of the principle modes of care, arguing that 'recognizing the needs of those around us, is a difficult task, and indeed, a moral achievement' ([1993] 2009: 127). Tronto argues for a radically restructured society that would recognise and value interdependency rather than revolve around the rights of the self-mastering neoliberal individual. To ensure that it is not just those 'who are already sufficiently powerful' who benefit from these radical changes, Tronto calls for new democratic processes structured around an obligation to '[listen] and to [include] care-receivers in determining the processes of care' ([1993] 2009: 172). Tronto's arguments suggest there is a radical need for an intervention into the dynamics of power in society that ensure that those for whom the structures of care are least effective are heard and attended to, and that action is taken accordingly.

Another core element of TVF is the practice of what feminist ethicist Nel Noddings describes as the quality of 'receptivity', which she argues is demonstrated in both caring for an other as well as in the way creative artists practice 'aesthetical caring' in their attempts 'to grasp or receive a reality rather than impose it' (2013: 21–2). Within TVF, the quality of engagement that is forged between the participants, the project practitioners and facilitators allows for some sense of the young people's reality to emerge in the aesthetic material that is formed. TVF facilitators must be 'present' and engaged in an attentive form of 'listening, watching, feeling, contributing' (Noddings, 2013: 22). The quality of receptivity, as we go on to discuss below, also infuses the practice and ethics of TVF verbatim performances, both in terms of how the performer delivers the recorded testimonies and in the way that audience members, of whom a large proportion work in social care, are inclined and encouraged to receive them.

It is important to state that our work is also determined by what Noddings describes as the 'problem of reciprocity' (2013: 69–74). For Noddings, as for our practitioners, this emerges when the care receiver does not recognise the care that is offered. For many of the young people who participate in TVF, care is not something that is administered in ways that feel caring, rather care is something that is measured out and often mediated by bureaucratic practice and social stigma. For many young people, encounters with caregiving from state carers often feels transactional and structured to ensure that official procedures are followed. These encounters do not resemble the unconditional loving that takes place within the parent–child relationships so often held up as the ideal and indeed the norm in society. In such cases, care may become something that is experienced by a young person as 'ugly', an encounter that does not alleviate a person's trials, but rather amplifies them. We would therefore argue that the act of caring within the TVF project has important ethical and political implications. By establishing performative, dialogical encounters that can recognise and responsibly attend to the 'ugliness' of caring that is articulated by young people who are 'care experienced', the project creates a space in which these ideas can be debated, challenged and explored safely in dialogue with professional carers.

'Apparently there is some big file on me in some cupboard somewhere' (Hannah, fifteen years old, TVF Audio Archive: 2015–18)

The accounts that our co-researchers have given and gathered during TVF reveal tensions between their perceptions of the care they are receiving and the focus on good listening that is emphasised in state provision. Since the adoption into UK law of the 1989 UN Convention on the Rights of the Child in 1992, corporate parents are legally obliged to give due regard to children's wishes and feelings in matters affecting them. The Department for Education and Department for Health document *Promoting the Health and Well-Being of Looked-After Children* (2015) specifies that local authorities should ensure that arrangements are in place that promote a culture 'where looked-after children are listened to' and that 'helps others [...] to understand the importance of listening to and taking account of the child's wishes and feelings' (2015: 7). Such advice recurs through many of the statutory documents and the regulatory discourse that surrounds the care system. The 2014 Children and Families Act also emphasises the importance of young people 'participating as fully as possible' (Children and Families Act, 2014: 18) in decisions that will affect their care. Furthermore, a survey by the Children's Commissioner for England (2015) whose terms were informed by the Act found that crucially, for children, what makes the difference between good or bad care is the experience of 'being listened to'. Yet, as Leah indicates in the epigraph at the start of this chapter, many care-experienced young people believe that they are being treated as a 'statistic' rather than a person and are often left feeling uncared for by the very state provision that is delegated as a source of support. Despite the activities of children in care councils – which exist in local authorities to provide a forum for young people – many of the TVF participants we worked with recounted incidents where they considered their feelings and perspectives were unheard and ignored. These accounts are not just related to emotional outbursts when an event did not go as they had hoped, but at more incisive moments where the young people experienced a particular manifestation of care that while seeming to be well intentioned was neither personal nor caring.

One example of this is a testimony given to us by a young woman, Stephanie, in her twenties, who described an incident that occurred in early adolescence that led her to take the extreme and dangerous step of absconding from her latest placement in foster care. 'There was an incident,' she explained, 'where I came back to one of my foster carer's house. I got there, and I saw a big black taxi, kind of cabbie thing outside.' Waiting inside the house, her foster carer and social worker had already packed up her things – 'her dirty laundry and everything' (Stephanie, TVF Audio Archive 2015–18). She was moving, for the first time in her young life away from London. Sadly, Stephanie describes an experience that is not uncommon. In 2015, 33 per cent of children in care were placed in more than one foster home and 10 per cent had three placements or more (Spring Consortium, 2016: 10). Stephanie's testimony is shocking not only because of the dehumanising way she recounts being treated, but because it reveals that she had not been consulted or even made aware of a decision about her care as is legally required. During the verbatim process, she explained that this was a key element of her experience, saying: 'It would have been nice for them to speak to me about it. Rather than it being like a set-up, and I'm like, what is going on?' (Stephanie, TVF Audio Archive, 2015–18). Stephanie's decision to abscond serves as evidence in the severe break down in her trust of the adults around her. She said: 'If they'd spoken to me, yeah maybe I'd have effed and blinded a little bit, but I would have understood. Give me the chance to … at least let me feel like I'm helping you make the decision' (Stephanie, TVF Audio Archive, 2015–18). Stephanie's anger and resignation were fuelled by feelings of powerlessness, something that many of the other young people we interviewed also experienced. TVF co-researchers have repeatedly testified to feeling frustrated about the ways their lives are described and documented by social workers in case notes they are not allowed to see. The very idea of having one's life narrated by another is seen as lacking in personal respect. There is also a feeling that their privacy is constantly being breached by social workers and other professionals sharing information that is not disclosed to the young person in question because of safeguarding regulation. As fifteen-year-old Hannah, one of the participants and co-researchers, told us: 'You don't know where the information that you're telling them is gonna go to … why should I put my trust in people at school because it ends up getting back to my social worker' (TVF Audio Archive, 2015–18).

Of course, securing the safety and well-being of these young people is paramount, but by fulfilling the legal requirements placed upon them, and in the wake of cases of deaths of young people such as Victoria Climbié and 'Baby P' in the care of local services, risk-averse social workers, it seems, continually enforce a system that young people experience as bureaucratic and dehumanising (Munro, 2011). As Hannah explains: 'Apparently there is some big file on me in some cupboard somewhere. You know, stuff that I don't even know about myself. And my past and all that' (TVF Audio Archive, 2015–18). Like many other young people we worked with, Hannah's anxiety about what her file says is heightened by her lack of access to it and a feeling that she has little or no control about how her life narrative is being constructed. The structures of safeguarding and child protection as experienced by Hannah seem to leave her feeling more vulnerable and insecure. She is aware that other adults may see the file before meeting her, and the narrative it tells will intercede on her behalf in a manner that is intimidating to her and not conducive to productive relations with adult professionals. Furthermore, the keeping of records by social workers and other agents of the state seems also to encourage young people to believe these narratives preclude any acknowledgement of their capabilities and potential – instead of recording positive achievements, the documentation of their cases tends to reinforce the idea that for young people in care, adults understand them as 'problems'. In state-orientated caring encounters, many of our co-researchers report a feeling that rather than following authentic caring practices, social workers 'erase them' with the use of a jargon of care. One example of this is the effect of being labelled as 'vulnerable', 'hard to reach' or 'non-compliant'. Many young people reported that this kind of language fuels feelings of anger and defensiveness, creating a sense of dehumanisation, which ultimately sabotages the potential of any relationship that may develop between young people and their foster carers or social workers. It was accounts such as Hannah's that led us to realise that listening is experienced by many young people in care not as caring but as a component of surveillance and part of a dehumanising statutory administration of record-keeping that feels far removed from a loving and trusting relationship with an adult. It is apposite to note here that that the anonymity of our verbatim practices, the licence the project grants young people to speak back to the system and the way it is administered, has greatly appealed to many of our participants.

For young people entering or leaving care, the shifting dynamics between 'dependence', 'interdependence' and 'independence' are desperately complex. In extremis, young people for whom state intervention has been deemed necessary have become emotionally dependent on family members who are unable to care for them or, in the worst cases, are their abusers. At the same time, the transition to becoming a 'looked-after child' can be experienced as brutal and traumatic. In many cases, acknowledging and accepting 'need' can contain enormous risk as well as being in itself a sign of an extraordinary capacity to adapt. In the TVF residentials, we have seen how some young people adopt a range of self-protective strategies, such as complete withdrawal of communication with adults, or in some circumstances violent rejection of any caregiving gesture, in order to protect themselves from further abuse, neglect or rejection. Such responses can be interpreted as a failure to compute or to recognise caring encounters, or being unable to trust others or allow oneself to be a care receiver. This accords with Noddings' account of the lack of responsiveness on behalf of the care receiver that negates the care relation (2013: 71). Such a negation occurs when the one being cared for does not feel that she is approached as a 'subject' but 'as an object to be manipulated' or 'data source' (Noddings, 2013: 72). It is this breakdown in communication between young people and their carers that leads to what the young people have described as the 'ugliness' of care.

The inversion of caring as something 'ugly' and destructive can impact both on young people and their social workers or foster carers. As child psychotherapist Peter Wilson reports, young people's negative feelings about care can become projected on to their carer, leading many carers to be 'shocked, insulted, aroused, provoked, rendered speechless' and made to feel as 'neglected, abused and abandoned' as the children they are caring for have been made to feel (2010: 13). Conversely, when the caring relation is working well, it is characterised by a fine attunement of the caregiver and the one who is cared for. If many of the testimonies that the TVF project has gathered have revealed young people's feelings of being unheard, we have also found examples of such attunement in the way that foster carers and social carers listen to the young people in their care. In fact, we have been struck by the similarities of their listening practices with the qualities of performance necessitated by the aural components of our verbatim processes. These adult professionals, who often find themselves dealing with the everyday ugly consequences of trauma and neglect, often find themselves engaged in multiple acts of listening as a mode of care for the young people they are looking after on a daily basis. The following testimony from a foster carer describes the highly skilled art of aural heed, akin to the somatic attention that many of our TVF facilitators and performers strive for. It is arguably a practice that exhibits the kind of 'receptivity' described by Noddings in her analogy between aesthetic engagement and the art of caring. In the following testimony, Sue, a foster carer, describes how she adopts an embodied form of caring and how she 'hears' without words being spoken by the other (Noddings, 2013: 22): 'All the time I listen with my eyes and my ears because I can read as much from the body as I can from what's being said, or what's not being said. So even at breakfast time, when the lad's going out the door, I check him over and talk to him, how you're doing and stuff. It's every day, it's all the time, it's part and parcel of everything' (TVF Audio Archive, 2015–18). Sue's mode of listening seems to suggest a practice that is beyond the gesture of a simple aural attention to what is being said. In her delicate sensory engagement, she is instinctively improvising care for her foster child's needs and recognising that listening becomes a source of support and stability through her adopting of a carefully nuanced attunement towards the young man she is caring for. This kind of holistic embodied attunement seems to exemplify and demonstrate the practices of good care advocated by many feminist care ethicists. It illustrates, for example, a form of 'motivational displacement', where the carer puts her own needs aside to act instead according to the needs of the one who is cared for (Noddings, 2013: 16–18). In this moment of caring, Sue's own needs are suspended as she engages with the young man in her care with complete commitment yet without an expectation that she will necessarily discover precisely what his needs are. In this sense, this act of listening and attunement is a striving towards an understanding of this young man's frame of reference rather than her own. Crucially, this mode of listening is multidimensional and to draw on Maurice Hamington's account of care, it is arguably also 'embodied' (2004: 108). Attentive to not only what he says, but to the non-verbal somatic cues of his whole body, all Sue's senses are holistically engaged in her interaction with the young man in her care. For Tronto, who draws on Simone Weil's understanding of the human capacity for attention as the opening to 'truth', 'attentiveness' is conceived as a profoundly active moral commitment and is a form of engagement with knowledge ([1993] 2009: 128). In this sense, Sue's artful and non-intrusive practice becomes a form of inquiry into the young man's well-being. Her act of listening and attuning herself to the state of his being performs a mode of attentiveness and care that is informed by profound personal and moral responsibility. Such an embodied and attentive commitment to the experiences of our co-researchers have informed the development of TVF, and, in the final sections of this chapter, we will explore how our own practices of embodied listening have sought to emulate the qualities of Sue's aesthetical caring.

'Doing her justice' (Sid, twenty-year-old facilitator-performer, TVF Audio Archive, 2015–18)

Following Noddings' cue that there are commonalities between the receptivity of aesthetic engagement and the practice of care whereby the artist like the caregiver is in a sense 'seized by the other's project or plight' (2013: 22), in the course of TVF, we have been exploring how the verbatim performer's aesthetic efforts in some ways resemble the caregiver's practices of attentiveness and receptivity. As we explain above, the decision to employ verbatim theatre techniques was initially due to the desire to use theatre-making strategies that would preserve the authority and integrity of the young people's own accounts of their experience of entering state care. As we developed our practice, we realised how effectively this mode of performance could be inflected with the ethics and practices of good care described by Tronto and Noddings and that is also evident in the account above from Sue. Tom Cantrell's research into the performance of verbatim material by professional actors reveals how it generates 'a sense of responsibility towards the representation' of the real-life figure that actors represent (2013: 5). It became clear to us that this sense of obligation was also a crucially important feature of the TVF project, especially given the powerlessness that many young people encounter when entering the state care system. After he performed with the TVF at the Wellcome Trust in 2015, Sid, a twenty-year-old male student, explained that it was only after several attempts at sharing the testimony of a fourteen-year-old girl that he felt he was able to begin to 'do her justice'. Far from attempting to speak *for* her, or use acting technique to somehow *become* her, Sid endeavoured to employ verbatim performance as a meticulous practice of attentiveness that *honoured* the original speaker through rigorous attention to her words and bodily rhythms.

Rather than adopting the approach taken by playwrights such as David Hare, in which a writer 'interferes' with verbatim material by rescripting and dramatising the text, we chose to draw on and adapt a genealogy of headphone verbatim theatre-making processes adopted by theatre makers such as Anna Deveare Smith, Mark Wing Davis, Alecky Blythe and Robin Oades (Haydon, 2013; Wake, 2013b). In TVF, the use of headphone performance generates a performance of 'care-full' attentiveness by requiring the performer *to attune* – via the recordings of interviews – to the original textures and cadences of the interviewee's speech, paying attention and reproducing the gaps in words, hesitations, vocal ticks, false starts and paralinguistic parts of speech such as laughs, sighs or groans. This mode of performance allows both the young people we work with and our facilitators to explore how the performer (albeit temporarily) can apply what anthropologist Thomas Csordas describes as a 'somatic mode of attention' to another person. As Csordas argues, this form of attention is a mode of embodied attentiveness where the body becomes a means of attending to another (2002: 137).

There is another analogy here between the creative processes of TVF and the act of caring, for as Noddings argues: 'caring involves stepping out of one's own personal frame of reference in to the other's' (2013: 24). We would suggest that in the practices of care that emerge in TVF, as in the caring encounter itself, the process of 'stepping out of one's own personal frame' is not simply a cognitive one. Rather, through 'care-full' listening and articulation, care and attunement to the other becomes physically *embodied*. To use the headphone technique successfully, the performer must be engrossed in or, to use Noddings' term, 'seized' by the sonic material itself, suspending temporarily their own physical needs. One adult TVF facilitator described how in the process of performing verbatim her whole being became engaged as she attempted to bring her body and voice into 'synch' with the voice she heard through her earphones. Trying to voice another's words accurately and responsibly, she reported, involved a recalibration of bodily rhythm and breathing – a temporary rearrangement and reprioritisation of her own physiological needs. In the meticulous observance and re-embodiment of the verbatim somatic score, the ethical and aesthetic dimensions of performance converge. For Sid, whom we quoted above, this sense of using a practice of listening to exercise responsibility for the speaker seemed to intertwine profoundly with the mode and shape of his delivery, leading to a heightened awareness of the prolonged, bodily attentiveness and responsibility that care requires.

In TVF, verbatim performance work is augmented and extended through our participatory and pedagogical practice, which includes extensive discussion with the young people, facilitators and performers around the ethics of this type of performance, the importance of respect for the words and voice of the speaker, and how the mediation of the material by the performer qualifies the extent to which it becomes possible to represent the original speaker 'truthfully'. As will by now be clear, we have found that many care-experienced young people have a nuanced awareness of and very strong feelings about the ways in which their care identities often become represented oversimplistically, through negative stereotypes, and in ways that exclude their input. Performance scholar Caroline Wake argues that headphone theatre 'does not so much "give voice" as "grant an audience"' (2013b: 321). Because audiences at a TVF event include the care-experienced participants themselves, a co-presence of adults and young people is created that engages all event participants in shared encounters that respect the acts of self-representation that verbatim theatre practice makes possible and that are honoured in the ways that we described above through headphone performance.

'I think I listened with a more open ear if that makes sense' (Rash, social worker, TVF Audio Archive, 2015–18)

During TVF performances, we have found that the 'care-full' and ethical receptivity of TVF performers and facilitators to the material gathered from our co-researchers has extended to the way audience members engage with it. Recounting his experience of attending a performance of Klaus Pohl's verbatim play *Waiting Room Germany* (1995), playwright and actor Robin Soans notes the tendency of audience members to become 'unselfconsciously involved' (Soans, quoted in Hammond and Steward, 2008: 23). This observation leads him to argue that 'in verbatim theatre the audience assumes an active rather than a passive role' and that audience members' responses are framed by a deep sense of 'responsibility' (Soans, quoted in Hammond and Steward, 2008: 23–4). This sense of active engagement has also been discussed by performance scholar Patrick Duggan with regard to the ethics of representation. In analysing theatre company Paper Birds' production of *Others* (2010), Duggan notes that though the subject of the performance was absent and therefore in danger of being misrepresented, 'the live performance event positions the spectator as ethical respondent to the presented work and the problems it is grappling with' (2013: 155). Because of its shortening of the distance between a member of the audience and the representation of the other, Duggan argues that verbatim theatre 'makes visible the ethical complexities of such representations' (2013: 158). In TVF performances, the importance of the ethics of representation that so preoccupy scholarship on verbatim theatre are animated in the performance and reception of the testimonies of young people to whom issues and practices of representation make a real difference to how their voices are heard, and to the care that they receive.

The use of the headphone technique, then, we argue, can foster recognition, respect and a sense of responsibility both in performers and among audience members towards the young people and their testimonies. Given what young people have told us about the extent to which their corporate parents are *not* listening, we think that our aesthetic and participatory practices will ultimately make an important intervention into the way that social workers reflect on young people's responses to their caregiving, especially in those moments when young people express anger, frustration or indifference. Importantly, the performances of the verbatim material disrupt the normal mode in which young people's voices are heard, and the aesthetics of the performance practice seek to position adults not as the arbitrators of the way young people's care is given, but as audience members who are invited to listen and take on some responsibility for what they hear. The performance of the testimony in TVF is thus not the end stage: the sharing and attentive listening it evokes leads to political and ethical reflection on the care of so-called 'looked-after' young people and invites further conversation, often without the urge for defensiveness or antagonism that adults might experience when they sense criticism of their practice or behaviour.

As noted above, the performances of TVF usually take place in the presence of audiences made up of social workers or other adults responsible for young people's care and education as well as the young people themselves. During our events, the testimonies are interspersed with facilitators' explanation of TVF participatory research practice. Placing young people centrally to the practice means they take an active role in choosing which testimonies

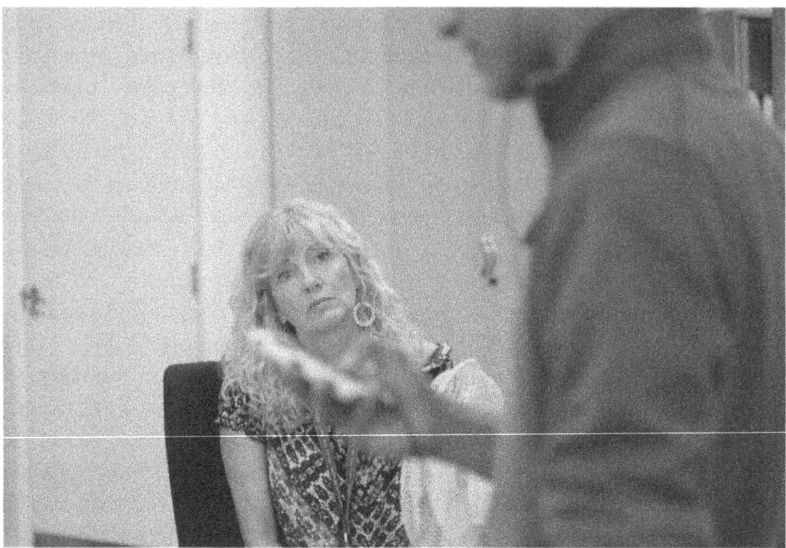

Figure 10.3 Sharing verbatim

to share and, during events, actively participate in extending discussion. This has often revolved around issues of representation, pertaining not only to the testimonies, but also to the meetings that young people must undergo as they enter care and the ways that their care identities are documented. In this sense, the performances of TVF establishes a new ground of representation under different terms, giving young people and adults the opportunity to discuss the extent to which the experiences that emerge in the testimonial material could lead to changes in areas of professional practice. By adopting an aesthetic process of caring, TVF establishes a dialogic opportunity for exchange between the young people and adults that feels very different from the confrontational exchanges that often occur in care settings. Feelings that are challenging and that might otherwise accrue blame are allowed to emerge and are mediated by the performance process itself. The caring, participatory, performative processes the project opens up generates spaces of communication that are far removed from the more transactional encounters of which young people have complained. The project's events can become an opportunity for professionals to reflect on how their own daily working practices can exacerbate the reasons why young people find it difficult to accept the care that they are offered. The young people themselves report feeling that their voices are being heard on more equal terms.

Social workers who have attended a TVF sharing have fed back that they were reminded of the impulse to care that led them to enter social work to begin with. They also tend to add that the project also reminded them of how difficult it is to do their job well or even adequately given the lack of time and resources within the system. Some social workers have also stated they intend to change their practice, by making more time to talk to a young person as an individual, for example, or trying to turn off their phone during a meeting with them so that they can listen better, or writing in a more positive light about the young people in their files. On their own, these acts may not seem significant but taken in a context that often feels dehumanising, these small acts speak volumes, not least because they tangibly demonstrate that, to some extent, the young people have finally been heard. After a conference TVF facilitated with and documented by the Young People's Peer Outreach team at a Greater London Authority conference in Care Week in 2015, one social worker delegate pledged to reach out to a care leaver she worked with: '[I promise to] meet up with a care leaver who I know is very lonely. I usually only meet him when he asks for support over a specific problem' (Peer Outreach Team, 2015). Such a change suggests the beginning of a process of 'humanising' care systems and helping to improve the quality of 'reciprocity' in the exchanges between care-experienced young people and the professionals working with them. Certainly, we hope that TVF performances can generate changes, however small, that cumulatively make it less likely that young people become distrusting of or disengaged from the adults who are their corporate parents. In pledging to make this change, this social worker committed herself to a sense of *honour*, promising to fulfil her obligations as a carer, taking responsibility for what she heard by making it action. Of course, if all corporate parents are to be empowered to identify and honour changes in their daily practice, their good intentions will both require personal commitment and need to be supported at a structural and policy level.

In facilitating this research, it has become clearer than ever to us that the 'care-full' art of attending to care-experienced young people requires extraordinary patience, persistence, subtlety and a strength of character that challenges the boundaries within which many artist practitioners or practice-based researchers tend to operate. In addition to being tender, respectful and generous, the act of giving and receiving care, we have discovered, can often feel ugly and involve psychologically and emotionally distressing aspects and incidents. We are also conscious that our own participatory practice sometimes risks replaying painful adult–child power dynamics that are all too familiar to the young people we work with and can therefore also become a further source of complaint. Yet while the realisation of a fully egalitarian and democratic practice remains an aspiration rather than a reality, we have found that TVF practices have led to effective moments of reflection for both the young people involved in the project and the adults who have been involved. Certainly, many social workers and fosters carers report shifts in understanding and perspective that seem likely to motivate them to make other small changes to their daily practices. We also hope that by sharing the issues in this way, the project helps to democratise and open up debate in relation to the problems the care system as identified above, which the young people have described as 'ugly' and from which adults might in other circumstances turn away. We believe that our methodologies, which aim to honour the experiences of care-experienced young people and share tools and opportunities for self-narration, are an important practical response to the statistics we introduced at the beginning of this chapter and to the damaging cultural narratives that situate those who need care as a drain on economic resources, where dependency is a 'condition to be overcome' (Tronto, [1993] 2009: 163). We firmly believe that far from being a deficit to society, young people who enter care have immense knowledge and potential from which we can all benefit.

If, like Csordas, we think of embodied experience as 'the starting point for analysing human participation in the cultural world' (2002: 135), then the corollary of this is that young people's affective and aesthetic transactions with carers and other adults can be used to diagnose much wider structural deficits in social relations and responsibilities. In other words, listening to the care-experienced voices of young people in public obliges adults to recognise the ugly, 'care-less' cultural structures and power dynamics that delimit a caring society and that ultimately lead many young people to believe that any dialogue with adults is both futile and inauthentic. The 'care-full' aural aesthetic of TVF is therefore not intended to create a social portrait of care for an audience of passive viewers, but to invite all those with an insight and connection with the care process to reflect collectively on how it functions and, crucially, how it can be enhanced. By facilitating an embodied somatic attentiveness to young people's voices, no matter how challenging or disturbing what they say, TVF facilitates socially responsible encounters and dialogue that perform a mode of caring that seeks to make the needs of care-experienced young people more audible and to place the onus on adults to meet their responsibilities more effectively.

Notes

1 The testimonies that are quoted in this chapter are part of *The Verbatim Formula* (TVF) Audio Archive, collected 2015–18. All names have been changed to protect and respect the identities of the original speakers.
2 The legal term for children in the 'care' of the state in the UK.
3 We are indebted in particular to Rosie Hunter and Renata Peppl at People's Palace Projects, to Priya Clarke and Sadhvi Dar at QMUL, to arts evaluator Mita Pujara, to our research assistants Shalyce Lawrence, Darcey Williamson, Michael Amaning, Henrietta Imoreh and Jerome Harvey-Agyei, and to Becs Colwell and Alfie Kingsnorth of the Peer Outreach Team at the Greater London Authority, who have all made invaluable contributions to this research.

Acts of care: applied drama, 'sympathetic presence' and person-centred nursing

Matt Jennings, Pat Deeny and Karl Tizzard-Kleister

The practices and principles of nursing have long been associated with kindness, respect and compassion (Nursing and Midwifery Council, 2015). Nursing pedagogy promotes these attributes as necessary for humanistic, 'person-centred', therapeutic practice. Professors Brendan McCormack and Tanya McCance, in the Person-Centred Nursing Framework (PCNF, see Figure 11.1), identify the importance of 'respecting the patient's rights as a person, building mutual trust and understanding and developing therapeutic relationships' (2017: 1). Such values resonate with a relational ethics of care, as described by Virginia Held (2006), Joan Tronto (2013) and Nel Noddings (2013). However, nurses sometimes struggle to maintain these principles in the face of increasingly 'mechanistic' paradigms of care (de Zulueta, 2013: 123), inadequate staffing levels and ever-changing challenges to patient safety (Louch *et al.*, 2016).

In the wake of critical reports on the UK National Health Service (NHS), there has been increasing concern about the quality of the 'patient experience'. A nationwide report into complaints against the NHS, which received more than 2,500 submissions, described 'many accounts of patients not being treated with dignity or respect' (National Archives, 2013: 16). The Belfast-based Patient Client Council Complaints Support Service, in their 2016–17 annual report, identified communication problems and staff attitude as the basis for 28.5 per cent of total complaints (PCC, 2017). The same report shows that the most effective methods for resolving complaints, all of which depend on interpersonal communication, account for 82.5 per cent of all resolutions. This evidence suggests that improved communication skills could resolve many of the issues faced within the NHS – and health

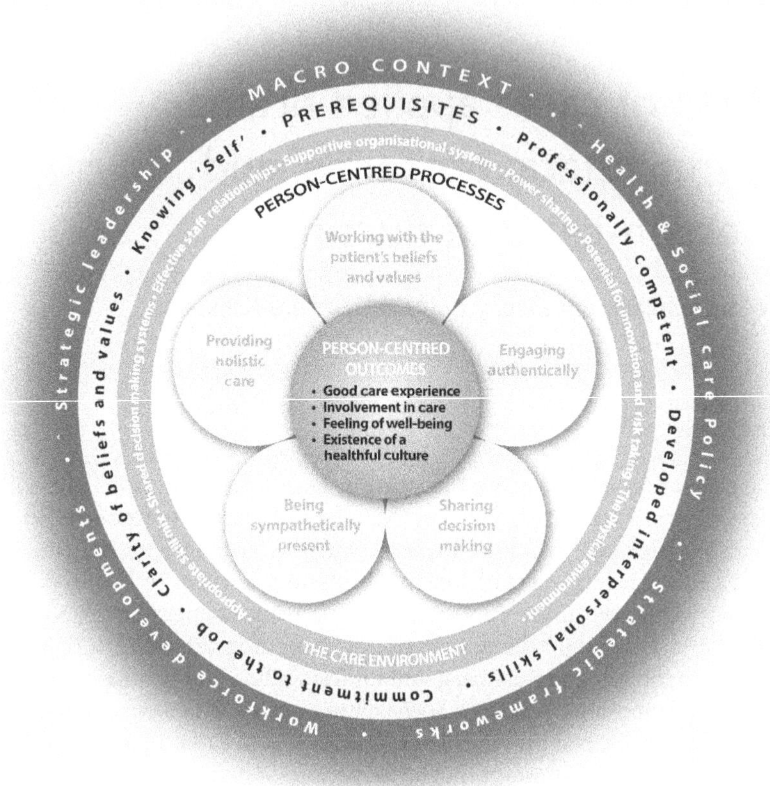

Figure 11.1 Person-centred nursing framework

care globally – yet these so-called soft skills are often neglected within medical and nursing training in favour of a focus on technical or hard skills (Monden *et al.*, 2016).

This chapter discusses an interdisciplinary teaching project at Ulster University (UU) that has attempted to address some of these issues through a combination of applied drama, actor training and simulation training. Through this pioneering collaboration, Drama lecturer Dr Matt Jennings has worked with nursing lecturers Pat Deeny and Mary Findon-Henry to improve the communication and interpersonal skills of UU adult nursing and mental health nursing students since 2013. The project initially intended simply to improve the nursing students' performance in the role-play assessments used to evaluate their clinical skills in the final year of their studies. However, as the project developed, it emerged that specific techniques derived from drama training provided nurses with a systematic approach to improving the performance of care in general.

Such a systematic approach to communication training appears to be an urgent necessity. Health care simulation is a global phenomenon, rich in potential as a pedagogical methodology (Aggarwal *et al.*, 2010), yet the research literature has repeatedly identified a need for more systematic approaches to training and evaluation in communication skills (Hallenbeck, 2012; Levett-Jones and Lapkin, 2014). A 2016 'review of reviews' covering dozens of international studies in the field of health care simulation, identified a widespread need for 'stronger simulation designs, standardization of the process from prebrief to debrief, and faculty training', particularly to address poor interpersonal communication (Doolen *et al.*, 2016: 301). Research in the field 'clearly indicates a need for specific training to address such deficiencies in communication [...] such training should start from undergraduate level and continue into postgraduate professional development, involving as many professions as realistically possible' (Siassakos *et al.*, 2011: 148).

Findings from this project suggest that drama training for health professionals could help to address such deficiencies. Drama training can provide a framework for reflecting and improving on interpersonal interactions – in simulation, in clinical practice and in everyday life – and a set of techniques with which to practise related skills. Our experience suggests that drama training for health professionals has great potential to improve current approaches to health care simulation and the performance of care within the wider health sector. This collaborative combination of applied drama with clinical skills training supports both cognitive and emotional approaches to improving communication and care relationships.

The chapter begins by outlining the place of this project within the broader field of arts and health, exploring the gaps and intersections between applied drama and health care simulation. It will then discuss some key principles of contemporary nursing pedagogy, such as the PCNF and 'sympathetic presence' (McCormack and McCance, 2010: 3). After this, it will examine key practices and moments that have emerged during the delivery of the project, as part of a qualitative investigation of its outcomes and impact.

Arts and health

In terms of interdisciplinary practice, arts and health (or 'arts in health') has become a rapidly expanding area of research and practice (White, 2009; Baxter and Low, 2017; Fancourt, 2017). According to Mike White (2009), creative arts interventions in health care settings help to build relationships, maintain resilience, create more comfortable and user-friendly clinical environments, and support holistic approaches to care. Arts activities are a means of 'nurturing and sustaining meaningful human relationships' in support of individual and social health and well-being (White, 2009: 3).

The UK government All-Party Parliamentary Group (APPG) report *Creative Health* (2017) presents substantial evidence that participation in the arts can be beneficial for mental and physical health, recovery and well-being. Veronica Baxter and Katherine Low (2017) argue for a deeper understanding of the impact that social factors (such as economic disadvantage, environmental pollution, geographic and psychological isolation) can have on health outcomes. From their perspective, arts interventions should aim to address social inequalities, political structures and other contextual factors, as well as supporting well-being through participation.

Emma Brodzinski (2010) examines a wide range of performance-based practices within the field of arts in health, including theatre in health education and health care simulation. Brodzinski discusses role play for training and evaluation, which has become a core element of health care training globally. One common approach is to use actors to play patients (known as 'standardised patients' or 'patient actors'), an internationally established practice since the 1960s (Barrows, 1993). For instance, Loth *et al.* (2015) describe a long history of specialised training for patient actors in Australia since 1975. The use of such patient actors allows health care students to simulate the practitioner–patient relationship in a consequence-free environment. This approach has become crucial to the assessment of students and practitioners of medicine and nursing. For instance, all UK-based health professionals must demonstrate their clinical skills through evaluation processes like the Objective Structured Clinical Examination (OSCE), which includes elements of simulation and role play.

There has been little crossover to date between the specific practice of health care simulation and the broader social practices of applied drama. Applied drama interventions that do engage with health care training often seek to support the development of creativity and empathy in general terms, in line with the idea that the medical humanities can help to humanise medicine (White, 2009; Baxter and Low, 2017; Fancourt, 2017). Yet few arts interventions have attempted to use applied drama techniques to address specific clinical problems in the performance of health care.

Some approaches have sought to narrow the gap between these potentially complementary performative techniques. The APPG report *Creative Health* (2017) cites the Performing Medicine project, developed by Clod Ensemble in London, as a rare example of an approach that involves close collaboration between artists and health practitioners to improve skills in clinical practice. Performing Medicine employs visual artists, dance and theatre practitioners to work with medical professionals, exploring clinical experiences, in order to develop new ways to resolve communication issues. These interdisciplinary teams use the circle of care model to improve 'nonverbal communication, self-care, spatial awareness, and appreciation of the person with an emphasis on understanding the perspectives and contexts of others' (Willson and Jaye, 2017: 643). Similarly, Reeves and Neilson (2018) discuss a project that used forum theatre to present interactive versions of simulated scenarios in palliative care, to improve nursing students' communication skills. In Sweden, the drama caring and reflection in nursing education model (DRACAR) has used drama workshops alongside traditional nursing teaching to address gaps between nursing theory and praxis. Students bring their own experiences of delivering or receiving health care into workshop sessions, where they use 'drama techniques such as improvisation, role-play, forum-theatre, and nursing-play' to rehearse alternative actions and behaviours (Ekebergh *et al.*, 2004: 625). Such arts and drama interventions could potentially begin to bridge the gap between arts in health practices and conventional health care simulation.

Health care simulation

The term 'health care simulation' is an umbrella term for all forms of simulation used in the preparation and training of health care students and professionals. There is abundant evidence that simulation training can improve clinical skills. For instance, Victor *et al.* (2017) have found that simulation training for nurses led to improvements in knowledge levels, critical thinking and clinical judgement. Health care simulation increasingly incorporates theatrical production elements, such as costumes, props, make-up and automated mannequins (Lateef, 2010; McAllister *et al.*, 2013; Reid-Searl *et al.*, 2014). Lateef notes a plethora of 'new techniques and equipment' improving practitioners' confidence and skills while avoiding patient risks (2010: 348–9). Mannequins for medical simulation are increasingly sophisticated, automated and technically specific; some are designed for needle insertion and airway management or feature rubber orifices for catheter insertion. However, a reliance on robotic mannequins can reinforce mechanistic paradigms of treatment, as against more holistic approaches (Brodzinski, 2010; de Zulueta, 2013; Reid-Searl *et al.*, 2014). Despite the technological innovations, the area of greatest need is still training in communication and interpersonal skills, both with patients and within health care teams (Siassakos *et al.*, 2011; Hallenbeck, 2012; Levett-Jones and Lapkin, 2014).

Brodzinski has also observed that there are limitations to the effectiveness of health care simulation in terms of credibility and commitment, arguing that role play can seem 'hyper-real', leaving students 'painfully aware of the false nature of the scenarios' (2010: 123–4). One consequence of this is that 'students may realise the setting is artificial and fail to fully engage, attend or remember' (McAllister *et al.*, 2013: 1453). In addition, Fidment (2012) highlights the intense levels of stress and anxiety experienced by students subjected to the OSCE examination process. While these studies focus on deficiencies in terms of realism and performance anxiety, other studies (see Bach and Grant, 2017; Gault *et al.*, 2017) urge a greater focus on kindness, respect and compassion within simulation training. For this to occur, health care simulation needs to promote a shift away from the primacy of technical skills and recognise the importance of interpersonal and communication skills, treating 'the person as a whole, concerned with the interrelationship of body, mind and spirit' (McEvoy and Duffy, 2008: 414).

PCP, sympathetic presence and empathy

One prime example of a more holistic approach to nursing is person-centred practice (PCP). The PCP approach hinges on the primary concept of 'personhood', whereby an individual is treated as someone with his or her own characteristics, values, beliefs, attitudes, unique life story and future goals. PCP models, such as the PCNF, provide guidance for inciting and sustaining cultural changes in health care environments. The framework addresses 'person-centredness' throughout the whole system of care, considering such *macro* elements as 'care environment' and 'health and social care policy', as well as *micro*-level factors, such as 'shared decision making' and 'providing holistic care' (McCormack and McCance, 2010: 3)

The framework also addresses empathy and its place within nursing practice, suggesting the alternative term 'sympathetic presence'. The PCNF defines sympathetic presence as 'an engagement that recognises the uniqueness and value of the individual, by appropriately responding to cues that maximise coping resources through the recognition of important agendas in their life' (McCormack and McCance, 2017: 102). When sympathetically present the nurse is 'in the moment' (McCormack and McCance, 2010: 104), paying attention to how other people feel, without trying to assume or share their emotional or physical state. As McCormack and McCance describe it, sympathetic presence involves a recognition that a conventional understanding of 'empathy' (i.e. to 'walk in another person's shoes') is neither desirable nor possible, as one person cannot 'fully comprehend another individual's particular experience' (2010: 102).

Meanwhile, attempts to improve the capacity for empathy among health care students have encountered significant challenges. For example, a study conducted by Nunes *et al.* (2011) showed that self-reported empathy scores for undergraduate medical and nursing students, based on questionnaire responses, significantly declined during the period of their training. There is also evidence that some attempts to improve empathy within health care education have been counterproductive. A study conducted by Ward *et al.* (2012) discovered that students exposed to situations designed to improve empathy, including interactions with real patients, had lower empathy scores after the interventions. A study by Heggestad and colleagues discovered that undergraduate nursing students appeared to suppress their personal responses to challenging clinical situations, through strategies of 'emotional immunisation' (2016: 11). Student responses became increasingly limited to the realm of 'cognitive empathy', 'the capacity to understand and imagine the lived experiences of other persons', as against 'affective empathy', which is 'both a bodily and spontaneous emotional experience' (Heggestad *et al.*, 2016: 2). These students, perhaps understandably, were better prepared to consider another person's situation through rational and practical understanding, rather than allowing themselves an emotional reaction to the suffering of another.

Nursing students and practitioners who resist or reject affective empathy might be trying to manage the demands of the emotional labour of care (Smith, 1992). Such emotional labour is seen as a crucial aspect of the nursing profession; yet it rarely features as an explicit element of traditional nursing education. The decline in empathy scores, as nurses try to immunise themselves against their patients' pain, may be a tactic to avoid emotional burnout. Heggestad *et al.* (2016) observe that although 'affective empathy' may be desirable, students can often experience 'empathic over-arousal', a term attributed to Hoffman (2000: 13), whereby 'affectivity becomes so overwhelming that it becomes uncontrollable for the person and clouds his or her judgments' (Heggestad *et al.*, 2016: 10). The question for this chapter is whether practical training in sympathetic presence can develop skills in both cognitive and affective empathy, encouraging nursing students to engage with the patient experience while supporting their own capacity to cope.

Alternatively, as the project has developed, we have considered whether it might be appropriate to abandon the conventional idea of empathy completely, as some drama practitioners have done. Political and applied theatre artists, since the early twentieth century, have rejected the perception that drama should generate empathy through identification with a hero, as originally suggested by Aristotle. Both Bertolt Brecht and Augusto Boal asserted that the traditional Aristotelian focus on the fate of the tragic individual – whereby audiences should identify with the suffering of the protagonist and cathartically 'feel their pain' – is coercive, limiting the capacity for independent critical thinking, social agency and collective action (Brecht, 1978; Boal, 1998; Nicholson, 2005).

Boal, trying to avoid such fixed narrative functions, developed theatrical techniques that allow spectators to intervene in the onstage action and take an active role in changing the story (1998: 33–5, 102–4). He titled this approach to socially conscious, interactive theatre making 'theatre of the oppressed' inspired by Paolo Freire's 'pedagogy of the oppressed' (Freire, 2000). Forum theatre, a core element of the theatre of the oppressed approach, is a format in which audience members can engage with performances devised to represent their own challenging experiences. We will discuss this technique in more detail later in the chapter. Both Brecht and Boal called for dramatic forms that encourage critical discourse and pragmatic community action, for theatre that supports actual social change.

One way that applied drama can transform health care training is to encourage a shift in the conception of care from fixed *adjectival* forms (such as 'I am a caring person' or the 'care system') towards more fluid and relational *verb* forms (such as 'I care for you' or 'we care for each other'). This shift supports a mutual and pragmatic recognition of vulnerability, interdependence and contingency, reflecting the debate between the paradigm of an ethics of care and more traditional virtue ethics. For example, Held (2006) characterises virtue ethics as emphasising the inherent attributes of the individual – the virtuous traits that an individual possesses – rather than the fundamental interdependence of human beings, encountered in the relational act of care.

Applied drama can help to understand the performance of care as a set of relational tasks, based on transitive verbs (e.g. 'to reassure', 'to comfort', 'to observe', 'to listen'). The performance techniques of Constantin Stanislavski (discussed in more detail later in this chapter) analyse the subtext of any given situation – the meaning of what is actually happening between people – as a set of such transitive actions and reactions. Basic actor training can improve the performance of such actions. In the process, actors can learn to attend more closely to the responses of other people. This 'attentiveness' is a key element of Tronto's model of care ethics, which posits it as a primary necessity in the delivery of care (2013: 34). The cultivation of conscious attentiveness can help carers to recognise and clarify their intentions (both conscious and subconscious) and the consequences of their actions within the caring relationship.

Framing sympathetic presence as a relational practice of attention and intention in the performance of care, means that it can be taught and learnt as a specific set of transferable skills, using time-honoured techniques drawn from actor training. While sympathetic presence is only one factor in the PCNF, it is the process whereby carers 'establish a therapeutic relationship', crucially described as 'the fabric that weaves together other person-centred processes' (McCormack and McCance, 2010: 103). Yet there is little detail in the research and teaching literature to explain how the process of sympathetic presence might actually be applied in practice. Acting techniques can improve communication in health care simulation and clinical practice, by providing a framework for understanding sympathetic presence in pragmatic terms, as a set of skills based in attentive interaction.

In keeping with the dialogical, contextual and relational conception of care, we have engaged in a continuous process of pedagogical collaboration and shared reflection with students and staff, from both nursing and drama, adapting to the needs and perspectives expressed by the participants and co-researchers as the project has developed. In this way, we have tried to model the processes of person-centredness in our teaching and research, as well as practice. The next section of the chapter highlights some of the key developments in this methodology as it has emerged over the last five years.

Developing practice in action: processes and moments

Early stages: role play and forum theatre 2013–15

This interdisciplinary project has seen many changes, adaptations and breakthroughs. It began with a workshop in June 2013, introducing UU nursing lecturers and tutorial assistants to applied drama, as a methodology to enhance their creativity in teaching. Dr Matt Jennings (first author of this chapter) facilitated the drama workshop. Senior nursing lecturer Pat Deeny (co-author of this chapter) saw the potential of drama training as an element of nursing pedagogy and suggested that it might help nursing students to perform their final year role-play assessments. While nursing students had been playing doctors, patients and family members, as well as nursing staff, in their simulation scenarios, many had been struggling with performance anxiety, particularly in front of a camera, and some found it hard to take the simulation seriously. Jennings and Deeny believed that drama might help the students with these issues and planned a workshop to explore the possibilities.

Initially, from September 2013, applied drama was introduced within the curriculum of a compulsory third-year nursing module, 'The Safe and Effective Nurse'. The module requires groups of nursing students to present a role-play scenario, based on real-world encounters, in order to demonstrate their technical and communication skills after a six-week period of clinical placement. Groups of eight nursing students are allocated one of three fictional scenarios, each of which includes three phases in the treatment of an individual patient, and are encouraged to prepare and rehearse their presentation before the assessment. The simulations are filmed on a fixed camera; afterwards, the students watch the footage and reflect on their performances in an essay assignment. In early iterations of the module, students had consistently expressed concern about the presence of the camera and a lack of belief in the verisimilitude of the scenarios and were often self-conscious about watching themselves on screen.

In September 2013, 240 final-year nursing students attended drama workshops facilitated by Matt Jennings, in groups of 60 students per one-hour session. The aim of the workshop was to ease their performance anxiety and support their ability to commit to a convincing realism in their role-play scenarios. Each workshop began with basic relaxation and breathing exercises drawn from yoga and martial arts, centring the participants in their bodies, followed by warm-up drama activities drawn from Boal's *Games for Actors and Non-Actors* (2002). The students then explored exercises associated with the 'method of physical action', as developed by Constantin Stanislavski (Carnicke, 2010: 16). While Boal is probably the most influential practitioner in the field (Babbage, 2004), Stanislavski's approaches to acting and actor training are less commonly associated with applied drama. The nursing students engaged in basic exercises in developing their ability to perform 'actions' and 'objectives', according to Stanislavski's understanding of sub-text (Benedetti, 1998). As mentioned above, an 'action' is a transitive verb, something that someone attempts to 'do' to someone else, while the 'objective' is the intended goal of those actions, often understood as the need or desire of a specific character within a set of given circumstances (Benedetti, 1998: 6). Through dramatic improvisation, nursing students explored playing actions on each other (such as 'I reassure you', 'I challenge you' and 'I observe you'), with clear objectives (such as 'I want you to trust me' or 'I want to get an accurate diagnosis'), within such given circumstances as a busy emergency ward or a patient's home.

Student responses following this introductory session were encouraging, although the lecturers felt that a more substantial intervention would be necessary in order to provide more context and explanation of its relevance to clinical practice. In the following academic year (2014–15), UG drama students taking an optional 'Theatre and Community' module joined the workshops and collaborated with nursing students as co-creators in a devised performance.

After an initial set of drama workshops with the full cohort of 220 nursing students, a small group of drama students devised a short forum theatre play, based on the experiences of a subgroup of nursing students during their clinical placements. In forum theatre, audiences watch a performance based on real-world problems encountered by members of their own community or collaboratively developed with other groups facing similar challenges. After the first presentation of the play, the actors perform selected scenes again; during this replay version, audience members can stop the action at any point and replace an actor in the scene, to try to change the outcome. In this way, forum theatre audiences transform themselves from passive spectators to active 'spect-actors' (Boal, 1998), enhancing their capacity for creative agency, through imagining and practising possible solutions to real-world problems.

From September to December of 2014, five drama students developed a forum theatre play drawn from weekly communication with twenty-five volunteers from nursing. The play presented the character of Jane as its protagonist, a nursing student on clinical placement who has experienced bullying, inappropriate behaviour and inadequate instruction from senior colleagues. In one scene of the forum theatre play, Jane encountered a character from one of the simulation scenarios presented in the 'Safe and Effective Nurse' module, John-Jo McKitray. According to the brief for the simulation scenario, John-Jo is an eighty-one-year-old farmer from North Antrim in the early stages of dementia. In the early phases of the scenario, John-Jo (played by one of the nursing students) has had a fall and fractured his hip, setting off a traumatic process of pain, confusion and distress over the following phases.

During one of the later phases of the scenario, a confused and vulnerable John-Jo demands to see his wife. John-Jo's wife has been dead for twenty years and the nursing students treating him are aware of this. In the simulation assessments, this moment often stumped the nursing students; later, watching the filmed footage of themselves, many realised that they had performed unhelpful actions or not paid enough attention to the patient in the moment. Some had lied to John-Jo, telling him that his wife was on her way or simply ignored his distress while concentrating on their clinical tasks. At this point, they began to understand the importance of sympathetic presence. This insensitivity was compounded by the surprise twist in the scenario – a moment of dramatic interaction not included in the brief – in which John-Jo's son or daughter (also played by a nursing student) suddenly arrives and becomes outraged that they have misled her father by telling him that his wife is still alive. After watching the footage, many students realised that their own discomfort had affected their performance of care, particularly when they tried to avoid the interpersonal challenges of the situation. Yet despite these realisations, many nursing students struggled to identify specific methods to overcome the challenge. The drama students decided to include the John-Jo scenario in the forum play, to see whether nursing students might be able to share constructive ideas for alternative courses of action.

The drama group performed the forum play for the third-year nursing students at the end of the semester, after the completion of their role-play assessments. In the final scene, Jane struggled to handle John-Jo's demand to see his wife and his escalating distress. The hospital staff were either unable or unwilling to help. The joker, or master of ceremonies (Luke Merritt, who contributed to the development of this chapter) encouraged nursing students from the audience to take over the role of Jane and demonstrate how they might handle these challenging 'given circumstances'. A few brave 'spect-actors' experimented with various strategies to change the outcome, while the drama student playing John-Jo (Harrison McCallum, who also contributed to this chapter) improvised and reacted to their actions.

One nursing student played a particularly effective set of actions, achieving their objective of soothing John-Jo while maintaining his trust. Instead of lying to him or rejecting the request to see his wife, the nursing student first spent some time engaging with John-Jo on a non-verbal level, attending to him 'in the moment' as he repeatedly asked for Margaret. During a pause in John-Jo's refrain, the nursing student responded: 'So, I hear that you're a farmer up in Antrim? How's that going these days?' The actor playing John-Jo stopped for a moment to consider his answer. At this point, the audience of nursing students erupted in laughter, and then applause. During the subsequent conversation about farming, the nurse guided John-Jo back to his bed, providing an instructive example to a hapless doctor character in the process, leading to further laughter. This laughter seemed to come from the moment of recognition, seeing a nursing student playing identifiable actions to achieve clear objectives; it also reflected the potential for aesthetic delight in live performance, when neither actor nor audience know what is going to happen next.

The value of this moment was not just in the creation of a comic scene. The nursing students witnessed one of their peers successfully demonstrate person-centred care in action, through sympathetic presence, within a familiar yet challenging clinical situation. In doing so, the 'spect-actor' showed that nursing students could demonstrate exemplary communication skills despite their relatively low status in the hospital hierarchy. In addition, the momentary pause provided a flash of non-verbal communication to the whole audience; it represented an eruption of uncontrolled and unpredictable agency, of 'liveness' in the performance of care, releasing the collective anxiety about technical competence. This performance of relational action showed that a carer could practice person-centred care while achieving clinical tasks in a challenging environment – crucially, in an unrehearsed, non-coded and spontaneously creative way. This was the point when Jennings and Deeny realised that applied drama had the potential to provide a set of techniques for teaching sympathetic presence as a specific practice, rather than a general concept or an inherent attribute of the professional carer. Prior to this, UU nursing staff and students had struggled to define sympathetic presence beyond the abstract PCNF definitions discussed above. Part of the purpose of this chapter is to suggest a fuller definition of sympathetic presence that bridges the gap between theory and practice.

Developing practice: 'presence', 'attention' and 'intention' 2016–18

The role-play assessments in 2013–14 and 2014–15, as well as the forum theatre presentation in 2014, confirmed that applied drama could both ease students' anxiety and provide a toolkit to support their understanding of the performance of person-centred care. We continued to develop the principles of the toolkit over the next two years, adapting our approach in response to feedback from students in their module evaluations, as well as tutorial assistants involved in the assessing of the simulations. Some nursing students had requested an earlier introduction to applied drama, in order to give them time to understand the principles and techniques before the pressure of final-year assessments. In 2016–17, the intervention was adapted to include an introductory drama workshop in the final semester of the second year of the nursing programme, to prepare students before their simulation assessments in the following semester. The same cohort received two further drama sessions during the first semester of their third (and final) year, prior to the role-play assessments. Matt Jennings delivered these workshops with the support of third-year drama students studying a module in 'Performance and Health'. The extra workshops also introduced basic techniques of puppetry and object theatre, using these skills to animate medical mannequins. We do not have space within this chapter to discuss the experiment with applied puppetry, although this will be the subject of a future publication.

In 2017–18, the two third-year workshops lasted an hour and a half, as against the previous sessions of forty-five minutes. Participant numbers for each workshop were also decreased (from sixty nursing students to thirty-five), to allow more time and attention for small groups and individual students. There was an extra follow-up session during the final week before their simulation assessments, where drama staff and students provided brief, but detailed, feedback to small groups of nursing students rehearsing their scenarios. The role of the drama team was to remind nursing students to play actions and objectives, paying attention to their interpersonal relations with patients, family members and each other. At this point, many nursing students had become primarily concerned with performing technical skills correctly, with a lesser focus on communication.

Next we will discuss four individual exercises from the training programme in detail. In particular, it will examine moments that have emerged during the delivery of the workshops that have stimulated significant critical reflection on the function of the methodology. These four moments challenged our thinking in ways that were productive and profound, yet occasionally problematic. These moments highlight the potentially fruitful intersections and collisions between nursing practice, care ethics, sympathetic presence and drama training. The first three moments are described from the point of view of co-author Karl Tizzard-Kleister, who has been researching this project for an interdisciplinary doctoral thesis since 2017 and are extracts from a first-hand report of Karl's observations while participating in the workshops led by Matt Jennings in June and September 2017, as well as his experience of facilitating an introductory workshop himself in June 2018. They describe the experiences of workshop participants as they encounter the three key concepts of 'presence', 'attention' and 'intention'.

Presence

After a brief introduction welcoming the nursing students to the session, the workshop begins with breathing exercises designed for relaxation and centring. The groups quickly find a collective awareness in exercises drawn from Aikido martial arts, which focus on synchronising breath and movement; the entire group simultaneously enact the same movements and breathing patterns. For every group who perform this exercise, an awkward and profound silence follows the final collective out-breath. This moment is held for as long as possible. This moment and atmosphere, the facilitator explains, represents 'presence'. The group are encouraged to offer what they think 'presence' might mean, beginning the dialogical learning that recurs throughout the workshop. Participants have the opportunity to explore their ideas, to embody them and reflect on them. Students tentatively offer thoughts on what 'presence' might be. Some say it is 'not having your mind elsewhere', others use the nursing terminology of 'sympathetic presence'. Most groups come to define presence as 'being here and now', which is shown to be related to the concept of 'stage presence', and indeed illustrates bodily what sympathetic presence might feel like. (Tizzard-Kleister, unpublished notes, 2017)

Attention

The concept of 'attention' is introduced through an 'image theatre' exercise (Boal, 1998) whereby two people stand still in freeze frame representing a handshake. This then changes into an image of one person turning their back on the other. These images provide a stimulus to discuss their understanding of space, physicality and relationality. It further deepens the engagement with dialogical pedagogy, as participants realise that each person's interpretation of the image is distinct and yet valid. After this, the group spilt into pairs and engage in activities, such as mirroring and Colombian hypnosis (Boal, 2002), which involve a leader and a follower. The students explore the sensitivity required to allow the follower to follow, as well as the consequences of certain actions as they explore and exchange leader/follower roles. The students express an embodied experience of control, resistance and power. Some participants find relinquishing control difficult, others say that being in control felt uncomfortable. Group discussions focus on how they may be required to take control of difficult situations or relinquish control to others in certain clinical circumstances. This consideration of the ability to take and relinquish control may allow them to recognise when patients might want to take control of their own care or when they might need another person, such as a nurse, to share this control with them. (Tizzard-Kleister, unpublished notes, 2017)

Intention

The next step in the workshop focuses on the importance of conscious and unconscious 'intentions' in interactions between subjects. In non-verbal activities and short improvisations, participants practice playing actions with objectives. One scenario involves two nurses ignoring a silent patient, who is begging for help, but is motionless and can only communicate with their eyes, while the nurses discuss what each other is wearing. Many of the students note that it is startlingly easy to ignore a silent person, although their 'presence' never entirely goes away. The interactions build in complexity, as the students explore a variety of tactics to achieve their 'intentions'. 'Given circumstances' are then added to these interactions, creating situations for the small groups to recreate, such as 'explaining complex treatment in a busy ward' or 'giving bad news to an anxious relative'.

The participants often remark surprise when they discover that what they say does not always convey what they mean in these situations. Those playing the patient characters are equally surprised at what they can learn from their peers' performance of care. For instance, the use of a patient's first name, though indeed a personal touch, can alienate the patient if it is overused or begins to sound formulaic. Similarly, physical contact may or may not be appropriate in different circumstances and with different people. This is interesting, because most of the students believe that sympathetic presence depends on maintaining eye contact, performing therapeutic touch or addressing the patient by their first name. Only when a student tries to play counter-intuitive or taboo actions, such as to ignore or intimidate a patient, do they realise how common – and damaging – these behaviours might be. In this way, the students are better able to understand the need to be sympathetically present, attentive and responsive in the moment. (Tizzard-Kleister, unpublished notes, 2017)

'I could be hurt by you'

The following section draws on the reflections of all the authors, in relation to a particularly powerful and affective exercise – known as 'I could be hurt by you' – that distils the essence of the approach and provides an intensely interpersonal encounter of shared vulnerability. It provokes an embodied and emotional understanding of what it means to depend on others for safety and well-being – an uncomfortable subjective position, yet deeply relevant to performing care in clinical practice.

The delivery of some drama exercises has remained the same since the beginning of the project (such as 'mirrors' and 'hypnosis'); others have been regularly revised and adapted at various stages, including 'I could be hurt by you'. This activity has been used in almost every workshop since the beginning of the applied drama intervention. The intention of the exercise is to create a moment of affect, a short performative act embracing an aesthetic of mutuality and care (Thompson, 2015). Matt Jennings first encountered it while training as an actor at the University of Western Sydney in the early 1990s and has adapted it for use in a wide range of community contexts ever since.

The activity involves pairs of partners, holding hands and looking into each other's eyes for the duration of the exercise. The facilitator asks the partners to think about each other's eyes in various ways – to imagine that they are looking into the eyes of a baby or the eyes of a very old person. They are also asked to love them, then to hate them and then to let their imagination run wild. Finally, they are asked to speak a simple line of dialogue to each other: 'I could be hurt by you'. They can deliver the line any way they wish, while continuing to hold hands and maintain eye contact. They must say it at least once, but they can repeat it as many times as they like. After some time, when all of the participants have uttered this phrase at least once, they then acknowledge the end of the task with a hug, a handshake or whatever exchange feels mutually comfortable for each person.

Some participants in the initial sessions in 2014 and 2015 reported feeling uncomfortable after the exercise. These participants were generally unable to articulate specific reasons for feeling this way, but some said that they felt intensely emotional after the exercise. For some, it was a profoundly moving experience; for others, it was awkward and confronting. Some said that it was both meaningful and uncomfortable at the same time. By 2017, it was clear that the project team needed to be sensitive to the range of potential responses to the exercise and to ensure that participants did not leave feeling hurt or troubled by the task. The value of the exercise as an aesthetic experience of care is difficult to define, but impossible to overlook. We wanted to ensure that the exercise aligned with what we intended to communicate – the interdependence and shared vulnerability of the caring relationship, and the emotional connection required to build such relationships.

Before the 2017–18 nursing workshops, the project team considered the feedback from previous years and extensively discussed the ethics and affective impact of this particular exercise, agreeing that we should adapt it in some way and provide 'trigger warnings' about the emotional risks. In addition, participants were told that if the actions 'to love' and 'to hate' seemed too confronting, then they could try to play the actions 'accept' or 'reject' instead. During the introductory workshop in June 2017, Matt

Jennings also added an extra element of instruction, in a moment of improvised facilitation. Instead of ending on the statement 'I could be hurt by you', he asked the participants to follow this with 'and you could look after me'.

The addition of the statement 'and you could look after me', after 'I could be hurt by you', acknowledges that while we might have the power to hurt each other, we also have the capacity to do the opposite. The sensation, as well as admission, of vulnerability is an integral part of the exercise. Students are encouraged to recognise and embrace the *necessity* of emotional interdependence with their partner. Students anecdotally and observationally responded favourably to the adaptations.

This simple task is still challenging for participants. They are asked to 'stay with the trouble', to borrow the evocative title of Donna Haraway's 2016 book. 'Staying with the trouble' means that we cannot solve problems independently of the messy and entangled contexts in which they occur. 'I could be hurt by you' asks participants to admit their own vulnerability and recognise the vulnerability of another in an affective relational exchange, in an aesthetic performance of an ethic of care.

Nursing is not traditionally associated with taking conscious risks; safety and contingency are the priorities in an intensely high-stakes profession (Dingwall *et al.*, 2017). However, practitioners are required to be open in their communication with those they care and are often required to advocate on their behalf. As the theorists of person-centred practice explain (McCormack and McCance, 2010, 2017), this is not possible until a nurse first 'knows themselves' and is comfortable with their own vulnerabilities. Feminist thinkers (see for example, Butler *et al.*, 2016), argue for a re-evaluation of vulnerability, away from ideas of victimhood and passivity. Political philosopher Martha Fineman (2008) suggests that far from being a state of lower status and victimhood, vulnerability is in fact a key ontological feature of being human.

Nicholson defines applied drama as providing a creative space where 'people feel safe enough to take risks and to allow themselves and others to experience vulnerability' (2005: 129). If nursing education struggles to provide such a 'safe space' for students to challenge the perception of vulnerability as a sign of 'victimhood', perhaps applied drama can provide the techniques and spaces to explore the emotional risk of 'person-centred' nursing practice. Through drama, nursing students can embrace their own vulnerability in safety.

Conclusion

This chapter makes the argument for collaboration between nursing and drama pedagogies, in order to deepen students' understanding of the relationships that they build with those in their care and provide methods to enhance their communication skills, both emotionally and cognitively. The scope for the application of drama training to health care simulation, within a person-centred curriculum, is clear and has great potential for further development.

This approach asks nursing students to develop skills in sympathetic presence through health care simulation, in order to enhance their ability to engage in caring relationships that are compassionate as well as technically competent. This collaborative approach to health care simulation and applied drama practice promotes an understanding of care as a fluid and formative relationship, not just a clinical task. Drama pedagogies can provide novel and effective methods to improve the performance of person-centred nursing. Training in these skills can also support the professional and personal resilience of the health practitioner. Drama training can provide opportunities to learn to look after oneself, as well as the people one cares for, by helping us to come to terms with the limits of our capacities, to acknowledge our shared vulnerability and to 'rehearse the transformation' of the caring relationship.

Taking care of the laundry
in care homes

Jayne Lloyd

This chapter discusses how artists' performative engagements with processes of caring for objects can establish new models of relational care with and for older people residing in care homes, especially those living with dementia. The chapter focuses on an art project I created and led in a care home in south London in 2014 as part of my PhD.[1] In my examination of what this project set out to do and what it achieved, I apply Fisher and Tronto's (1990) definition of 'caring about' and 'caregiving' to processes of caring for objects. I consider how relationships with everyday objects and certain acts of domestic labour became meaningful acts of self-care for an elderly care home resident living with dementia who participated in the project. Fisher and Tronto define caring about as involving 'paying attention to our world in such a way that we focus on continuity, maintenance, and repair' (1990: 40). They define caregiving as the labour involved in that maintenance and repair and include objects in the scope of what can be cared for, but it is not the focus of their research. In this chapter, I argue that the care of objects could form an important part of care ethics because the performance of the processes involved in their maintenance and repair can be an important vehicle for caring for the self and other people. I want to make the claim that to build a more caring, nurturing – identity-enhancing – life in care homes, residents need to experience a performed engagement with the care of objects that was part of their everyday routines before they entered institutionalised care.

The project I discuss included a series of ten-hour-long weekly sessions that took place in a care home living room. It was attended by a group of eight residents and two paid caregivers. It was the second in a series of five projects I designed in response to sessions I observed that were delivered by the Age Exchange Theatre Trust who developed 'reminiscence arts' sessions. The reminiscence arts sessions combined a range of arts practices, including drama, dance, music and visual arts, and aimed to support individuals and groups of care home residents and professional caregivers in their exploration and communication of stories about their lives. I observed that many of the stories told verbally or embodied in actions and interactions drew on everyday domestic activities such as gardening, cooking and cleaning that involved caring for objects and environments as well as people. My research aimed to interrogate and further develop aspects of Age Exchange's performance of everyday practices and develop an understanding of how the tasks and activities people regularly perform as part of their daily lives could become artistic practices. I wanted to understand how these practices retained a relevance to people's identity once they had moved into care, where the tasks involved in maintaining the care home were usually performed for them instead of by or with them. I designed and delivered five of my own projects themed around different everyday practices: doing the laundry, walking in different weather and environments, cooking, walking a dog and sharing meals. In the sessions, I brought in objects and materials used in these everyday practices and created simple sensory environments that evoked the lighting, texture, colour and smell of aspects of the processes and environments in which they took place. These were combined with arts materials and art-making activities.

I am a visual artist and researcher and collaborated with Christina Argyropoulou on the project, a dancer who facilitated some of the Age Exchange sessions I observed. The theme of the project was walking in different weather conditions and environments but this chapter focuses on how Betty, a care home resident living with dementia who participated in the project, introduced a different theme by performing the act of doing the laundry in the sessions.[2] My first PhD project focused on laundry processes, but it was not a theme I expected to engage with in this project. The following is a description of how Betty interpreted arts materials and props included in the sessions for other purposes to perform actions involved in doing the laundry and other cleaning processes:

> Christina Argyropoulou and I hung a white sheet up in front of the small group of care home residents, back lit it and began moving cut-outs of people, plants and animals behind it to create silhouettes. It was part of a session themed around night-time. Before we had finished our story, Betty, a member of the group, who, only seconds earlier, was laughing and watching the shadows intently, stood up and began unpegging the sheet. Understanding her action from previous sessions, we brought our performance to a close and transitioned into folding the sheet with Betty. I took the other end of the sheet and followed her lead in shaking and folding it, before thanking her and putting it away on a table with the other props and art materials. Betty's folding of fabric formed part of most of our ten sessions together. We would facilitate an interaction with a piece of dark-coloured bejewelled fabric to evoke a starry sky or blue fabric to evoke a summer's day or swimming pool and, at some point, Betty would get up and that would mark the end of the performance and the start of a new one that involved clearing away. Betty never verbally told us anything about her actions; we knew, however, from Betty's other interactions with objects and materials in the sessions, for example, using paint sponges to clean

umbrellas or sweeping up flour we were shaking over stencils, that it was a form of domestic cleaning and, in the case of the sheet folding, part of the process of doing the laundry.

Betty's performance of doing the laundry in the arts sessions did not contribute to the continuity, maintenance or repair of clothing or fabrics in the care home. I propose instead that it was a form of self-care that involves the performance of care for objects and materials as a way of maintaining and providing some continuity and, perhaps, repair of Betty's identity, which could be considered incomplete if activities that form and express aspects of who she is are lost on entering institutional care. The way I propose Betty cared for herself through performing processes that cared for objects suggests that interactions with the material world have a role to play in caring for the self and other people. One way to conceptualise the relationality between people and processes that care for objects is to include objects as an integral part of the existing concept of a relationship-centred approach to care. A relationship-centred approach is already applied to care practices, although not as prevalently as a person-centred approach that focuses on the individual's care needs rather than placing an emphasis on the network of relationships that support people's lives. A relationship-centred approach to care proposes that 'relationships are critical to the care provided by nearly all practitioners (regardless of discipline or subspecialty) and a source of satisfaction and positive outcomes for patients and practitioners' (Tresolini and the Pew-Fetzer Task Force, 1994: 11). The relationships they propose are particularly important to the quality of care relationships between people. This chapter proposes that the integration of objects into relationship-centred care could make a contribution to improving practices and concepts of care by recognising that the web of relations that support a person's sense of self goes beyond interactions between people. Further, the inclusion of objects could make a contribution to care ethics by productively developing Held's relational concept of care ethics that, in a similar way to the relationship-centred approach to care, asserts that '[t]he values of caring are especially exemplified in caring relations, rather than in persons as individuals' (2006: 42).

In the remainder of the chapter, I discuss Betty's engagement with laundry practices in the art sessions to further explore how a relational approach to care that involves the performance of care for objects can support care home residents' identities and to build an understanding of the specific role artistic processes can play in care. First, I identify how the role of looking after objects is lost when older people, especially those living with dementia, enter institutional care and I argue that this loss can have a significant impact on their sense of self. Second, I propose an important role for framing everyday domestic practices as performances in art sessions. I argue that enacting aspects of certain domestic processes in this context supports tacit skills and knowledge that are embedded in these processes and that form part of care home residents' identities to be communicated and valued. Third, I propose that there is a focus with which artists pay attention, value and respond to care home residents' interactions with material processes that is specific to their artistic processes and has the potential to have wider implications for concepts of care and care practices.

Institutionalised care and the loss of the care of objects

On entering institutionalised care, Betty lost the role of looking after objects, including her clothing that she no longer laundered. Yet Betty performed the actions involved in doing the laundry during the art sessions, suggesting these seemingly redundant processes still held a significance for her. Tasks involved in caring for objects could be important to her because before entering care they were part of her ongoing creation of home, which supported aspects of her sense of self. If these actions are no longer completed the skills, knowledge and associations embodied in them stop being renewed and brought into the present through their enactment. The loss of the maintenance of a home and the objects and materials that comprise it therefore can signify the decline of a resident's sense of identity. This loss is, in part at least, a result of entering 'total institutions', a term Goffman first applied to care homes in 1961. He defines total institutions as 'a place of residence and work where a large number of like-situated individuals, cut off from wider society for an appreciable period of time, together lead an enclosed, formally administered round of life' (Goffman, 1990: 11).

On entering these closed communities, Goffman describes how practices from their previous 'home world' are discarded as the residents are inducted into the routines and practices of the institution. The everyday practices of older people, especially those living with dementia, are likely to begin to change and diminish before entering care as levels of care and support are introduced prior to their admission. Now 'batch living' (Goffman, 1991), however, their daily routines must conform much more abruptly to those set by the institution, and they are treated and expected to behave similarly to their co-residents, despite having life experiences and domestic practices that were established before entering it. There was no place for Betty's enactments of the laundry process in the care home laundry or in working alongside the paid staff who were responsible for the maintenance of the care home and the care of its residents. Further, Betty's enactment of actions involved in laundry practices could be understood as the performance of an 'occupational remnant' (Gibson, 2006), an action developed by someone living with dementia before entering care that can in the absence of its previous context appear out of place. This can lead to the actions being misunderstood, dismissed and discouraged.

Sarah Pink's (2012) research into the laundry practices of middle-aged women who maintained their own homes gives an insight into the important role laundry practices can play in the ongoing formation of a person's identity and how laundry practices are developed as part of the creation and maintenance of a material, social and multi-sensory home. I introduce her research here to begin to build an understanding of how the care of objects is entwined with self-care and to highlight how aspects of identity that are supported by the completion of these processes are lost when someone enters institutional care. Her research into laundry practices was conducted following the principles and methodologies of her sensory ethnography practice, which pays close attention to the performance and multi-sensorality of everyday practices in order to understand the personal and social meanings they hold. She carefully listens with all her senses to her research participants' verbal and non-verbal descriptions of their laundry as they take her on tours of their homes.

Pink coined the term 'laundry lines' to describe how clothing, soft furnishing, towels and other washable items move *in* the home before, after and during washing as part of a domestic cycle. The concept of laundry lines extends what is categorised as laundry by expanding the duration of time an item is considered to be laundry beyond clothing and other items when they are in the washing machine or hanging on the washing line, to items at different stages of cleanliness in use in the home and beyond; for example, the curtains hung at the window or the shirt a research participant is wearing or is folded in their drawer. Following the laundry lines through their cycles highlights how the act of doing the laundry relates to other aspects of the research participants' lives and uncovers how laundry contributes to the 'multi-sensory home' and the identity of its inhabitants (Pink, 2012). Pink describes how laundry is a relational process that plays an important part in the ecology of a home:

> [L]aundry is moved through a home it is *not* moving *in* the home, but is moving as part of the home, and in relation to the other things that make up home. Laundry is part of the ecology of things that make the textures, smells and visual appearance of home and the affective affordances of home and it is embedded in the socialities of home. Laundry practices therefore are integral to the constitution of the sensory home. The laundry lines that these practices are interwoven with thus participate in the making of home as a place-event. (2012: 76–7, original emphasis)

The laundry lines of a domestic home are specific to the inhabitants that continuously create and maintain them and, as Pink's research attests, integral to the ongoing formation of an individual's home. In care homes, the inhabitants do not do their own laundry. The laundry lines are disjointed as different aspects of the laundry process are performed by different people often out of view of the residents who only encounter the laundry when it is in use as part of their environment or clothing. The process of caring for the laundry is further removed from the residents because in care homes most domestic labour is a backroom activity (Goffman, 1991) spatially segregated from the residents' living quarters. Betty's enactments of aspects of the laundry process are instances of a resident engaging with a domestic activity in a communal area of a care home. However, her actions did not form part of the laundry lines or everyday maintenance of the home. This prompts questions that I engage with in the following section about the specific role performing certain domestic processes in the context of an art session can play in supporting care home residents' sense of identity.

Framing domestic performances in art sessions

There were important differences between how Betty's laundry practice was framed in the context of an art session and how laundry is done in everyday life. Her laundry practice had become performative: her actions had lost their practical application, she repurposed materials and spaces that were available to her in the session to improvise a version of her laundry practice, and she was observed by a small audience that included other care home residents and professional caregivers participating in the group, my co-facilitator and myself. Her performance enabled the qualities of the laundry process to be paid attention by her audience who watched and were encouraged by Christina Argyropoulou to mirror her actions and mime parts of their own laundry practices in response. This kind of attention is rarely paid to everyday practices, which are often overlooked. The context of an art session, therefore, can provide an opportunity for a different and, perhaps, deeper engagement with certain domestic processes than is possible in everyday life.

The processes undertaken to care for objects in everyday life are embodied experiences and the tacit skills and knowledge required to complete them are rarely consciously considered, voiced, shared or even acknowledged or understood. Pink's research is relevant again here. It highlights that the complex multi-sensory actions, skills and knowing involved in everyday domestic practices that are integral to the creation and maintenance of home remain tacit and unacknowledged, even by those who complete the tasks: 'Doing the laundry is one of the skilled multisensory practices of everyday domestic life. It involves embodied knowing, sensing, ways of doing that are rarely articulated verbally, but that are essential to the successful accomplishment of its various stages and to the constitution of the home as place' (Pink, 2012: 71).

A similar lack of understanding and interest in understanding the embodied and tacit knowledge involved in care is identified by Fisher and Tronto (1990). They account for the lack of attention paid to how caring processes are accomplished by citing the incredible wealth of experience of caring for others that women accumulate in their everyday lives. They write:

> [N]one of these images of carers fully examined caring itself; they were focussed much more on the actors than on the activity. There are two main reasons for this lack of attention to caring itself: one is the tremendous fund of everyday experience that women especially have concerning caring. This experience encourages us to think that we already 'know' what caring is. (Fisher and Tronto, 1990: 36)

There are limitations to what can be communicated and understood about the context of Betty's actions in a non-verbal performance, and I do not have any other information about her laundry practices than what was expressed through her enactments of them. Her dementia had impaired her ability to communicate verbally but she was still able to confidently perform an embodied recollection of these practices. Through her performances, the tacit skills and knowledge Betty needed to have developed to complete the processes were made explicit in the sessions. This happened because, as described at the start of this section, the everyday practice became performative and was witnessed and responded to by an audience. An attention was paid to her enactment of an everyday practice that valued the experience it embodied. Performing actions that care for objects in an art session can offer a space to appreciate the specific qualities of these caring acts. Further, the change in context of Betty's laundry practice from the everyday to an art session shifted not only how it was viewed and valued but also what Betty cared for through her actions. The laundry processes Betty used to complete before entering residential care would have provided maintenance, continuity and repair of clothing and other fabrics and can be understood as a form of caring about and caregiving as defined by Fisher and Tronto (1990). When they were enacted in the group, however, they did not support the maintenance or continuity of the care home. What was being cared for through Betty's interactions in the group was her identity. The value the audience's engagement with her laundry practice placed on her performance had the potential to support her sense of self. Performing her laundry practice for her caregivers and fellow care home residents has the potential to strengthen her relationships with them by enabling them to know more about her and through her seeing that they are paying attention to what she was communicating about herself.

I have argued in this section that it is the context of the art session that frames domestic acts that care for objects in such a way that they become performative and this enables attention to be paid to them by those participating in the group. Artists can be instrumental in establishing contexts for themselves and others to share in a type of attention that enables reciprocal processes that support caring relationships. Chrissie Tiller (2017) proposes that artists can be particularly skilled at revealing the tacit skills of communities and if these can be uncovered and valued then they can support members of communities to recognise how they are contributing to the collaboration. She observes that when artists engage with communities, reciprocity is important in moving towards an equality of exchange. She argues that reciprocity depends on both parties believing they have something equally important or useful to give and to gain. In the next section, I explore what is specific about artists' processes that enables them to create a space for reciprocal caring interactions that involve people and objects.

The role of artistic processes in relational care

In one of the sessions, I folded a sheet with Betty. Folding a sheet with her raised my awareness of the role of my own embodied knowledge in the activity and it gave me an understanding of how the materials and objects with which we interacted affected our engagement with each other. In this section, I consider this act to discuss how folding a sheet is a relational process that involves the movements of people and objects. I propose that the sensory attunement and aesthetic sensibility I have developed as part of my art practice enabled me to understand and respond to this everyday act in a way that facilitated a specific kind of relational care.

Holding the opposite end of the sheet to Betty, I was connected to her through its material. As she moved to fold the sheet lengthways twice before folding it in half the other way, I instinctively moved to fold it in half first. I realised this was different to my usual laundry practice. When she shook the sheet, I had to tune in to her rhythms to enable the sheet to move freely between us and to stop the flow of my laundry practice disrupting hers. We both held very specific embodied knowledge of this process, and we needed to respond to each other and the material and spatial qualities of the sheet in order to share in the activity. Before folding the sheet with Betty, I had not thought about or even consciously known how I folded a sheet. By making me pay attention to my actions Betty had taught me, not only about her laundry practice, but also about my own. I realised that the interaction provided the opportunity for mutual care and learning. It was not only about caring for Betty's identity but by raising my awareness of my tacit knowledge of my laundry process I could gain an understanding of an aspect of my own identity. This awareness has applications to my sense of self in my everyday life and builds on my knowledge as an artist of the performative, material and collaborative qualities of everyday acts. In the example of my interaction with Betty, we both uncovered each other's tacit skills.

While this encounter could have happened between two people who were not artists, I argue that the level of care and attention that I paid to the details of the materiality, movement and meaning of the interaction happened because of how I engage with the world through the processes I use to make artwork. My artistic practice includes materials, and this helped me to recognise that the reciprocity of my exchange with Betty happened not only through our relationship to each other but also in relation to the sheet, which was a vital aspect of the exchange. My interaction with Betty and the sheet could be conceptualised as a non-verbal conversation through which we communicated our embodied knowledge to each other. Understood in this way, it illustrates how artists can initiate a form of communication that is mediated through an engagement with objects and materials. Artists are able to communicate in this way because they look at the world with an attentiveness and care that breaks down what they see.

In his essay, *Eye and Mind* (1964), Merleau-Ponty explains how and why painters view the world differently to most other people. He argues that for painters to create a representation of the world on a canvas they must become aware of what they see in front of them. People who are not painters are not required to see in the same way and, therefore, overlook a lot of what painters train themselves to become aware of. He proposes that people see in light. However, the light is instinctively reconstructed into a spatial vision of material objects with texture and form. Therefore, only the object is perceived, not the light and shadow that make it visible. He describes the process of seeing as follows:

> Everyone with eyes has at some time or other witnessed this play of shadows, or something like it, and has been made by it to see things and a space. But it worked in them without them; it hid to make the object visible. To see the object, it was necessary not to see the play of shadows and light around it. The visible in the profane sense forgets its premises; it rests upon a total visibility which is to be recreated and which liberates the phantoms captive in it. (Merleau-Ponty, 1964: 133)

Tim Ingold's extension of Merleau-Ponty's experience of the world through vision to other senses is helpful in applying Merleau-Ponty's ideas about how painters see to how artists with more performative and multi-sensory practices interact with the world. Ingold proposes that if, as Merleau-Ponty argues, we see in light then an equivalent of what goes for vision should also go for auditory and tactile perception.

> If we can see things because we first can see, so too, we can hear things because we first can hear, and touch things because we first can feel. The sight, hearing and touch of things are grounded in the experience, respect- ively, of light, sound and feeling. And if the former force us to attend to the surface of things, the latter, by contrast, redirect our attention to the medium in which things take shape and in which they may also be dis- solved. (Ingold, 2011: 135)

Drawing on Ingold, if painters break down the process of seeing to enable them to understand what they are looking at and, in turn, to paint it, is it not, therefore, possible that sculptors and craft artists do the same with materials, musicians with sound and dancers with movement? The atten- tiveness Merleau-Ponty and Ingold propose that artistic processes involve, I argue, can be employed in art sessions to mediate a form of communication with other people. This can be understood as the sensory attunement and aesthetic sensibility of the artistic process enabling 'total communication' (Fox and Macpherson, 2015). Fox defines 'total communication' as a careful listening with and through materials and gestures (Fox and Macpherson, 2015). The practice of making art together enables a prolonged focused atten- tiveness on the participants and an openness in listening and responding to what is being communicated. Folding the sheet with Betty is an example of 'total communication' in which we carefully 'listened' with and through the movements and materiality of the sheet to each other's embodied stories. Further, I propose that the way Betty's laundry process was engaged with in the art sessions illustrates how relational care built on an understanding, valuing of and response to another person's tacit skills and knowledge can be practised. Not only valuing the meaningfulness these tacit skills and know- ledge hold for care home resident's identity but also what they can bring to an exchange in terms of enabling an understanding of and engagement with one's own skills and knowledge is particularly important because it enables care home residents to give something – to provide care. This is significant to a relational approach to care because care home residents have paid care-givers to attend to their personal care needs but they have few opportunities to care for others or to share their skills and knowledge.

The performative care of objects in institutional care settings

In this chapter, I have argued for a relational approach to care that recognises how engaging with everyday domestic processes that care for objects can play an integral role in self-care and caring for other people. I have proposed that opportunities to perform processes that care for objects should be part of the care received by older people living in residential care homes. This assertion is a response to the significant impact entering institution-alised care can have on older people's sense of identity, particularly those living with dementia. A decline in a care home resident's sense of self can, in part, be the result of the lack of opportunities they have to care for others or look after their own home by completing certain domestic processes that involve the maintenance and repair of objects. Residential care provision is round-the-clock, and the types of processes I am concerned with are completed regularly as an integral part of the day-to-day maintenance of a home. Supporting residents to participate in the everyday domestic processes that maintain the care home would be the most obvious solution to addressing the loss of these activities in their lives. In this chapter, however, I have made a different proposition. I have argued that there is a specific benefit to these processes being performed and framed in the context of an art session.

Betty's performance of her laundry practice is one small example of how a meaningful interaction can be mediated through an object. Concepts and practices of care cannot be changed on the strength of such a small moment of practice; however, this small moment does illustrate the powerful way attentiveness to the embodied skills of residents can help facilitate a form of relational care. The performances bring domestic processes that are usually backroom activities into the heart of the care home and introduce into the place in which they currently reside aspects of care home residents' lives that are lost when they enter institutional care. Enacting these practices in the context of an art session has a specific role to play in enabling the tacit skills, knowledge and embodied experiences required to accomplish them to be communicated and valued. The art session frames them as a performance and as part of an artistic process in which the performative, material, sensory and aesthetic qualities of the process can be shared. Through the perform-ance and witnessing of these acts, a reciprocal form of care can take place during which those involved learn something about and from each other.

Fisher and Tronto propose that 'skills in perception and trained attention may shape what we care about' (1990: 42). Art processes and performances of everyday activities make otherwise overlooked and undervalued processes of caring explicit, and this could have wider application than the specific art session context I have discussed. This way of engaging with and understanding the world is the contribution I propose artists engaging with everyday acts can make to care. There are significant challenges and further considerations that are beyond the scope of this chapter to applying a practice developed in an art session to the context of the everyday life of institutional care. The sensory and aesthetic orientation of the artistic processes I have discussed have been developed over time as part of an art practice and cannot be quickly and easily acquired. It is likely, therefore, that while it may be desirable to adapt and embed care practices that involve the care of objects as a form of self-care in the everyday life of the care home, there is still an ongoing role for artists' performative engagements with and within care.

Notes

1 My research was part of *Reminiscence Arts and Dementia Care: Impact on Quality of Life* (RADIQL, 2012–15), a three-year programme of creative activities for and with care home residents living with dementia. It was funded by Guy's and St Thomas' Charity and delivered by Age Exchange Theatre Trust.
2 Name changed to conceal identity in accordance with the ethical approval the research received.

Performing the 'aesthetics of care'

James Thompson

In this chapter, I develop some of the thinking introduced in an article I wrote in 2015 around what I described as an 'aesthetic of care' (see Chapter 2 of this edited collection). To speak of care as a mode of aesthetics is to make two related claims. First, that reciprocal acts of caring, whether formal, informal, interpersonal or collective, have a sensory, crafted quality that could be called an aesthetic. Caring, thus, I suggest, has an artistry and there are inspirational carers who exhibit a virtuosity in the way they care for and with others. As Maurice Hamington argues, 'this does not suggest that care givers are artists […] but it does suggest that care givers are artists in terms of being aesthetically attuned to the bodies, actions, and relations of themselves to others' (2015: 279). I am locating the aesthetics here in the shape, style, action and interaction between two people, and I propose that in that focused attention between bodies we can recognise an artfulness that is too rarely acknowledged. The second claim is that arts processes, and I am concerned principally with community-based or applied theatre practices here, can be caring or uncaring. In process, design and execution, the arts, I suggest, can promote or exhibit inter-human forms of care that demonstrate a mutually reliant, selfless and constructive form of sociality – and, of course, they can do precisely the opposite of this. Both the first and second claims have a related politics – the first, in suggesting that carers have an artistry, is also a comment on care that fails to exhibit any relational, sensory quality. So care in an institutional health setting, for example, that pays limited attention to felt or embodied relations between people, or is forced to pay limited attention due to social or financial constraints, is likely to be unsatisfactory and a potential source of injustice. The second claim, that community-based art practices can be more or less caring, suggests that processes and products/productions that fail to acknowledge the importance of care, and the quality of relations that are part of different projects, can also be the source of injustice, no matter the claims of those who lead them. In summary, care practices need attention to their aesthetics, and community-based arts programmes need an understanding of care, if either is to make claims to be contributing to social justice. In making, and therefore linking, these two claims, I am asserting that care aesthetics is concerned with how to develop successful arts projects, for example, in homes for the elderly, but I am also recognising the artistry that is already demonstrated by those who live and work in these different community settings. While this chapter accepts that there is more work to be done on the aesthetic, artistic and crafted practices of caregivers in health and other related settings, this will not be the focus here. In my 2015 article, I outlined a broad case for an *aesthetics of care*, whereas here, I will describe a number of micro-examples to illustrate what this focus reveals about certain arts practices. In the second half of the chapter, I examine three examples of theatre practice that, I suggest, demonstrate intricate ways that performance can be said to generate care for one another. Two of these examples draw on projects by the London Bubble Theatre – one linked to the devising of their show *The Grandchildren of Hiroshima*, and the other a drama workshop programme for Year 1 (five-year-old) primary schoolchildren called *Speech Bubbles*. The third example comes from a performance of *Ruff* (2013) by Peggy Shaw and directed by Lois Weaver. In my engagement with these examples, I demonstrate how arts practices can produce or strengthen important interdependent social relations between groups and communities. By foregrounding these relationships in performance these projects invite us to recognise the importance of interdependence within socially engaged performance and to rethink what constitutes artistry and efficacy. The argument is that practices that acknowledge their presence in networks of interdependent care can build communities of affective solidarity, supporting the development of what Judith Butler terms a 'sensate democracy' (2015: 207) – that is, a society that is more just, caring, mutually supportive and crafted with a collaborative, joyous sense of artistry. A *sensate democracy* here is understood as the contribution of artistic, and more broadly aesthetic, activity to the political arena. It is also, however, in the sense I am using it here, the end result of artistic activism that produces a democratic arrangement that properly values the full sensory life of different communities. Butler's term will be connected later in the chapter to Rancière's idea of the *distribution of the sensible* (2004), where a redistribution of sensory relations becomes a priority for enabling the democratic arrangements that Butler is proposing.

The case for interdependency

To understand the ethics, and then aesthetics, of care proposed here, I want to link what Hamington calls a 'performance of care' (2015: 288) to Eva Kittay's and Judith Butler's accounts of interdependency. The case to make is that well-crafted care does not 'end with a particular act of kindness' but starts from a broader 'dramatic rehearsal, a habituation of going out and learning about others in varied, humble, open, and meaningful ways' (Hamington,

2015: 288), which can then be part of a wider 'struggle for an egalitarian social and political order in which a livable interdependency becomes possible' (Butler, 2015: 69). The perspective on interdependency here, with its insistence on the reality of mutual reliance, does not somehow validate relations of dependence as automatically positive, but does insist they are, to use Kittay's term, 'inextricable' (2015). Eva Kittay, in an extended feminist critique of individualised ethics, suggests that 'at best our independence is relative, but at heart it is really a fiction' (2015: 55). The argument is that those who claim their ability or right to act autonomously, or aspire for human independence as a social good, are in fact denying those dependencies on which their apparent freedoms rely. So while we are all dependent on networks of care and infrastructures of support, *those dependencies* are frequently elided, and in our current society access to enabling structures are rarely distributed equally. Paradoxically, often those who are most strident in their assertion of an individual's freedom to act as they choose are those that most benefit from dependent relations distributed unequally along class, gendered and racial lines. Working-class communities, women and people from minority or migrant backgrounds take a substantially higher proportion of the frequently poorly paid care burden. It is not that seeking a realm of independent action is an automatic negative, but it is based on the fiction that denies, and frequently hides, those social and communal supports that make one's independence possible. And the arts are, of course, not immune from promoting this fiction. Of course, the other side to that denial is the tendency of those who advocate self-reliance as a fundamental social good, to seek to undermine those very structures of dependency and infrastructures of social care that make many lives possible. This is the vision of a neoliberal campaigner proposing the cutting of support for public provision of childcare, while privately paying for their own that makes their 'independent' presence in the public sphere possible. A campaign for justice and a fairer society does not deny that unequal distribution of different sustaining care and solidarity practices. Instead, it acknowledges the dependencies on which we all rely, and then, 'by removing the political social, and economic disadvantages that attach to dependency' seeks to make them a source of value (Kittay, 2015: 67). They then become 'a source of connection, an occasion for developing our capacities for thought, empathy, sensitivity, trust, ingenuity, and creativity; in short, as providing for us the conditions of our distinct human dignity' (Kittay, 2015: 67).

It is, therefore, the unequal distribution of dependency that is the problem and not dependency itself. The claim here is that recognition of our dependency helps it become a potential source for developing the capacities outlined by Kittay, but also any process that fosters 'empathy, sensitivity, trust, ingenuity, and creativity' will itself promote the beneficial aspects of living in dependent relations with others (Kittay, 2015: 67). These processes – which the argument here suggests can be found in arts projects with a well-developed aesthetics of care – can maintain and strengthen those mutually supportive human relations and promote the more equitable 'conditions of our distinct human dignity' that we all need (Kittay, 2015: 67).

Judith Butler in her work on a 'performative theory of assembly' (2015) argues similarly for us to take account of the paradoxical status of dependency. It is a given that 'everyone is dependent on social relations and enduring infrastructure in order to maintain a livable life' but at the same time, she argues, it is important to recognise that while dependency is 'not the same as a condition of subjugation, [it] can easily become one' (Butler, 2015: 21). The perspective advocated by Butler, and developed in this account, is not to deny that dependent relations might be the source of injustice or the unequal exercise of power, but to affirm and seek out human activity where those forms of dependency might become sources for mutual support and solidarity. The argument here seeks to value these as the foundation of movements that aim to counter the ethos of radical, selfish individualism. The denial of inextricable interdependency and the concomitant avowal of self-sufficiency as a 'moral ideal' (Butler, 2015: 14) is the foundation of a neoliberal ideal of entrepreneurial self-sufficiency. And, while proponents of individual responsibility delegate, and often hide, their dependency on others, they simultaneously support the undermining of those sustaining inter-human and social infrastructures that make lives liveable.

To link this perspective to the ethics of care proposed in this edited collection, therefore, is to recognise our dependency on others, and acknowledge the inequalities in how that dependence is distributed, organised and experienced. Starting from this position, particular forms of caring solidarity and care-filled political action become necessary: when life 'is understood as both equally valuable and interdependent, certain ethical formulations follow' (Butler, 2015: 43). Subsequently, it is important to critique those activities that deny interdependency and reproduce the social conditions that undermine the productive forms of dependency that make more equal forms of social life likely. This critique of 'that unacknowledged dependency' (Butler, 2015: 206) suggests the search for a 'sensate democracy' (Butler, 2015: 207) that demands forms of 'improvisation in the course of devising collective and institutional ways of addressing induced precarity' (Butler, 2015: 22). My argument is that these 'collective' and 'institutional' approaches can be system wide but also of a much smaller scale – and can be evoked and developed to different degrees within art projects as will be argued in the next section of the chapter. They can be part of what Hamington calls 'the performance of care' exhibited within a 'dramatic rehearsal, a habituation of going out and learning about others' (2015: 288). Felt, embodied, careful collaborative acts of mutual reliance are the minute building blocks of that more caring, just society and examples of what sociologist Christian Smith would call 'the microfoundations of social life' (2015: 2). These, I will suggest, are made visible in the examples of practice outlined below.

Aesthetics of care in action

This section outlines three examples of aesthetics of care. Since I started writing on this theme, and in particular during earlier work on my 2015 article, I have searched for moments or glimpses of care aesthetics in practices that I encountered both personally and professionally. So here, the patting down of masking tape by five-year-olds in a *Speech Bubbles* workshop, a trust game in a London Bubble Theatre workshop and a spoken intervention from director Lois Weaver during a performance of Peggy Shaw's one woman show *Ruff*, become my chosen examples. My argument is that they illustrate ways that the arts can promote and perhaps produce inter-human relations with deeply embedded mutual care. In each example, the art is being made with and between people, in one sense modelling forms of a caring relationship that might be an inspiration for a more cooperative form of social arrangement, but also crucially enacting that relationship in the moment of the art making. My argument here is that an aesthetics of care can be a demonstration, a showing of caring, but, more significantly, it can be the actual moment of building a more just distribution of caring and increase participants' capacity to care and be cared for.

The understanding of aesthetics here is, on the one hand broad, signalling aesthetic in the sense of the appreciation of something crafted, artistic or beautiful. However, on the other hand, I am also using it in a more particular sense borrowed from the work of Jacques Rancière and his framework of the 'distribution of the sensible' (see Rancière, 2004: 12–19). If, according to Rancière, politics 'revolves around what is seen and what can be said about it, around who has the ability to see and the talent to speak', then 'aesthetics practices' are an intervention in those ways of 'doing and making' (Rancière, 2004: 13). Aesthetic practices are, therefore, always part of the processes by which capacities for seeing, doing, making and speaking are organised and these practices will, to varying degrees, maintain or undermine different 'distributions of the sensible'. So the examples I offer here might inspire as examples or representations of caring relations, but they are also actual interventions in political distributions of 'ways of doing and making as well as the relationships they maintain to modes of being and forms of visibility' (Rancière, 2004: 13). In building new sensory relations, caring interactions and less familiar patterns of mutual support, they are interventions in existing, and frequently iniquitous distributions of, *ways of doing*. They are acts of redistribution that are vital if we are to create a more caring, just world: a more 'sensate democracy' in Butler's terms. While the examples I examine here are small in scale, somehow these moments opened up something wider and therefore, they suggest something grander as potential sources for gentler, kinder forms of inter-human relations. They were glimpses of an aesthetics of care, and, maybe, hints of a more hopeful, equitable way of being together.

The Grandchildren of Hiroshima

In April 2015, the London Bubble Theatre was working on a new performance piece in Hiroshima, Japan called *The Grandchildren of Hiroshima* as part of a project to commemorate the 70th anniversary of the bombing of the city in August 1945. I have written elsewhere about the broader project (Thompson, 2017) and here will only focus on one exercise from a workshop early in the process. I want to demonstrate how the playing of games, and this game in particular, in a devising workshop can exhibit, but then importantly practice and build a form of artful care. It can stage and ultimately produce the interdependencies discussed above. This was particularly important in this context, as the project was intergenerational, bringing young children into contact with elders in a programme that asked questions about how young Japanese could connect with the experiences of the war generation: how they could value and learn from their mutual dependency. Playing with each other became a symbol of that connection, an actual moment of connecting and also a memorial act as, through this process, elders remembered themselves as children at the time of the nuclear attack.

Games within community-based theatre have numerous purposes, including the sensitising of participants to their own and others' bodies, the rekindling of a capacity for and comfort with play so vital for collaborative theatre making and to enhance an embodied sense of connection and trust with one's fellow participants. Play can be joyous, disruptive and anarchic, as well as rule-bound, disciplinary and, of course, controlling. The intention here is not to offer a detailed analysis of play within community performance, but to argue that its relational qualities can both prepare and perhaps rehearse groups for attentiveness to the other and also can be actual examples of that bodily interdependence. They can be part of a process by which groups of individuals enhance their caring capacities, identified by care ethicist Jean Tronto as including 'attentiveness, deep reflection on responsibility [...] and responsiveness both to care receivers and to the process and effectiveness of care itself' (2015: 262). Attentiveness, in terms of the arguments of this chapter, is, therefore, a central capacity through which interdependencies are realised and strengthened. While I have no doubt that games can be used to exclude and divide, the account here suggests that they can also develop a capacity for inter-human care, engendering, in Tronto's words, 'the qualities of solidarity and trust' (2015: 262) that are a crucial part of the case for an aesthetics of care.

Early in one of the group's first workshops, the director of London Bubble, Jonathan 'Peth' Petherbridge, chose an exercise that required the group to work in pairs. The participants, a mix of Japanese children, young adults and elders, were all working on a performance piece about the experience of people on the day of the atomic bombing of Hiroshima. This particular exercise was broken into several stages, becoming more challenging as it progressed. The first stage required one person 'A' in the pair to rest his or her hand on the 'B' partner's shoulder and then with the other hand hold the partner's left hand gently. 'A' was then asked to guide 'B' around the space with 'B' keeping her or his eyes shut. After a short period of the pairs taking tentative – careful – steps around the space, they were asked to swap over so 'B' took on the 'A' role, and the process was repeated.

At all times, Peth encouraged people both to explore the space, but also ensure that the person with their eyes closed was marshalled gently around without bumping into other people or objects. After this first element of the exercise, the partners briefly discussed how they felt about it – was this safe, scary or enjoyable? The next stage increased the challenge and the lead partner no longer held the other's hand but just placed his or her single hand on the shoulder of their collaborator. There was the same close process of directing someone around the space, but the connection was lighter. After both had done this variant, it was changed once again, so that the lead now kept her or his hand on the shoulder only to direct movement but took it off otherwise, leaving the partner to move around the space with no contact. The hand was only returned to the shoulder to redirect, slow down or stop a person: that is, to keep them safe from the other players and obstacles in the room. The final stage changed again with the instruction for the leaders to make eye contact with other leaders and, when they took their hands off a partner's shoulder, they swapped partner and moved their hand to a new shoulder. Ideally the person with their eyes closed hardly noticed the switch, as they were conducted around the room with different partners just making gentle shoulder touches to stop, turn and carefully orientate them only when absolutely necessary. In the playing, this final section lasted longest with the group quietly and relatively effortlessly allowing the walkers their space with the leaders pivoting between different individuals allowing them to explore the room safely.

This final stage was almost balletic – as a lead partner moved stealthily around the room to catch a new person and then pirouette around another. Each needed to be minutely connected with other leaders to ensure that all remained safe, at the same time as watching closely for her or his particular partner and partners they would soon be assisting. The exercise built a particular (not of course completely unproblematic – of which, more later) model of care. First, there was an intimate connection to the direct partner as the person quietly led him or her around the space. Second, as the touch became slighter, there was the experience of the reciprocal nature of that touch as the person being led had to respond to the feel of the fingers and had to concentrate on the quality of the connection to understand what it sought. And finally, there was an ensemble moving in a combined act of care that shared responsibility for ensuring people could move safely around the space. In this final stage, just as a person released the touch from one person, she or he moved on to support another – and the exercise built to the point where relative independence was assured by the sensation that, if someone shifted too close to an edge or to a table, she or he would be retrieved by someone in the group; by a sense of collective responsibility. As the exercise developed, the somewhat functional, perhaps over protective hand-on-shoulder-hand-in-hand relationship became replaced with more relaxed, gentler movements of the eye-closed partner. This was coupled with the dance of care around the different partners as the others moved to support each other, balancing and shifting physically through the space with an artful set of movements whose objective was to ensure the collective safety of all players. And this was a display, a choreography of care, as the fluid movements had a shape and pattern: it was dance-like as one person caught another, but then moved to someone else, shifting a body around the space to ensure the network of care and support was not broken. But of course, it also was not a display, in the sense of being for someone outside the group to witness. It existed in its own right as a mutual and relational experience for the group that modelled, and built, that subtle trust needed for quality ensemble work. It was, to rephrase Rancière, an act of redistributing the sensible relations between members of this group.

As I note above, there is a danger in assuming that this is a complete metaphor for an aesthetic realisation of a caring relationship. Requiring one person to close their eyes, hints at the disabling metaphor at the centre of the exercise. There is, of course, the danger of paternalism in the relationship between the carer and the 'blind' cared for, where one ultimately maintains the direction and power over the other. Care ethics, as discussed above, is concerned with the inequalities and imbalances in caring relations as much as the potential for forging more just relations based on mutual interdependency. Butler warns that attention must be paid to modes of dependency based on forms of subjugation but, in doing so, she does still assert that interdependence can form the basis for more just relations (2015: 21). A response to this problem did, however, emerge here. As the exercise developed, we witnessed some surprising acts of support, for example, between a smaller child and an adult or between a teenager and an elder, and between women and men. The exercise in fact could be viewed as one that shifted the dynamics of interpersonal care and dependency, and reassembled caring relations in ways that broke some of the expected, more familiar relations between children and elders, between the young and the old. A trust game that was part of the process of building up a theatre-making ensemble thus made new forms of mutual awareness, interdependency and interpersonal solidarity possible.

In this example, caring expertise – that grew through the exercise – had an artistry, a physicality and sensory quality. It was not the perhaps clumsy touch of the opening stage (which was a literal aiding of a partner and, of course, a metaphor for multiple different interpersonal relationships) that was valued, but the emergent delicate touch, release and sharing of responsibility for collective care. In a way, this mirrored the shift in care ethics from one-to-one caring relationships (for example, parent to child) to more social models of caring exemplified in the work of Virginia Held (2006) and Jean Tronto ([1993] 2009) on care's politics. For both these authors, there is an important move in care ethics from the assumed ground of a primarily private set of interpersonal relations, to the social and ultimately political implications of a broader vision of a more caring social order. The shift was made visible through the exercise in a process of increased difficulty and increased focus on the collective responsibility for multiple, interrelated acts of care. Significantly for an argument about aesthetics, the success of this more collective stage required the interdependent care to be valued in part, of course, for its gracefulness. A child lightly touched the shoulder of an older woman to keep her safe; a teenage girl coaxed a middle-aged man to move gently across the room. The game demonstrated that the execution of care for the other required practice, rehearsal in the theatrical sense, as well as networks of connectedness and mutual support. However, it also showed that it required craft, attention to minute differences in inter-human physicality and a sense of awareness of the body in space and its rhythms of connection to others. The significance for community-based theatre is that this was a key *outcome* that was realised within the process itself and was not merely a moment of preparation for a final performance. So, in fact, this was not care 'like' a dance, as if the dance were a metaphor for or representation of care. Instead, high-quality care was shown in and of itself to be embodied in and have the aesthetic dimensions of dance – and the more graceful the dance, the higher quality the care. The exercise built the group's capacity to respond and then enabled them to enjoy dancing their care for each other.

While it is not the primary purpose of this chapter to discuss the broader connections this exercise made with the intergenerational performance project between elders and youth in the context of the memorialisation of the nuclear bomb, this small moment did illustrate the wider project's ambition to demonstrate and perhaps prefigure new modes of connection between older Japanese and the contemporary young citizens of the city of Hiroshima. Exercises such as the one described here practised, exhibited and then permitted the group to experience the mutual care between members. This enabled a group to create a performance piece that showed *and developed* collaborative and caring ways of working and listening between older and younger actors. The point to emphasise, for an account of the *aesthetics of care*, was that there was not a linear move from rehearsals where care was practised to the presentation of a play in which care was performed. In multiple moments across the devising, workshopping, rehearsing and performing of *The Grandchildren of Hiroshima* caring relations were built, felt and experienced. The play was, following Rancière (2004), *about* new 'modes of being and forms of visibility', but the example here also suggests that that at multiple micro-moments, the process was an actual intervention in the distribution of 'ways of doing and making' – a game, that briefest of exercises in the rehearsal room, allowed new interdependencies to be realised.

Ruff

Peggy Shaw is a performance artist celebrated for her work with Lois Weaver in the duo Split Britches. Pioneers of the queer and experimental performance scene in New York in the 1960s and 1970s, they have, since the 1980s, drawn on contemporary, classical and popular forms to create performance projects dealing with a huge range of lesbian, feminist and other themes. Peggy Shaw, in particular, is known for her one-woman shows dealing with the many characters, stories, inspirations and personal experiences that have shaped her life. In response to her stroke in 2011, she developed a new show, *Ruff*, directed by Lois Weaver, dealing with the impact of the event on her life, her body and her memories. It explored her subsequent recovery, her ability to recall stories and her new found capacities and struggles. *Ruff* toured the UK in 2013 and 2014, visiting Manchester's Contact Theatre where I saw it with an audience of young people, stroke survivors and medical professionals.

Peggy took her post-stroke memory challenges as inspiration to construct a show that used monitors, green screen and other technological memory aids, including the presence of director Lois Weaver in the audience, to enable her to move her way through its multiple sections and stories. The presence of a mobile screen on stage laid bare the support structures that are often made invisible in many performance pieces – almost in homage to a Brechtian desire to make visible the mechanics that makes the theatre possible. In a straightforward way, there was an honesty about the structures of care that were needed to make this particular performance possible, which acted as a commentary on the way theatre more usually hides the means by which the performers are supported in order to come on to, and stay safe, onstage. There was no independent, entirely autonomous autobiographical performer here, but a person acutely aware of their own vulnerability and joyously presenting the tools needed to transform that vulnerability into a live presentation. The performance was not a story of an individual with extraordinary power to overcome, but a demonstration of the inevitable need for people to draw on the care and support of others, to make, in Butler's terms, 'life liveable'. Peggy told stories from her stroke, her hospital care, her recovery and her past, including relations with friends and family. Fragmentary accounts of tea with friends, hospital stays and her sister's wedding, interspersed with sound from 'her band' and green-screened images, built up a moving and comedic account of the stroke's impact on her life. While the monitors positioned around the front of the stage were in one sense the machinery of care – they were also, by being present with the actor, given an aesthetic presence. They were co-performers (along with Lois, see below) with Peggy, giving the care that she needed to make the show an onstage form. Their presence enacted a refusal to deny the performer's dependency, and in so doing made visible something of the interdependency of all performance, and of course, all performers.

This sense of laying bare and giving form to care in performance, however, was realised most directly in a couple of moments in the show I saw in Manchester, which, for me, placed care at the centre of the event in a way that further emphasised something of the vulnerability of all performers. At a couple of points in the show, Peggy looked up to ask: 'Am I in the right place?' and 'Where do I go now?' As an audience member, being hyper-aware of the medical history that Peggy was presenting, my immediate thought when this first happened was that something was going terribly wrong. However, from the semi-obscurity of the audience a voice was heard giving reassurance, saying, 'yes that's right', 'you're fine' and 'yes, just there'. Unbeknown to me, and I assume others, director Lois Weaver was close to the front of the auditorium, ready to provide orientation and gentle guidance if the screens and other technical prompts failed to provide it. She made audible the usually unheard process of directorial guidance and signalled the care that was part of the labour inherent in it. There was something profoundly moving about this voice from the darkness. It seemed to express what was acutely present, but unspoken, in the audience; that is, an overwhelming sense of willing Peggy's success as she travelled through her complex, multilayered story telling. During the performance, there was a nervous anticipation, an almost collective holding of breath, as those watching urged Peggy to remain in control of the show. Lois' words of encouragement voiced the unspoken care of this particular director for her actor, a responsibility that is by no means ubiquitous, but in an argument for the importance of care aesthetics should be more central to a director and actor's relationship. While some theatre traditions might be prepared to tolerate less caring relations between directors and actors, the argument here insists that there should not be a means-justify-ends logic in theatre making and also that in applied theatre or community-based performance, means and ends are indistinguishable. As demonstrated in the example from Hiroshima, mutual care between participants should not be seen as optional but a potential, vital outcome of each workshop, rehearsal and performance moment.

Lois' interjections also voiced the audience's desire to connect with and support the unfolding narrative of Peggy's performance. Her ad libs both illustrated that the facilitating human technology behind this exceptional performance was a relationship of care and that in being voiced from the auditorium, she gave that care audible form: she made it present in the show. The support structure became part of the artistry of the event – something admitted and celebrated rather than something denied – and a structure that drew those in the audience into a relationship of care with the performer. The aesthetics of care, here, is in laying bare the relationship between audience and stage to make us all aware of the sensation of mutual regard, and care, which make successful performances possible. We witnessed a solo performer as a dependent person, relying on visible technologies and invisible spoken assurances – on networks of affective solidarity. This was not dependency as a source of subjugation, following Butler's concerns, but dependency that through mutual support became a display of productive and inspiring 'human dignity' (Kittay, 2015: 67).

The formulation of aesthetics of care that I am arguing for, therefore, insists that the aesthetic successes and failures of the show are not located solely in what takes place on the stage, but in the sensations of mutual reliance and concern between audience and performers, and between performers and their creative support teams. And, in the example of Peggy Shaw and Lois Weaver's *Ruff*, this involved ensuring that the crafted care that allowed Peggy to perform successfully became visible and part of what was appreciated about the performance. Lois' care for Peggy in that 'you're fine' became part of the moving, care-filled beauty of this piece, and spoken from within the audience, it brought those of us watching into the relationship of care that she expressed. Lois demonstrated for the audience something of Butler's 'ethos of solidarity' (2015: 22) that is based firmly in an acknowledgement of mutual dependency. While there was a singular relationship here between performer and director, her position within the audience seemed to share that responsibility with a group of spectators who were then, in turn, called upon to care. The dance of collective care from the exercise in *Hiroshima* was here the collective, heightened attention of a caring audience, drawn into a relationship with a performer who allowed her dependency to be made visible and audible. The fact of that dependency is not an impediment to living well but should be regarded, to repeat the quotation from Kittay, 'as a source of value: a source of connection, an occasion for developing our capacities for thought, empathy, sensitivity, trust, ingenuity, and creativity' (2015: 67). Interdependency, therefore, so movingly demonstrated within this performance piece, becomes a touchstone for intimate forms of human justice, where the arts can be an occasion for developing those resources of care that make collective dignity more likely.

Speech Bubbles

London Bubble Theatre, the creative force behind the *The Grandchildren of Hiroshima* performance piece, also run a programme called *Speech Bubbles* for Year 1 and Year 2 schoolchildren (five- to seven-year-olds) who have communication issues, such as speech delays, both near their base in London and across the UK. It is a school-based, year-long intervention with a group of ten children who are selected by the school and spend forty-five minutes each week, out of their classes, joining in a series of drama workshops focusing on whole-body communication. There are multiple reasons for their selection, relating to problems with their verbal and non-verbal contribution to their classroom studies; from speech impediments, selective mutism, English as a second language to struggles with verbalisation, sentence formation and other forms of verbal and participation anxiety. Each *Speech Bubbles* workshop is run by a lead drama worker supported by a member of support staff from the local school, either a teaching assistant or learning support assistant, who will know the children from her or his work with the different classes within the school.

A *Speech Bubbles* workshop follows a familiar pattern, slightly varying depending on the style of the drama worker and the particular needs of the young people. Broadly, they will start with a welcome game, including a name exercise and then some simple theatre games that support the children in their use of their bodies and their confidence in verbal and physical expression. Games that support taking turns, listening to each other and expressing themselves make up the first section of the workshop. The second half concentrates on acting out a story that one of the children will have had noted down the previous week. This includes laying out a story square on the floor with masking tape, large enough for roughly three children to sit along each side. The space outside the square is for attentive audience members and inside is for the performers. Once the square has been established, one child's story will be acted out within the acting area with different children (and teachers and visiting adults!) being encouraged by the drama workshop leader to play the various characters and objects that make up the story. The child whose story it is is given an opportunity to take the role they want to, but otherwise the story is collectively worked on, expertly marshalled by the drama worker to ensure all have an opportunity to take on different acting challenges. Some stories are fantastical with talking animals and wondrous creatures, some are based on contemporary popular culture (from the latest animated or comic hero films) and others might be based on the familiar worlds of five-year-olds, with parents, siblings and other family members appearing as the leading characters. Once the story is finished, the workshop ends with a few concluding exercises. This includes a routine to 'wash off' the story, showering away the varying roles the child will have played, a group sharing of their favourite moments of the day and then a final song. In most *Speech Bubbles* sessions, one child stays behind to tell a story to the drama worker for the following week and that story is taken word for word into the *Speech Bubbles* notebook.

The playwright and young people's theatre expert Noël Greig, when running devising sessions, used to explain his approach as a process that moved 'from limitation to stimulation' (Personal communication, 1992). This was his formula for expressing how restrictions or constraints can inspire creative responses in making theatre with young people. In many ways, this ethos could be assumed to run through *Speech Bubbles* as the precisely chosen and repeated structure shapes the involvement of the children each week. What I want to argue here, however, is thinking about structure in theatre workshops in terms of 'restriction' or 'constraint' fails to account for how structure might be a particular route to taking good care of participants. The case to make is that *structure as care* provides an alternative, perhaps more productive, register. Debates about theatre workshop shape can become about how tightly or freely they are planned, and whether a strictness with timing and the format of exercises should be replaced with a greater openness or free-flowing process. For the argument I am making here, and in the case of *Speech Bubbles*, I want to explore how a structure that was repeated with almost ritualised elements actually provided a framework of care that held, maintained and made possible the play and delight of the children. Here, therefore, far from being a constraint, structure enabled the performance of care to emerge and this is what made possible the young people's creative success. For *Speech Bubbles*, the format of the workshop was not something simply to make the theatre possible – to limit in order to stimulate. The shape *and the content* of the workshop were owned by the children in such a way that both constituted the art of this particular form of drama work – they combined as the aesthetic of this practice of care.

When it is time for the story square to be delineated on the carpet with sticky masking tape, the drama worker pulls the tape and constructs the basic outline, but the children relish patting down the lines and ensuring that it is properly aligned. This happened in every session I witnessed, in different schools. Once the square was properly stuck down, the children would then enthusiastically sit in place behind the lines. They repeatedly showed a sense of consideration and protection for the boundary that was both part of the structure of this section of the workshop and was visible on the floor in front of them. The frame was present, and it allowed them both to tell their stories and watch them being made. Children knew that when moving into the square they became the characters of that day's story – animals, super-heroes, family members – and then, with a 'whoosh', they would jump out of the circle and sit back just behind the line. The workshop felt like a container of these young people, holding them in place, in safety, ushering them in certain directions, prompting their somewhat uneasy vocalisations, but also handing on that shape for the participants to claim themselves.

The structure was not so much a limitation, in Greig's terms, as a form of gently holding in place – for young people who had multiple, different and, at times, challenging means of being present in that space. The *hold* had a sensory quality as the tape on the carpet provided an almost magical line across which startling things were made possible. I would argue there was a caring pattern to the workshop that, in being repeated, constantly visible and shared with the children, had a sensory, affective and aesthetic quality. The workshop structure or form was part of the felt delight and excitement the children had for the session itself. The patterns were visible through the words of the drama worker, on the floor and in the actions and movements of the children – all becoming enabling features of its success. Feeling the tape on the floor was a process of sensing the shape or the care provided by the workshop. This was also the case with other exercises and workshop moments, which the children delighted in knowing the structure of and the order in which they appeared. Again, this places the care process – that supported these young people who were struggling for multiple reasons in their first year of primary school – as one that was practised, precisely crafted and collaboratively developed. The pattern had a certain beauty, artistry and ritualised quality in the way that it held these young people and sustained them through the workshop process. A *Speech Bubbles* workshop was, therefore, a set of mutually reinforcing exercises that gently prompted the participants and allowed them also to take hold of the workshop structure themselves. They were invited to have ownership of the workshop's shape – to pat it down – to take control, in a small way, of the mutual support that would make them feel more confident and excited about expressing themselves and making themselves part of their wider school experience.

Conclusion

The examples shared here are, of course, small scale. They are illustrations that art making can build powerful forms of interdependent care that have a quality and beauty – and that these aesthetic elements are as vital to the art as they are to the experiences of those involved. The examples model forms of embodied, mutually reliant relationships, then rehearse and develop those relations and finally share or display them. They exhibit caring, artful structures that are integral to the performance on display – whether it is the balletic drama exercise, the one-women show or the children's workshop. The art processes are richer and more moving because of their display of the interdependencies that give them their strength. Art making here is not an independent practice of the specifically trained or talented, but rather a practice that in being embedded in more interpersonal, caring processes, points to a world where mutual dependency is a source of less self-centred or unequal relations.

This chapter has aimed to articulate an *aesthetics of care* as a counter to the valuing of autonomy and independence, both within arts practices and the wider world in which they take place. It has also suggested that projects that enable well-crafted sensory, mutually supportive artistic experiences can become interventions that prefigure a fairer society, where art making actively redistributes the sensible in favour of more equitable arrangements to allow people's interdependent flourishing. It has made the case that rehearsals, demonstrations, performances and workshops where these care aesthetics are realised become places through which more care-filled social relations and just interdependencies are experienced. The ritualised caring structure owned by the children participants in *Speech Bubbles*, the graceful care ballet of the simple exercise in *Hiroshima* and the sensation of affective solidarity between audience, director and performer in *Ruff*, all showed how caring artistry provides glimpses of more mutually sustaining social relations. The arts and artists are, thus, not valued primarily for their capacity to comment independently, to awaken understanding or challenge the world, however important these qualities may be. Instead, they are valued for the intimate way they connect people with each other in mutually supportive communities. In a world that seems endlessly in the thrall of individualised prowess, privatised responsibility and wanton disregard for the welfare of others, beautiful moments of inter-human artful care perhaps hint that there is a better mode of being human and living well together.

References

Abraham, N. and Busby, S. (2015) *Celebrating Success: How Has Participation in Clean Break's Theatre Education Programme Contributed to Individuals' Involvement in Professional or Community Arts Practices?* London: Central School of Speech and Drama.

Abu-Rish, Z. (2015) Garbage politics. *Middle East Report* 277(December).

Aggarwal, R., Mytton, O. T., Derbrew, M., Hananel, D., Heydenburg, M., Issenberg, B., MacAulay, C., Mancini, M. E., Morimoto, T., Soper, N., Ziv, A. and Reznick, R. (2010) Training and simulation for patient safety. *BMJ Quality & Safety*, 19(suppl. 2), pp. i34–i43.

Ahmed, S. (2000) *Strange Encounters: Embodied Others in Post-Coloniality*. London and New York: Routledge.

Alhayek, K. (2015) 'I must save my life and not risk my family's safety!': untold stories of syrian women surviving war. *Syria Studies* 7(1), pp. 1–30.

Ali, M. (2015, 20 March) The reality of Chris Grayling's probation revolution: '£46 goes nowhere'. *Guardian*. Available at: www.theguardian.com/society/2015/mar/20/chris-grayling-probationrevolution-prisoners-reoffending (accessed 12/10/17).

All-Party Parliamentary Group (APPG) (2017) *Creative Health: The Arts for Health and Wellbeing*. London: All-Party Parliamentary Group. Available at: www.artshealthandwellbeing.org.uk/appg-inquiry/Publications/Creative_Health_Inquiry_Report_2017_-_Second_Edition.pdf (accessed 30/10/18).

Almog, N. (2016) *Outcomes of Störung*. Available at: https://hafraah.wordpress.com/2016/01/26/outcomes-of-storung (accessed 15/02/16).

Al-Saadi, Y. (2014) Attacks on Syrians in Lebanon: scapegoating, par excellence. *Al-Akhbar*. Available at: http://english.al-akhbar.com/node/21557 (accessed 13/02/17).

Amans, D. (ed.) (2008) *An Introduction to Community Dance Practice*. London: Palgrave Macmillan.

Amin, A. (2012) *Land of Strangers*. Cambridge, UK: Polity Press.

Anderson, P. (2017) *Autobiography of a Disease*. Abingdon, UK: Routledge.

Anonymous (2016) Financial prosecutor charges Sukleen in corruption case. *Daily Star*. Available at: www.dailystar.com.lb/News/Lebanon-News/2016/Mar-02/340293-financial-prosecutor-charges-sukleen-in-corruption-case.ashx (accessed 02/03/16).

Aylesworth, G. (2015) Postmodernism. In Zalta, E. N. (ed.) *The Stanford Encyclopedia of Philosophy*. Available at: https://plato.stanford.edu/entries/postmodernism (accessed 28/02/18).

Babbage, F. (2004) *Augusto Boal.* Abingdon, UK: Routledge.

Bach, S. and Grant, A. (2017) *Communication and Interpersonal Skills in Nursing* (2nd ed.) London: Sage.

Balfour, M. (2016) The art of facilitation: 'taint what you do (it's the way that you do it). In Preston, S. (ed.) *Applied Theatre Facilitation: Pedagogies, Practices, Resilience.* London: Bloomsbury Methuen Drama, pp. 151–65.

Balsamo, A. M. (1999) *Technologies of the Gendered Body: Reading Cyborg Women.* Durham, NC: Duke University Press.

Barad, K. (2007) *Meeting the Universe Halfway: Quantum Physics and the Entanglement of Matter and Meaning.* Durham, NC: Duke University Press.

Barad, K. (2012) On touching. *Differences: A Journal of Feminist Cultural Studies* 23(3), pp. 206–23.

Barnes, M. (2006) *Caring and Social Justice.* London: Palgrave Macmillan.

Barnes, M. (2012) *Care in Everyday Life: An Ethic of Care in Practice.* Bristol: Polity Press.

Barrows, H. S. (1993) An overview of the uses of standardized patients for teaching and evaluating clinical skills. *Academic Medicine* 68(6), pp. 443–51.

Bartholomew, R. (2009, 18 March) Manifesto for maintenance: a conversation with Mierle Laderman Ukeles. *Art in America.* Available at: www.artinamericamagazine.com/news-features/interviews/draft-mierle-interview (accessed 11/12/17).

Bartula, M. and Schroer, S. (2003) *On Improvisation: Nine Conversations with Roberto Ciulli.* Brussels: Peter Lang.

Batson, G. (2010) Feasibility of an intensive trial of modern dance for adults with Parkinson's disease. *Complementary Health Practice Review* 15, pp. 65–83.

Bauman, Z. (1993) *Postmodern Ethics.* Oxford: Blackwell.

Bauriedel, G. Q. (2016) Pig iron: disponibilité and observation. In Evans M. and Kemp, R. (eds.) *The Routledge Companion to Jacques Lecoq.* London: Routledge, pp. 356–62.

Baxter, V. and Low, K. (2017) *Applied Theatre: Performing Health and Wellbeing.* London: Bloomsbury.

Bel, J. (2015) Interview with Jérôme Bel: 'it's all about communication'. In Umathum, S. and Wihstutz, B. (eds.) *Disabled Theater.* Zurich-Berlin: Diaphanes, pp. 163–74.

Benedetti, J. (1998) *Stanislavski and the Actor.* London: Methuen Drama.

Bennett, J. (2010) *Vibrant Matter: A Political Ecology of Things.* Durham, NC: Duke University Press.

Bishop, C. (2012) *Artificial Hells: Participatory Arts and the Politics of Spectatorship.* London: Verso.

Boal, A. (1998) *Theatre of the Oppressed.* Pluto Press: London.

Boal, A. (2002) *Games for Actors and Non-Actors* (2nd ed.). Translated by Jackson, A. London: Routledge.

Bourriaud, N. (2002) *Relational Aesthetics.* Translated by Pleasance, S. and Woods, F. with Copeland, M. Dijon, France: Les Presses du Réel.

Bradshaw, S. (2002) *Gendered Poverties and Power Relations: Looking Inside Communities and Households.* Managua, Nicaragua: ICD, Embajada de Holanda, Puntos de Encuentro.

Brecht, B. (1978) *Brecht on Theatre.* London: Methuen.

Brodzinski, E. (2010) *Theatre in Health and Care.* Basingstoke, UK: Palgrave Macmillan.

Bruce, D. (2017) *Hear*. London: Clean Break. [Unpublished play text.]

Bruce, D., Ikoko, T., Lomas, L., Odimba, C. and Sarma, U. (2015) *Joanne*. London: Nick Hern Books.

Butler, J. (2015) *Notes Toward a Performative Theory of Assembly*. Cambridge, MA: Harvard University Press.

Butler, J., Gambetti, Z. and Sabsay, L. (eds.) (2016) *Vulnerability in Resistance*. London: Duke University Press.

Calvert, D. (2014) 'Actual idiocy' and the sublime object of Susan Boyle. In Chow, B. and Mangold, A. (eds.) *Žižek and Performance*. Basingstoke, UK: Palgrave Macmillan, pp. 178–95.

Cantrell, T. (2013) *Acting in Documentary Theatre*. Basingstoke, UK: Palgrave Macmillan.

Caputo, J. D. (1993) *Against Ethics*. Bloomington: Indiana University Press.

Carers UK (2015) Valuing carers. Available at: www.carersuk.org/news-and-campaigns/campaigns/we-care-don-t-you/value-my-care/valuing-carers-2015 (accessed 12/12/17).

Carnicke, S. M. (2010) Stanislavsky's system: pathways for the actor. In Hodge, A. (ed.) *Actor Training*. Abingdon, UK: Routledge, pp. 28–53.

Carper, B. (1978) Fundamental patterns of knowing in nursing. *Advances in Nursing Science* 1, pp. 13–24.

Cayley, D. (2005) *The Rivers North of the Future: The Testament of Ivan Illich as told to David Cayley*. Toronto: Anansi Press.

Chandler, K. (2016) *Spent*. London: Clean Break. [Unpublished play text.]

Children and Families Act (2014) Available at: www.legislation.gov.uk/ukpga/2014/6/pdfs/ukpga_20140006_en.pdf (accessed 29/10/18).

Children's Commissioner for England (2015) *State of the Nation: Report 1: Children in Care and Care Leavers Survey 2015*. Available at: www.childrenscommissioner.gov.uk/sites/default/files/publications/Care%20monitor%20v12.pdf (accessed 28/11/16).

Chit, B. and Nayel, M. A. (2016) Understanding racism against Syrian refugees in Lebanon. Civil Society Knowledge Centre, Lebanon Support. Available at: http://civilsociety-centre.org/PAPER/UNDERSTANDING-RACISM-AGAINST-SYRIAN-REFUGEES-LEBANON (accessed 13/02/17).

Clean Break (2018) *Business Plan 2018–2022*. London: Clean Break. [Unpublished.]

Clean Break Associate A (2015, 16 March) [Unpublished transcript of a Long Table on Clean Break, Kentish Town, London].

Code, L. (2015) Care, concern, and advocacy: is there a place for epistemic responsibility? *Feminist Philosophical Quarterly* 1(1), pp. 1–20.

Coleman, R. (2009) *The Becoming of Bodies: Girls, Images, Experience*. Manchester: Manchester University Press.

Collins, S. (2015) *The Core of Care Ethics*. New York: Palgrave Macmillan.

Connell, R. W. (2005) *Masculinities* (2nd ed.). Cambridge, UK: Polity Press.

Corbett, K. (2009) *Boyhood: Rethinking Masculinities*. New Haven, CT: Yale University Press.

Corston, J. (2007) *The Corston Report: A Report by Baroness Jean Corston of a Review of Women with Particular Vulnerabilities in the Criminal Justice System*. London: Crown Copyright.

Coyle, A. (2003) *Humanity in Prison: Questions of Definition and Audit*. London: International Centre for Prison Studies.

Coyle, A., Fair, H., Jacobson, J. and Walmsley, R. (2016) *Imprisonment Worldwide: The Current Situation and an Alternative Future*. London: Policy Press.

Critchley, S. (2007) *Infinitely Demanding: Ethics of Commitment, Politics of Resistance.* London: Verso.

Csordas, T. (2002) *Body/Meaning/Healing.* Basingstoke, UK: Palgrave Macmillan.

Cull, L. (2011) Attention training immanence and ontological participation in Kaprow, Deleuze and Bergson. *Performance Research A Journal of the Performing Arts* 16(4), pp. 80–91.

Cull, L. (2013) Philosophy as drama: Deleuze and dramatization in the context of performance philosophy. *Modern Drama* 56(4), pp. 498–520.

Cull, L. (2014) Performance philosophy: staging a new field. In Cull, L. and Lagaay, A. (eds.) *Encounters in Performance Philosophy.* New York: Palgrave Macmillan, pp. 15–38.

Cull, L. (2015) Doing performance philosophy: attention, collaboration and the missing '&'. Keynote presented at the Performance and Interdisciplinarity Conference, University of Malta.

Dalmiya, V. (2002) Why should a knower care? *Hypatia* 17(1), pp. 34–52.

Dance for PD (2017) *About Us.* Available at: https://danceforparkinsons.org/about-the-program (accessed 05/12/17).

Deleuze, G. and Guattari, F. ([1972] 1983) *Anti-Oedipus: Capitalism and Schizophrenia.* Translated by Hurley, R., Seem, M. and Lane, H. R. Minneapolis: University of Minnesota.

Department for Education and Department for Health (2015). *Promoting the Health and Well-Being of Looked-After Children: Statutory Guidance for Local Authorities, Clinical Commissioning Groups and NHS England.* London: Department for Education. Available at: www.gov.uk/government/publications/promoting-the-health-and-wellbeing-of-looked-after-children--2 (accessed 08/03/19).

de Raeve, L. (1998) The art of nursing: an aesthetics? *Nursing Ethics* 5, pp. 401–11.

de Zulueta, P. (2013) Compassion in 21st century medicine: is it sustainable? *Clinical Ethics* 8(4), pp. 119–28.

Dingwall, L., Fenton, J., Kelly, T. B. and Lee, J. (2017) Sliding doors: did drama-based inter-professional education improve the tensions round person-centred nursing and social care delivery for people with dementia? A mixed-method exploratory study. *Nurse Education Today* 51, pp. 1–7.

Doolen, J., Mariani, B., Atz, T., Horsley, T. L., Rourke, J. O., McAfee, K. and Cross, C. L. (2016) High-fidelity simulation in undergraduate nursing education: a review of simulation reviews. *Clinical Simulation in Nursing* 12(7), pp. 290–302.

Douglas, M. (ed.) (2016) *Performing Mobilities* [symposium publication]. Melbourne, Australia: RMIT School of Architecture & Design.

Drinko, C. D. (2013) *Theatrical Improvisation, Consciousness, and Cognition.* New York: Palgrave Macmillan.

Driscoll, C. (2002) *Girls: Feminine Adolescent in Popular Culture and Cultural Theory.* New York: Columbia Press.

Duggan, P. (2013) Others, spectatorship, and the ethics of verbatim performance. *New Theatre Quarterly* 29(2), pp. 146–58.

Education Committee (2016). *Mental Health and Well-Being of Looked-After Children: Fourth Report of Session 2015–6.* London: House of Commons.

Ekebergh, M., Lepp, M. and Dahlberg, K. (2004) Reflective learning with drama in nursing education: a Swedish attempt to overcome the theory praxis gap. *Nurse Education Today* 24, pp. 622–8.

Engster, D. and Hamington, M. (eds.) (2015) *Care Ethics and Political Theory.* Oxford: Oxford University Press.

Enosh, S. (2016) *Outcomes of Störung*. Available at: https://hafraah.wordpress.com/ 2016/01/26/outcomes-of-storung (accessed 15/02/16).

Fancourt, D. (2017) *Arts in Health: Designing and Researching Interventions*. Oxford: Oxford University Press.

Feder, E. and Kittay, E. (2002) Introduction. In Feder, E. and Kittay, E. *The Subject of Care: Feminist Perspectives on Dependency* (Kindle ed.). Lanham, MD: Rowman & Littlefield, pp. 2–12.

Federici, S. (2012) *Revolution at Point Zero: Housework, Reproduction, and Feminist Struggle*. Oakland, CA: PM Press.

Fevered Sleep (2017) *Men & Girls Dance* newspaper (London ed.). Available at: www.menandgirlsdance.com/newspaper (accessed 26/01/18).

Fevered Sleep (2018) *Men & Girls Dance* video. Available at: www.menandgirlsdance.com (accessed 18/12/18).

Fidment, S. (2012) The objective structured clinical exam (OSCE): a qualitative study exploring the health care student's experience. *Student Engagement and Experience Journal* 1(1), pp. 1–18.

Fineman, M. (2008) The vulnerable subject: anchoring equality in the human condition. *Yale Journal of Law & Feminism* 20(1), pp. 1–25.

Fisher, B. and Tronto, J. (1990) Towards a feminist theory of caring. In Abel, E. K. and Nelson, M. K. (eds.) *Circles of Care: Work and Identity in Women's Lives*. Albany: State University of New York Press, pp. 35–62.

Fisher, T. (2015) Thinking without authority: performance philosophy as the democracy of thought. *Performance Philosophy* 1, pp. 175–84.

Fitch, C., Hamilton, S., Bassett, P. and Davey, R. (2011) The relationship between personal debt and mental health: a systematic review. *Mental Health Review Journal* 16, pp. 153–66.

Foster, E., Golden, L., Duncan, R. P. and Earhart, G. M. (2013) Community-based Argentine Tango dance program is associated with increased activity participation among individuals with Parkinson' s disease. *Archives of Physical Medicine and Rehabilitation* 94(2), pp. 240–9.

Fox, A. and Macpherson, H. (2015) *Inclusive Arts Practice and Research: A Critical Manifesto*. Oxford: Routledge.

Franzmann, V. (2014) *Pests*. London: Nick Hern Books.

Franzmann, V. (2014) *Sounds Like an Insult*. London: Clean Break. [Unpublished play text.]

Fraser, N. (2016) Contradictions of capital and care. *New Left Review* 100, pp. 99–177. Available at: https://newleftreview.org/II/100/nancy-fraser-contradicti0ons-of-capital-and-care (accessed 14/09/17).

Freeman, B. (2016) Theatre for a changeable world or making room for a fire. In Gallagher, K. and Freeman, B. (eds.) *In Defence of Theatre: Aesthetic Practices and Social Interventions*. Toronto, ON: University of Toronto Press.

Freire, P. (2000) *Pedagogy of the Oppressed* (30th anniversary ed.) New York: Continuum.

Frichot, H. (2014) Introduction: following the material, or materially situated learning. In Preston, J. *Performing Matter: Interior Surface and Feminist Actions*. Baunauch, Germany: Architecture Art and Design Research/Spurbuchverlag, pp. 9–14.

Fritsch, K. (2010) Intimate assemblages: disability, intercorporeality, and the labour of attendant care. *Critical Disability Discourse*. 2, pp. 1–14. Available at: https:// cdd.journals.yorku.ca/index.php/cdd (accessed 09/04/18).

Frost, A. and Yarrow, R. (2016) *Improvisation in Drama, Theatre and Performance: History, Practice, Theory* (3rd ed.). London: Palgrave Macmillan.

Gallagher, K. (2014) *Why Theatre Matters: Urban Youth, Engagement, and a Pedagogy of the Real.* Toronto, ON: University of Toronto Press.

Gallagher, K. (2018) Love, time, reflexivity, and the methodological imaginary. In Gallagher, K. (ed.) *The Methodological Dilemma Revisited: Creative, Critical, and Collaborative Approaches to Qualitative Research for a New Era.* London: Routledge, pp. 91–111.

Gallagher, K., Jacobson, K. and Mealey, S. (2018) Accuracy and ethics, feelings and failures: youth experimenting with documentary practices of performing reality. *Theatre Research in Canada* 40(1), pp. 58–76.

Gallagher, K. and Mealey, S. (2018) Staging our selves: towards a theory of relationality, possibility, and creative youth selfhood. In Burgoyne, S. (ed.) *Creativity in Theatre: Theory and Action in Theatre/Drama Education.* Dordrecht, the Netherlands: Springer, pp. 133–52.

Gallagher, K., Wessels, A. and Yaman Ntelioglou, B. (2012) Verbatim theatre and social research: turning towards the stories of others. *Theatre Research in Canada* 33(1), pp. 24–43.

Gardner, L. (2016, 1 November) Children storm the stage with awkward questions for grownups. *Guardian.* Available at: www.theguardian.com/stage/theatreblog/2016/nov/01/children-storm-the-stage-with-awkward-questions-for-grownups (accessed 18/03/19).

Garland, D. (2018) *Punishment and Welfare: A History of Penal Strategies.* New Orleans, LA: Quid Pro, LL.

Gault, I., Shapcott, J., Luthi, A. and Reid, G. (2017) *Communication in Nursing and Health Care: A Guide for Compassionate Practice.* London: Sage.

Gauntlett, D. (2011) *Making Is Connecting: The Social Meaning of Creativity, from DIY and Knitting to YouTube and Web 2.0.* Cambridge, UK: Polity Press.

Geras, N. (1998) *The Contract of Mutual Indifference: Political Philosophy After the Holocaust.* London: Verso.

Gibson, F. (2006) Life factors influencing present behaviour. In Marshall, M. and Kate A. (eds.) *Dementia: Walking Not Wandering: Fresh Approaches to Understanding and Practice.* London: Hawker, pp. 61–7.

Gilligan, C. (1982) *In a Different Voice: Psychological Theory and Women's Development.* Cambridge, MA: Harvard University Press.

Gilligan, C. (1995) Hearing the difference: theorizing connection. *Hypatia* 10(2), pp. 120–7.

Gilrain, J. (2016) The mimo-dynamics of music, poetry, and short story: Lecoq on Bartók. In Evans, M. and Kemp, R. (eds.) *The Routledge Companion to Jacques Lecoq.* London: Routledge, pp. 127–35.

Glenn, E. N. (2010) *Forced to Care.* Cambridge, MA: Harvard University Press.

Glisovic, S. (2016) Bit-u-men-at-work [respondent review]. In Douglas, M. (ed.) *Performing Mobilities* [symposium publication]. Melbourne: RMIT School of Architecture & Design, pp. 77.

Godder, Y. (2015a) In discussion with Monica Gillette. *The Space Between.* Available at: https://hafraah.wordpress.com/2015/12/10/the-space-between (accessed 06/12/17).

Godder, Y. (2015b, 19 December) Public discussion with Godder: winter conversations, *Störung/Hafra'ah.* Theatre Freiburg.

Godder, Y. (2016a) *Common Emotions.* Available at: https://hafraah.wordpress.com/2016/06/12/common-emotions (accessed 15/10/16).

Godder, Y. (2016b) *Outcomes of Störung.* Available at: https://hafraah.wordpress.com/2016/01/26/outcomes-of-storung (accessed 15/02/16).

Goffman, E. (1990) *The Presentation of Self in Everyday Life.* London: Penguin.

Goffman, E. (1991) *Asylums.* London: Penguin.

Goodley, D. (2014) *Dis/ability Studies.* Oxford: Routledge

Gorman, S. (2017) Performing failure? Anomalous amateurs in Jérôme Bel's *Disabled Theater* and *The Show Must Go On 2015. Contemporary Theatre Review* 27(1), pp. 92–103.

Graham, J., Nosek, B. A., Haidt, J., Iyer, R., Koleva, S. and Ditto, P. H. (2011) Mapping the moral domain. *Personal Social Psychology* 101(2), pp. 366–85.

Gunnison, E. and Bernat, F. (2016) *Women, Crime and Justice: Balancing the Scales.* Chichester, UK: Wiley Blackwell.

Hackney, M. E. and Earhart, G. M. (2009) Effects of dance on movement control in Parkinson's disease: a comparison of Argentine tango and American ballroom. *Journal of Rehabilitative Medicine* 41, pp. 475–81.

Hackney, M. E. and Earhart, G. M. (2010) Effects of dance on gait and balance in Parkinson's disease: a comparison of partnered and nonpartnered dance movement. *Neurorehabilitation and Neural Repair* 24, pp. 384–92.

Hafra'ah (2017) Available at: https://hafraah.wordpress.com (accessed 18/02/19).

Hallenbeck, V. J. (2012) Use of high-fidelity simulation for staff education/development: a systematic review of the literature. *Journal for Nurses in Staff Development* 28(6), pp. 260–9.

Hamera, J. (2013) Response-ability, vulnerability, and other(s') bodies. In Johnson, E. P. (ed.) *Cultural Struggles: Performance, Ethnography, Praxis.* Ann Arbor: University of Michigan Press, pp. 306–10.

Hamington, M. (2004) *Embodied Care: Jane Addams, Maurice Merleau-Ponty, and Feminist Ethics.* Urbana: University of Illinois Press.

Hamington, M. (2015) Politics is not a game: the radical potential of care. In Daniel, E. and Maurice, H. (eds.) *Care Ethics and Political Theory.* Oxford: Oxford University Press, pp. 272–93.

Hamington, M. and Miller, D. (eds.) (2006) *Socializing Care: Feminist Ethics and Public Issues.* Oxford: Rowman & Littlefield.

Hammond, W. and Steward, D. (eds.) (2008) *Verbatim Verbatim.* London: Oberon.

Haraway, D. (2008) *When Species Meet.* Minneapolis: University of Minnesota Press.

Haraway, D. (2016) *Staying with the Trouble: Making Kin in the Chthulucene.* Durham, NC: Duke University Press.

Hardt, M. (1999) Affective labour. *Boundary 2* 26(2), pp. 89–100.

Harpin, A. (2018) *Madness, Art and Society: Beyond illness.* Abingdon, UK: Routledge.

Harrison, D., Jahangard, R. and Duffy, K. (2016) *Dear Home Office.* [Unpublished.]

Haydon, A. (2013) Theatre in the 2000s. In Rebellato, D. (ed.) *Modern British Playwriting: 2000–2009.* London: Bloomsbury, pp. 40–96.

Heddon, D. (2007) *Performance and Autobiography.* Basingstoke, UK: Palgrave Macmillan.

Hedge, N. and Mackenzie, N. (2012) Beyond care. *Journal of Philosophy of Education* 46(20), pp. 192–206.

Heggestad, A. K. T., Nortvedt, P., Christiansen, B. and Konow-Lund, A. (2016) Undergraduate nursing students' ability to empathize: a qualitative study. *Nurse Ethics* 25(6), pp. 786–95.

Heiberger, L., Maurer, C., Amtage, F., Mendez-Balbuena, I., Schulte-Mönting, J., Hepp Reymond, M. and Kristeva, R. (2011) Impact of a weekly dance class on the functional mobility and on the quality of life of individuals with Parkinson's disease. *Frontiers in Aging Neuroscience* 3(14), pp. 1–15.

Held, V. (1993) *Feminist Morality: Transforming Culture, Society, and Politics.* Chicago: University of Chicago Press.

Held, V. (2005) Taking care: care as practice and value. In Calhoun, C. (ed.) *Setting the Moral Compass: Essays by Women Philosophers.* Oxford: Oxford University Press, pp. 59–71.

Held, V. (2006) *The Ethics of Care: Personal, Political, and Global.* Oxford: Oxford University Press.

Hims, K. (2013) *Billy the Girl.* London: Nick Hern Books.

Hochschild, A. (2003) *The Commercialization of Intimate Life: Notes from Home and Work.* Berkeley: University of California Press.

Hochschild, A. (2012) *The Managed Heart: Commercialization of Human Feeling.* Berkeley: University of California Press.

Hodgson, J. and Richards, E. (1966) *Improvisation.* London: Eyre Methuen.

Hoffman, M. L. (2000) *Empathy and Moral Development: Implications for Caring and Justice.* Cambridge, UK: Cambridge University Press.

hooks, b. (1994) *Teaching to Transgress: Education as the Practice of Freedom.* New York; London: Routledge.

Houston, B. (1990) Review: caring and exploitation. *Hypatia* 5(1), pp. 115–19.

Houston, S. (2014) Moved to dance: socially engaged dance facilitation. In Anderson, M. E. and Risner, D. (eds.) *Hybrid Lives of Teaching Artists in Dance and Theatre Arts: A Critical Reader.* New York: Cambria Press, pp. 133–54.

Houston, S. (2015) Feeling lovely: an examination of the value of beauty for people dancing with Parkinson's. *Dance Research Journal* 47(1), pp. 26–43.

Houston, S. and McGill, A. (2013) A mixed-methods study into ballet for people living with Parkinson's. *Arts & Health: an International Journal for Research, Policy and Practice* 5(2), pp. 103–19.

Houston, S. and McGill, A. (2015) *English National Ballet Dance for Parkinson's: An Investigative Study 2, a Report on a Three-Year Mixed-Methods Research Study.* London: English National Ballet.

Howard League (2016, 8 November) Ten years after the *Corston Report*, is this the end of women's centres? Available at: https://howardleague.org/news/isthistheendofwomenscentres (accessed 12/12/17).

Hughes, J. and Nicholson, H. (2016) Applied theatre: ecology of practices. In Hughes, J. and Nicholson, H. (eds.) *Critical Perspectives on Applied Theatre.* Cambridge, UK: Cambridge University Press, pp. 1–13.

Human Rights Watch (2017) *Lebanon: Refugees.* Available at: www.hrw.org/world-report/2017/country-chapters/lebanon (accessed 30/11/17).

Illich, I. (2001) *Tools for Conviviality.* London: Marion Boyars.

Ingold, T. (2011) *Being Alive: Essays on Movement, Knowledge and Description.* Oxford: Routledge.

Isin, E. F. and G. M. Neilson (eds.) (2007) *Acts of Citizenship.* London: Zed Books.

Jackson, N. and Shapiro-Phim, T. (eds.) (2008) *Dance, Human Rights and Social Justice: Dignity in Motion.* Lanham MD: Scarecrow Press.

Jackson, S. (2004) *Professing Performance: Theatre in the Academy from Philology to Performativity.* Cambridge, UK: Cambridge University Press.

Jackson, S. (2011) *Social Works: Performing Arts, Supporting Publics.* London: Routledge.

Jackson, S. and Scott, S. (1999) Risk anxiety and the social construction of childhood. In Lupton, D. (ed.) *Risk and Sociocultural Theory: New Directions and Perspectives.* Cambridge, UK: Cambridge University Press, pp. 86–108.

Jeffers, A. (2012) *Refugees, Theatre and Crisis: Performing Global Identities.* Basingstoke, UK: Palgrave Macmillan.

Johnson, M. (1987) *The Body in the Mind: The Bodily Basis of Meaning, Imagination, and Reason.* Chicago: University of Chicago Press.

Kaplan, C. (1996) *Questions of Travel: Postmodern Discourses of Displacement.* Durham, NC: Duke University Press.

Kennedy, H. (1993) *Eve Was Framed.* London: Vintage.

Kester, G. (2011) *The One and the Many: Contemporary Art in a Global Context.* Durham, NC: Duke University Press.

Khalaf, S. and Kongstad, P. (1973) *Hamra of Beirut: A Case of Rapid Urbanization.* Leiden, the Netherlands: E. J. Brill.

Kirkwood, L. (2009) *it felt empty when the heart went at first but it's alright now.* London: Nick Hern Books.

Kittay, E. F. (1999) *Love's Labor: Essays on Women, Equality, and Dependency.* Abingdon, UK: Routledge.

Kittay, E. F. (2002) When caring is just and justice is caring: justice and mental retardation. In Feder, E. and Kittay, E. (eds.) *The Subject of Care: Feminist Perspectives on Dependency* (Kindle ed.). Lanham, MD: Rowman & Littlefield, pp. 257–75.

Kittay, E. F. (2010) The personal is philosophical is political: a philosopher and mother of a cognitively disabled person sends notes from the battlefield. In Kittay, E. F. and Carlson, L. (eds.) *Cognitive Disability and Its Challenge to Moral Philosophy.* Malden, UK: Wiley-Blackwell, pp. 393–413.

Kittay, E. F. (2013) The body as the place of care. In Cruz-Pierre, A. and Landes, D. A. (eds.) *Exploring the Works of Edward S. Casey: Giving Voice to Place, Memory, and Imagination.* New York: Bloomsbury, pp. 205–15.

Kittay, E. F. (2015) A theory of justice as fair terms of social life given our inevitable dependency and our inextricable interdependency. In Engster, D. and Hamington, M. (eds.) *Care Ethics and Political Theory.* Oxford: Oxford University Press, pp. 51–72.

Klaver, K. and Baart, A. (2011) Attentiveness. *Nursing Ethics* 18(5), pp. 686–93.

Klein, N. (2017, 28 September) A new shock doctrine: in a world of crisis, morality can still win. *Guardian.* Available at: www.theguardian.com/commentisfree/2017/sep/28/labour-shock-doctrine-moral-strategy-naomi-klein (accessed 12/10/17).

Kuppers, P. and Robinson, G. (eds.) (2007) *The Community Performance Reader.* London: Routledge.

Lateef, F. (2010) Simulation-based learning: just like the real thing. *Journal of Emergencies, Trauma and Shock* 3(4), pp. 348–52.

Lecoq, J. (2000) *The Moving Body: Teaching Creative Theatre.* London: Methuen.

Leonard, K., Hafford-Letchfield, T. and Couchman, W. (2016) The impact of the arts in social work education: a systematic review. *Qualitative Social Work* 17(3), pp. 1–9.

Lepper, J. (2017, 20 February) Council to end funding for universal youth services. *Children and Young People Now.* Available at: www.cypnow.co.uk/cyp/news/2003208/council-to-end-funding-for-universal-youth-services (accessed 18/05/18).

Levett-Jones, T. and Lapkin, S. (2014) A systematic review of the effectiveness of simulation debriefing in health professional education. *Nurse Education Today* 34, pp. e58–e63.

Levinas, E. (1969) *Totality and Infinity: An Essay on Exteriority*. Translated by Lingis, A. Pittsburgh, PA: Duquesne University Press.

Lewis, W. W. and Tulk, N. (2016) Editorial: why performance as research? *PARtake: The Journal of Performance as Research* 1(1), pp. 1–7.

Løgstrup, K. E. (1997) *The Ethical Demand*. Notre Dame, IN: University of Notre Dame Press.

Loth, J., Andersen, P. and Mitchell, P. (2015) Acting for health: effective actor preparation for health-care simulations. *Applied Theatre Research* 3(3), pp. 285.

Louch, G., O'Hara, J., Gardner, P. and O'Connor, D. B. (2016) The daily relationships between staffing, safety perceptions and personality in hospital nursing: a longitudinal on-line diary study. *International Journal of Nursing Studies* 59, pp. 27–37.

Love, C. (2016, 7 April) *Men & Girls Dance*: the show fighting paranoia around child abuse. *Guardian*. Available at: www.theguardian.com/stage/2016/apr/07/men-girls-dance-fevered-sleep (accessed 18/03/19).

Lynch, K., Lyons, M. and Cantillon, S. (2007) Breaking silence: educating citizens for love, care and solidarity. *International Studies in Sociology of Education* 17(1), pp. 1–19.

el Mabsout, D. (2015a) 'Nightingale', in *Fleeing and Forgetting* [exhibition]. Mansion, Beirut, 5 December.

el Mabsout, D. (2015b) 'Still Lives', in *Fleeing and Forgetting* [exhibition]. Mansion, Beirut, 5 December.

el Mabsout, D. (2015c) 'Home', in *Fleeing and Forgetting* [exhibition]. Mansion, Beirut, 5 December.

Madison, D. S. (2018) *Performed Ethnography and Communication: Improvisation and Embodied Experience*. London: Taylor & Francis.

Mahmood, S. (2005) *Politics of Piety: The Islamic Revival and the Feminist Subject*. Princeton, NJ: Princeton University Press.

Mauer, M. (1999) *Race to Incarcerate*. New York: New Press.

Mauer, M. (2016) Thinking about prison and its impact in the twenty-first century. *Ohio State Journal of Criminal Law* 2, pp. 607–18.

Mayseless, O. (2016) *The Caring Motivation: An Integrated Theory*. New York: Oxford University Press.

McAllister, M., Searl, K. R. and Davis, S. (2013) Who is that masked educator? Deconstructing the teaching and learning processes of an innovative humanistic simulation technique. *Nurse Education Today* 33(12), pp. 1453–8.

McBrinn, R. (2015) *Preface to Joanne*. London: Nick Hern Books.

McCormack, B. and McCance, T. (2010) *Person-Centred Nursing: Theory and Practice*. Chichester, UK: Wiley-Blackwell.

McCormack, B. and McCance, T. (eds.) (2017) *Person-Centred Practice in Nursing and Health Care* (2nd ed.) Chichester, UK: Wiley-Blackwell.

McDonagh, P. (2008) *Idiocy: A Cultural History*. Liverpool: Liverpool University Press.

McEvoy, L. and Duffy, A. (2008) Holistic practice: a concept analysis. *Nurse Education in Practice* 8(6), pp. 412–19.

McGill, A., Houston, S. and Lee, R. (2014) Dance for Parkinson's: a new framework for research on its physical, mental, emotional and social benefits. *Complementary Therapies in Medicine* 22(3), pp. 426–32.

McGill, A., Houston, S. and Lee, R. (2018) Effects of a ballet-based dance intervention on gait variability and balance confidence of people with Parkinson's. *Arts & Health: An International Journal of Research, Policy and Practice*. Available at: www.tandfonline.com/doi/abs/10.1080/17533015.2018.1443947?casa_token=a7JiI_fFiA4AAAAA:jHQzgcHMw7GYtxOpjTZ5V4HtcWujmDohTuJHzIRkzyh-r-nGFBp5TU8dTC2zJ36DqkGRBR3K7RrEQ (accessed 06/03/18).

McKenzie, J. (2001) *Perform or Else: From Discipline to Performance*. London: Routledge.

McLaughlin, C. (2017) 'They don't look like children': child asylum-seekers, the Dubs amendment and the politics of childhood. *Journal of ethnic and Migration Studies* 44 (1), pp. 1757–73. Available at: www.tandfonline.com/doi/abs/10.1080/1369183X.2017.1417027 (accessed 19/09/17).

Merleau-Ponty, M. (1964) *'Eye and Mind': The Primacy of Perception and Other Essays on Phenomenological Psychology, the Philosophy of Art, History and Politics*. Edited by Edie, J. M. Translated by Cobb, W. Evanston, IL: Northwestern University Press.

Mikdashi, M. (2015) Lebanon, August 2015: notes on paralysis, protests, and hope. *Jadaliyya*. Available at: www.jadaliyya.com/Details/32403 (accessed 18/02/19).

Miller, G. (2007) A wall of ideas: the 'taboo on tenderness' in theory and culture. *New Literary History* 38(4), pp. 667–81.

Mills, D. (2016) *Dance & Politics: Moving Beyond Boundaries*. Manchester: Manchester University Press.

Mind the Gap (2016) *Contained*. [Unpublished script.]

Monden, K. R., Gentry, L. and Cox, T. R. (2016) Delivering bad news to patients. *Baylor University Medical Centre Proceedings* 29(1), pp. 101–2.

Morris, Hargreaves, McIntyre (2017) *Complexity with Care: Evaluation of Fevered Sleep's 'Men & Girls Dance'*. [Unpublished.]

Moving Communities. (2018, 18–19 January) Conference organised by Yasmeen Godder, Mandel Cultural Center, Jaffa, Israel. Available at: www.yasmeengodder.com/Parkinson/moving-communities-conference/moving-communities-conference-schedule (accessed 03/03/18).

Mroue, M. (2014) Anti-Syrian sentiment in Lebanon. *openDemocracy*. Available at: www.opendemocracy.net/arab-awakening/mahmoud-mroueh/antisyrian-sentiment-in-lebanon (accessed 13/02/17).

el Mufti, K. (2014) Official response to the Syrian refugee crisis in Lebanon: the disastrous policy of no-policy. Civil Society Knowledge Center, Lebanon Support. Available at: http://civilsociety-centre.org/paper/official-response-syrian-refugee-crisis-lebanon-disastrous-policy-no-policy (accessed 13/02/17).

Munro, E. (2011) *The Munro Review of Child Protection, Final Report: A Child-Centered System*. London: Department for Education.

Murray, S. (2004) *Jacques Lecoq*. London: Routledge.

Myers, E. (2013) *Worldly Ethics: Democratic Politics and Care for the World*. Durham, NC: Duke University Press.

Nadasen, P. (2016) The care deficit. *Dissent Magazine*. Available at: www.dissentmagazine.org/article/care-deficit-hta-domestic-worker-organizing-history (accessed 12/04/18).

National Archives, Records of GOV.UK (2013) *A Review of the NHS Hospital Complaints System: Putting the Patient Back into the Picture*. Available at: https://assets.publishing.service.gov.uk/government/uploads/system/uploads/attachment_data/file/255615/NHS_complaints_accessible.pdf (accessed 30/10/18).

National Audit Office (2015) *Care Leavers' Transition to Adulthood*. London: Department for Education.

Neimanis, A., Åsberg, C., and Hedrén, J. (2015). Four problems, four directions for environmental humanities: toward critical posthumanities for the Anthropocene. *Ethics & the Environment* 20(1), pp. 67–91.

Nicholls, T. (2012) *An Ethics of Improvisation: Aesthetic Possibilities for a Political Future*. Lanham, MD: Lexington Books.

Nicholson, H. (2002) The politics of trust: drama education and the ethic of care. *Research in Drama Education: The Journal of Applied Theatre and Performance* 7(1), pp. 81–91.

Nicholson, H. (2005) *Applied Drama: The Gift of Theatre*. Basingstoke, UK: Palgrave Macmillan.

Nicholson, H. (2016) A good day out: applied theatre, relationality and participation. In Hughes, J. and Nicholson, H. (eds.) *Critical Perspectives on Applied Theatre*. Cambridge, UK: Cambridge University Press, pp. 248–68.

Nield, S. (2006) On the border as theatrical space: appearance, dis-location and the production of the refugee. In Kelleher, J. and Ridout, N. (eds.) *Contemporary Theatres in Europe: A Critical Companion*. Abingdon, UK: Routledge, pp. 61–73.

Noddings, N. [1984] (2013) *Caring: A Relational Approach to Ethics and Moral Education* (2nd ed.). Berkeley: University of California Press.

Noddings, N. (1992) *The Challenge to Care in Schools: An Alternative Approach to Education*. New York: Teachers College Press.

Noddings, N. (1999) Caring and competence. In Griffen, G. (ed.) *The Education of Teachers*. Chicago: National Society of Education, pp. 205–20.

Noddings, N. (2002) *Starting at Home: Caring and Social Policy*. Berkeley: University of California Press.

Noddings, N. (2010a) *The Maternal Factor: Two Paths to Morality*. Berkeley: University of California Press.

Noddings, N. (2010b) Complexity in caring and empathy. *Abstracta* 5(special issue V), pp. 6–12.

Noddings, N. (2010c) Moral education in an age of globalization. *Educational Philosophy and Theory* 42(4), pp. 390–6.

Nolas, S. M. (2013) Exploring youth people's and youth workers' experiences of spaces for 'youth development': creating cultures of participation. *Journal of Youth Studies* 17(1), pp. 26–41.

Nunes, P., Williams, S., Sa, B. and Stevenson, K. (2011) A study of empathy decline in students from five health disciplines during their first year of training. *International Journal of Medical Education* 2, pp. 12–17.

Nursing and Midwifery Council (NMC) (2015) *The Code for Nurses and Midwives*. NMC: London. Available at: www.nmc.org.uk/globalassets/sitedocuments/nmc-publications/nmc-code.pdf (accessed 30/10/18).

Parkinson's UK. (2014) *About Parkinson's*. Available at: www.parkinsons.org.uk/content/about-parkinsons (accessed 18/11/14).

Parliamentary and Health Service Ombudsman (2011) *Care and Compassion? Report of the Health Service Ombudsman on Ten Investigations into NHS Care of Older People*. London: HMSO. Available at: www.ombudsman.org.uk/sites/default/files/2016-10/Care%20and%20Compassion.pdf (accessed 09/09/19).

Patient Client Council (PCC) (2017) *Quality Report 2016/2017*. Belfast: PCC. Available at: www.patientclientcouncil.hscni.net/uploads/research/Q2020_report_2016_17.pdf (accessed 30/10/18).

Peer Outreach Team (2015) *Pledges.* London: Greater London Authority. [Unpublished internal report.]

Perman, L. (2016, 6 December) *Interview with the Author.* London: Clean Break.

Perman, L. (2018, 6 July) *Interview with the Author.* London: National Theatre.

Peters, G. (2009) *The Philosophy of Improvisation.* Chicago: University of Chicago Press.

Peters, G. (2016, 20 September) Repetition and rehearsal. Presented at the Philosophy and Performance Conference, Ljubljana, Slovenia.

Peters, G. (2017) *Improvising Improvisation: From Out of Philosophy, Music, Dance, and Literature.* Chicago: University of Chicago Press.

Philips, J. (2007) *Care.* Cambridge, UK: Polity Press.

Pink, S. (2012) *Situating Everyday Life: Practices and Places.* London: Sage.

Preston, J. and Archer-Martin, J. (2015, 6–8 October) *Bit-u-men-at-work* [live art performance]. Performed by Julieanna Preston in Melbourne, a pavement outside Margaret Lawrence Gallery.

Preston, S. (2016) A conceptual framework. In *Applied Theatre Facilitation: Pedagogies, Practices, Resilience.* London: Bloomsbury Methuen Drama, pp. 17–87.

Pollock, D. (2005) *Remembering: Oral History Performance.* New York: Palgrave Macmillan.

Puar, J. K. (2009) Prognosis time: towards a geopolitics of affect, debility and capacity. *Women & Performance: a Journal of Feminist Theory* 19(2), pp. 161–72.

Puar, J. K. (2017) *The Right to Maim: Debility, Capacity, Disability.* London: Duke University Press.

Puig de la Bellacasa, M. (2012) 'Nothing comes without its world': thinking with care. *Sociological Review* 60(2), pp. 197–216.

Ramsbotham, D. (1997) *Women in Prison: A Thematic Review by Her Majesty's Chief Inspector of Prisons.* London: Home Office.

Rancière, J. (2004) *The Politics of Aesthetics*, Translated by Rockhill, G. London: Continuum.

Randall, P. (1991) *24%.* London: Clean Break. [Unpublished play text.]

Reeves, A. and Neilson, S. (2018) 'Don't talk like that: it's not just what you say but how you say it': the process of developing an applied theatre performance to teach undergraduate nursing students communication skills around paediatric end-of-life are. *Journal of Applied Arts & Health* 9(1), pp. 99–111.

Reich, W. (1995) *Encyclopaedia of Bioethics 2* (Vol. 5). New York: Simon & Schuster.

Reid-Searl, K., Mcallister, M., Dwyer, T., Krebs, K., Anderson, C., Quinney, L. and McLellan, S. (2014) Little people, big lessons: an innovative strategy to develop interpersonal skills in undergraduate nursing students. *Nurse Education Today* 34, pp. 1201–6.

Renold, E. (2005) *Girls, Boys and Junior Sexualities: Exploring Children's Gender and Sexual Relations in the Primary School.* London: RoutledgeFalmer.

Ridout, N. (2009) *Theatre and Ethics.* Basingstoke, UK: Palgrave Macmillan.

Robinson, F. (1999) *Globalizing Care: Ethics, Feminist Theory, and International Relations.* Boulder, CO: Westview Press.

Rowe, N. (2010) *Raising Dust: A Cultural History of Dance in Palestine.* London: I. B. Tauris.

Sahni, U. (2017) *Reaching for the Sky: Empowering Girls Through Education.* Washington, DC: Brookings Institution Press.

Salford City Council (2012) *Adult Social Care: Market Position Statement.* Available at: www.salford.gov.uk/d/Adult_social_care_market_position_statement.pdf (accessed 07/07/17).

Schechner, R. (1998) What is performance studies anyway? In Phelan, P. and Lane, J. (eds.) *The Ends of Performance*. New York: New York University Press, pp. 357–62.

Schechner, R. (2013) *Performance Studies: An Introduction* (3rd ed.) Abingdon, UK: Routledge.

Schmidt, Y. (2015) After *Disabled Theater*: authorship, creative responsibility and autonomy in *Freie Republik HORA*. In Umathum, S. and Wihstutz, B. (eds.) *Disabled Theater*. Zurich-Berlin: Diaphanes, pp. 227–40.

Seaton, S. (2016) House. In Seaton, S. and Odimba, C. (2016) *House + Amongst the Reeds*. London: Nick Hern Books, pp. 1–46.

Seidman, S. (2012) The politics of cosmopolitan Beirut: from the stranger to the other. *Theory, Culture & Society* 29(2), pp. 3–36.

Sellars, P. (2016) Forward. In Cox, E. (ed.) *Theatre and Migration*. Basingstoke, UK: Palgrave Macmillan, pp.viii–xii.

Sennett, R. (2012) *Together: The Rituals, Pleasures and Politics of Cooperation*. London: Allen Lane.

Shafir, U. (2016) *Outcomes of Störung*. Available at: https://hafraah.wordpress.com/2016/01/26/outcomes-of-storung (accessed 15/02/16).

Shalom, H. (2016) *Outcomes of Störung*. Available at: https://hafraah.wordpress.com/2016/01/26/outcomes-of-storung (accessed 15/02/16).

Shem-Tov, N. (2015) Improvisation is the heart of creativity. *RiDE: The Journal of Applied Theatre and Performance* 20(3), pp. 306–9.

Shohat, E. (1991) Imaging terra incognita: the disciplinary gaze of empire. *Public Culture* 3(2), pp. 41–70.

Siassakos, D., Bristowe, K., Hambly, H., Angouri, J., Crofts, J. F., Winter, C., Hunt, L. P. and Draycott, T. J. (2011) Team communication with patient actors: findings from a multisite simulation study. *Simulation in Health Care: Journal of the Society for Simulation in Health Care* 6(3), pp. 143–9.

Siegmund, G. (2015) What difference does it make? Or from difference to in-difference. *Disabled Theater* in the context of Jérôme Bel's work. In Umathum, S. and Wihstutz, B. (eds.) (2015) *Disabled Theater*. Zurich-Berlin: Diaphanes, pp. 13–30.

Siegmund, G. (2017) *Jérôme Bel: Dance, Theatre and the Subject*. London: Palgrave Macmillan.

Simone, A. (2004) People as infrastructure: intersecting fragments in Johannesburg. *Public Culture* 16(3), pp. 407–29.

Slote, M. (2007) *The Ethics of Care and Empathy*. Abingdon, UK: Routledge.

Smith, C. (2015) *To Flourish or Destruct: A Personalist Theory of Human Good, Motivations, Failure, and Evil*. Chicago: University of Chicago Press.

Smith, P. (1992) *The Emotional Labour of Nursing: Its Impact on Interpersonal Relations, Management and Educational Environments*. Basingstoke, UK: Palgrave Macmillan.

Smith, P. (2012) *The Emotional Labour of Nursing Revisited: Can Nurses Still Care?* (2nd ed.) Basingstoke, UK: Palgrave Macmillan.

Sodha, S. (2018, 25 March) Fathers want to take care of their children, too, but our very culture is against them. *Guardian*. Available at: www.theguardian.com/commentisfree/2018/mar/25/paternity-leave-women-equality-gender (accessed 18/03/19).

Solimeo, S. (2009) *With Shaking Hands: Aging with Parkinson's Disease in America's Heartland*. New Brunswick, NJ: Rutgers University Press.

Spence, J. (2007) Support. In Robb, M. (ed.) *Youth in Context: Frameworks, Settings and Encounters*. London: Sage, pp. 287–320.

Spolin, V. (1963) *Improvisation for the Theatre: A Handbook of Teaching and Directing Techniques.* Evanston, IL: Northwestern University Press.

Spring Consortium (2016) *Children's Social Care Innovation Programme: Interim Learning Report January 2016.* London: Department for Education.

Steinhauer, J. (2017, 10 February) How Mierle Laderman Ukeles turned maintenance work into art. *Hypoallergic.* Available at: https://hyperallergic.com/355255/how-mierle-laderman-ukeles-turned-maintenance-work-into-art (accessed 11/12/17).

Stern, V. (2006) *Creating Criminals: Prisons and People in a Market Society.* London: Zed Books.

Stromme, L. (2016, 20 October) 'Beards are a giveaway': these migrants are NOT unaccompanied minors, ex-UKIP MEP blasts. *Express.* Available at: www.express.co.uk/news/uk/723143/Beards-migrants-not-unaccompanied-minors-ex-UKIP-MEP-blasts (accessed 14/03/19).

Suttie, I. [1935] (2005) *The Origins of Love and Hate.* Abingdon, UK: Routledge.

Taylor, D. (2016) *Performance.* Durham, NC: Duke University Press.

Theater HORA (2015) Interviews with the actors of Theater HORA: on acting and spinning. In Umathum, S. and Wihstutz, B. (eds.) *Disabled Theater.* Zurich-Berlin: Diaphanes, pp. 85–94.

Thompson, J. (2004) Digging up stories: an archaeology of theatre in war. *TDR: The Drama Review* 48(3), pp. 150–64.

Thompson, J. (2009) *Performance Affects: Applied Theatre and the End of Effect.* Basingstoke, UK: Palgrave Macmillan.

Thompson, J. (2015) Towards an aesthetics of care. *Research in Drama Education: The Journal of Applied Theatre and Performance* 20(4), pp. 430–41.

Thompson, J. (2017) No more bystanders: 'Grandchildren of Hiroshima' and the 70th anniversary of the atomic bomb. *TDR: The Journal of Performance Studies* 61(2) (T234), pp. 87–104.

Thompson, N. (ed.) (2012) *Living as Form: Socially Engaged Art 1991–2011.* Cambridge, UK: Creative Time Books.

Tiller, C. (2017) *Power Up.* London: Creative People and Places. [Unpublished report.]

Tilsen, J. (2018) *Narrative Approaches to Youth Work: Critical Skills for a Conversational Practice.* New York: Routledge.

Tracey, D. (2017) *With the Witnesses: Poetry, Compassion, and Claimed Experience.* Montreal, Canada: McGill-Queens University Press.

Tresolini, C. P. and the Pew-Fetzer Task Force (1994) *Health Professions Education and Relationship-Centred Care.* San Francisco, CA: Pew Health Professions Commission.

Tronto, J. C. [1993] (2009) *Moral Boundaries; A Political Argument for an Ethic of Care* (2nd ed.) Abingdon, UK: Routledge.

Tronto, J. C. (2012) Democratic care politics in an age of limits. In Razavi, S. and Staab, S. (eds.) *Global Variations in the Political and Social Economy of Care.* New York: Routledge, pp. 29–41.

Tronto, J. C. (2013) *Caring Democracy: Marketing, Equality, and Justice.* New York: New York University Press.

Tronto, J. C. (2015) Theories of care as a challenge to Weberian paradigms in social science. In Engster, D. and Hamington, M. (eds.) *Care Ethics and Political Theory.* Oxford: Oxford University Press, pp. 252–72.

Turiel, E. (1983) *The Development of Social Knowledge: Morality and Convention.* Cambridge, UK: Cambridge University Press.

Turner, V. (1985) *Dramas, Fields and Metaphors: Symbolic Action in Human Society.* Ithaca, NY: Cornell University Press.

Turner-King, R. (2018) Creating welcoming spaces in the city: exploring the theory and practice of 'hospitality' in two regional theatres. *Research in Drama and Applied Theatre: The Journal of Applied Theatre and Performance* 23(3), pp. 421–37.

Ukeles, M. L. (1969) *Manifesto for Maintenance Art 1969! Proposal for an Exhibition: 'CARE'* [published online by Arnolfini in 2013]. Available at: www.arnolfini. org.uk/blog/manifesto-for-maintenance-art-1969/Ukeles_MANIFESTO.pdf (accessed 11/12/17).

Ukeles, M. L. (2015) *Mierle Laderman Ukeles: Seven Work Ballets.* Amsterdam: Kunstverein.

Umathum, S. (2015) Actors, nonetheless. In Umathum, S. and Wihstutz, B. *Disabled Theater.* Zurich-Berlin: Diaphanes, pp. 99–112.

Umathum, S. and Wihstutz, B. (eds.) (2015a) *Disabled Theater.* Zurich-Berlin: Diaphanes.

Umathum, S. and Wihstutz, B. (2015b) Prologue. In Umathum, S. and Wihstutz, B. (eds.) *Disabled Theater.* Zurich-Berlin: Diaphanes, pp. 7–9.

UNHCR (2018a) Syria regional refugee response: Beirut. Available at: https://data2. unhcr.org/en/situations/syria/location/83 (accessed 17/06/18).

UNHCR (2018b) Syria regional refugee response: Lebanon. Available at: https:// data2.unhcr.org/en/situations/syria/location/71 (accessed 17/06/18).

UNHCR (2018c) Syria regional refugee response: Bekaa. Available at: http://data2. unhcr.org/en/situations/syria/location/71 (accessed 17/06/18).

Valentine, G. (2014) *Inequality and Class Prejudice in an Age of Austerity.* Sheffield: Sheffield Political Economy Research Institute.

van Gennep, A. (1977) *The Rites of Passage.* London: Routledge and Kegan Paul.

van Heugten, K. (2011) *Social Work Under Pressure: How to Overcome Stress, Fatigue and Burnout in the Workplace.* London: Jessica Kingsley.

Victor, J., Ruppert, W. and Ballasy, S. (2017) Examining the relationships between clinical judgment, simulation performance, and clinical performance. *Nurse Educator* 42(5), pp. 236–9.

Wacquant, L. (2011) The punitive regulation of poverty in the neoliberal age. *openDemocracy.* Available at: www.opendemocracy.net/en/5050/punitive-regulation-of-poverty-in-neoliberal-age (accessed 11/03/19).

Waddell, M. (2018) *On Adolescence.* Abingdon, UK: Routledge.

Wainwright, P. (2000) Towards an aesthetics of nursing. *Journal of Advanced Nursing* 32(3), pp. 750–6.

Wake, C. (2013a) Between repetition and oblivion: performance, testimony, and ontology in the refugee determination process. *Text and Performance Quarterly* 33(4), pp. 326–43.

Wake, C. (2013b) Headphone verbatim theatre: methods, histories, genres, theories. *New Theatre Quarterly* 29(4), pp. 321–35.

Wang W.-J. (2010) An exploration of the aesthetics of an oral history performance developed in the classroom. *Research in Drama and Applied Theatre: The Journal of Applied Theatre and Performance* 15(4), pp. 563–77.

Ward, J., Cody, J., Schaal, M. and Hojat, M. (2012) The empathy enigma: an empirical study of decline in empathy among undergraduate nursing students. *Journal of Professional Nursing* 28(1), pp. 34–40.

Westheimer, O., Mcrae, C., Henchcliffe, C., Fesharaki, A., Glazman, S., Ene, H., Bodis-Wollner, I. (2015) Dance for PD: a preliminary investigation of effects on motor function and quality of life among persons with Parkinson's disease (PD). *Journal of Neural Transmission* 122(9), pp. 1263–70.

White, M. (2009) *Arts Development in Community Health: A Social Tonic.* Oxford: Radcliffe.

Wihstutz, B. (2015) '… and I am an actor': on emancipation in *Disabled Theater.* In Umathum, S. and Wihstutz, B. (eds.) *Disabled Theater.* Zürich, Switzerland: Diaphanes, pp. 35–50.

Wilson, P. (2010) Foreword. In Nicholson C., Irwin M. and Dwivedi, K. N. (eds.) *Children and Adolescents in Trauma: Creative Therapeutic Approaches.* London: Jessica Kingsley, pp. 11–13.

Willson, S. and Jaye, P. (2017) Arts-based learning for a circle of care. *Lancet* 390(10095), pp. 642–3.

Women in Prison (2017) *The Corston Report 10 Years On: How Far Have We Come on the Road to Reform for Women Affected by the Criminal Justice System?* London: Women in Prison.

Yoxall, M. (2018) At the 'frontiers' of humanitarian performance: refugee resettlement, theatre-making and the geo-politics of service. *Research in Drama Education: The Journal of Applied Theatre and Performance* 23(2), pp. 210–27.

Zamir, T. (2014) *Acts: Theater, Philosophy and the Performing Self.* Ann Arbor: University of Michigan Press.

Zayed, Y. and Harker, R. (2015) *Briefing Paper 04470: Children in Care in England – Statistics.* London: House of Commons Library.

el Zein, R. (2017) Resisting 'resistance': on political feeling in Arabic rap concerts. In Sabry, T. and Ftouni, L. (eds.) *Arab Subcultures: Transformations in Theory and Practice.* London: I. B. Tauris, pp. 87–112.

Index

EU authorised representative for GPSR:
Easy Access System Europe, Mustamäe tee 50,
10621 Tallinn, Estonia
gpsr.requests@easproject.com

www.ingramcontent.com/pod-product-compliance
Ingram Content Group UK Ltd.
Pitfield, Milton Keynes, MK11 3LW, UK
UKHW021826150726
7214IPUK00017B/337